Psychological Stress in the Workplace

Psychological Stress in the Workplace is the most up-to-date and comprehensive account of research on occupational stress. It identifies the sources, consequences and treatments of stress in the workplace from the perspective of organizational psychology and makes clear recommendations for future work in this area.

Terry Beehr discusses how role ambiguity and conflict act as stressors in the workplace, and discusses the characteristics of the job and the organization itself that can adversely affect performance. He examines the effects of stress in the workplace and describes methods that can be used to alleviate the problem, both at the individual and organizational level.

In addition, the book is illustrated with many examples from field research over the author's twenty years of experience in studying the workplace. *Psychological Stress in the Workplace* will be of considerable interest to students and researchers in occupational psychology, as well as managers and trainers.

Terry A. Beehr (PhD in Organizational Psychology, the University of Michigan, 1974) is a Professor in the PhD Program in Industrial/Organizational Psychology at Central Michigan University. He has previously co-authored *Human Stress and Cognition in Organizations: An Integrated Perspective* as well as dozens of articles in a variety of scholarly journals, covering issues such as occupational stress, leadership, employee motivation and job design, careers, employee gender, and other organizational behavior topics.

People and organizations
Series editor: Sheldon Zedeck
Department of Psychology, University of California, Berkeley

The study of organizations has increased significantly in recent years. In recognition of the growing importance of behavioural science research to our understanding of organizations, *People and Organizations* is a new series devoted to advanced research in industrial and organizational psychology, and organizational behaviour.

The books in the series are derived from empirical programmatic research on topics related to organizations and the ways in which people interact, respond to, and cope with the organization. Topics of special interest include: organizational culture, work and family, high technology, organizational commitment, careers, and studies of organizations in international markets. Books in the series are theoretically grounded and include specific guidelines for future research.

Already available:

Leadership and Information Processing
Linking Perceptions and Performance
Robert G. Lord and Karen J. Maher

Role Motivation Theories
John B. Miner

Volunteers
The Organizational Behaviour of Unpaid Workers
Jone L. Pearce

Psychological Stress in the Workplace

Terry A. Beehr

London and New York

First published 1995
by Routledge
11 New Fetter Lane, London EC4P 4EE

Simultaneously published in the USA and Canada
by Routledge
29 West 35th Street, New York, NY 10001

Typeset in Garamond by LaserScript Ltd, Mitcham, Surrey
Printed and bound in Great Britain by
T.J. Press (Padstow) Ltd, Padstow, Cornwall

British Library Cataloguing in Publication Data
A catalogue record for this book is available from the British Library

Library of Congress Cataloging in Publication Data
A catalog record for this book has been requested

ISBN 0-415-09426-7

To
Karen, Dana, Matthew, Alison, the MPSG,
and the Lincoln Research Institute

Contents

Figures

Tables

Preface

Occupational stress is a fascinating topic in many ways. We know much about it, there is much we do not know, and there is almost certainly much that we "know" about it that is not true. This volume is written after my first twenty years, more or less, of research on work-related stress and before my next twenty years of research on it. Two decades hence, some of the concepts discussed here will no doubt have become common knowledge, while others will have become yesterday's misunderstandings. The trick is to determine which concepts are which. In 1994 we cannot.

Stress has many different meanings, both in its public usage and in its technical, professional, and scholarly usages. The focus here is on work-related stress as opposed to life stress or stress in any non-work domain. The terms job stress, work-related stress, occupational stress, and organizational stress are used interchangeably in the book. This is done not because jobs, work, occupations, and organizations are indistinguishable concepts, but simply to reduce my writing fatigue and your reading fatigue due to too frequent redundancy of phrases.

Since a pair of review articles I wrote about fifteen years ago with John Newman (Beehr and Newman, 1978; Newman and Beehr, 1979) in *Personnel Psychology*, a great deal of new research has been done on occupational stress. It is remarkable, however, that some of the conclusions of those two articles would change only a little. Although progress has been made, there is still a need for more longitudinal and field experimental research designs, for better measurement, including more use of physiological measures, and for research testing theories, as the following chapters attest.

The general approach to occupational stress taken here is only one of many. It is the organizational psychology approach identified by Beehr and Franz (1987). This means especially that the environmental causes of interest here, the stressors, are primarily social psychological elements of the workplace. Keeping that as a main theme, the volume is divided into parts and research in each part's domain is discussed in relation to this organizational psychology approach to job stress.

The first part is the introduction, in which job stress and its major elements are defined, a theoretical approach to it is described, and research techniques are discussed. The second part describes the causes or stressors in the workplace. Two of the earliest and most often studied job stressors are given a single chapter of their own to share, while the others share a separate chapter. The third part describes what we know about the outcomes of occupational stress and these are divided into outcomes that are more immediately relevant to the individual and those more clearly affecting the organization. The fourth part of the book discusses research on the treatments of organizational stress, giving attention in a separate chapter to social support. Research on social support has made it one of the favorite, most intriguing, and most confusing treatments in the organizational psychology approach to job stress. The final chapter concludes that more research is needed and especially research following certain themes noted throughout the book. Twenty years from now, we might be able to review the research and determine which of these themes were most valuable.

Part I

Introduction to occupational stress

Occupational stress is studied and treated by many disciplines and these disciplines have tended to define it, study it, and treat it in their own separate ways. In addition to the professions' treatments of it, stress is now a common word in the English language and the general public has a variety of ways of using the term. It is therefore necessary to define it carefully before any discussion of it. Failure to do this will result in inaccurate communication.

In this section, the terms involved in occupational stress are defined and examined, a theory is described that uses the terms in a consistent way, and a few observations about methods of research are examined for their strengths and weaknesses in studying this topic. Chapter 1 outlines a model describing the program of empirical research and theory development in which my colleagues and I have been engaged for about the last twenty years. The remainder of the book describes that program.

Chapter 1

The many faces of occupational stress

> Unfortunately his initial studies involving hypoglycemia were unsuccessful because a change in the brain metabolism was only observed when the stress produced death.
>
> (From a letter recommending promotion in academia; Short Subjects, 1990: 8.)

Stress has many faces, perhaps due in part to the interest the topic generates among people with widely varying perspectives. The general public has always used the word stress in some sort of commonsense manner, so that researchers who are new to the topic might already believe they know what it is before examining past research on it. This could lead to operationalizations that are different from existing research. While this might result in innovation, it causes problems when one tries to compare results across studies.

The stress causing a change in brain metabolism noted in the quotation above seems to have come from a biology- or physiology-related study. The incident no doubt caused some stress in the researcher as well as in the research subject. Beehr and Franz (1987) noted that several very different research specializations have a logical interest in stress, albeit for different reasons and from different starting points and assumptions. Because of these various faces of stress, definitions of it vary widely and it is important to remember that any two people talking or writing about the topic may not always be referring to the same thing. This is true of work-related stress and of stress in general. Limiting the topic to work-related or occupational stress does not seem to help reach common definitions.

There is a consensus that job stress is important. Figures are often cited estimating that many billions of dollars are lost in the United States each year due to occupational stress (e.g. Beehr and Bhagat, 1985b). These "losses" are due to increased costs of medical insurance to employers and employees, excess pressure on the medical facilities and professionals who could otherwise work with other patients and illnesses, lost productivity due to illness, and so forth. No accurate estimate of national cost can be made, however, due to two considerations: since there are differing definitions of occupational stress, it is not easy to decide which one to use in making an estimate; and even when a definition is agreed upon, there is usually no clear research that would allow accurate estimates.

At an individual level, if work-related stress causes an individual to be ill, it is certainly important to that individual, however. At a societal level, we know that many illnesses are costing a great deal of money and many of these illnesses are thought capable of being partially caused by a stressful work environment (e.g. coronary heart disease and mental illnesses). In order to estimate the cost to society, however, the proportion of such illnesses that is actually due to stressful working conditions would have to be known. There are no clear estimates of this. More hard data can be found if we look at claims for workers' compensation. Corey and Wolf (1992) note that through most of the 1980s, there was a 540 percent increase in mental stress claims in California's worker compensation system, even though work-related injuries as a whole declined during the same period. The cost of these California claims in 1987, for example, was 383 million dollars. It is clear that there are some monetary costs for work-related stress, although the exact price is probably unknowable.

A SAMPLE OF FOUR APPROACHES TO OCCUPATIONAL STRESS

One thing most people agree about is that occupational stress is widespread. Of course, since there are so many different definitions of stress, it might be easy to find it in one form or another in many jobs. Ivancevich and Matteson (1980) even compared stress to sin, since both of these are emotionally charged topics that mean different things to different people. Beehr and Franz's (1987) analysis concluded that there are at least four broad fields of specialization that approach stress with their own assumptions and using their own research skills and orientations. Since the fields are broad, it is difficult to give precise labels to them, but the following have been suggested: medicine, clinical psychology, engineering psychology, and organizational psychology (Beehr and Franz 1987). Among other things, medicine would include physiological approaches in general, clinical psychology would include counseling and most of the human service oriented fields, engineering psychology would include human factors specialties and some experimental psychology, and organizational psychology would include organizational behavior and management.

To preview the chapter and the book, it can be stated here that my own approach to occupational stress research is the one labeled organizational psychology. Since organizational psychology can be considered the social psychology of organizations (Katz and Kahn, 1978), this book describes an approach that examines the links between social psychological characteristics of the workplace and harmful psychological or physical outcomes for the individual. The workplace characteristics are usually labeled stressors and the individual outcomes are collectively known as strains. The chapters herein are the result of a twenty-year program of research in which these links are examined in a variety of ways and in which other variables are explored for their association with stressors and strains.

Each empirical research project described herein examined slightly different aspects of the organizational psychology approach to job stress, but the one constant was the link between stressors and strains. Subjects of the projects always worked for pay, but there have been a large variety of occupations, from low to high in socioeconomic status, from poorly to richly paid, from those requiring little or no formal education to those requiring doctorates, from both service and manufacturing organizations, from both private and public sector organizations, from both US and foreign sites, and so forth. A few thousand people have participated in these studies at over thirty research sites. The people studied come in all shapes and sizes. That is, they range in age from barely old enough to hold paying jobs to old enough to retire if they wanted, and they are of different races and both sexes. Some of these individual differences have occasionally been a focus of the research, but one interesting overall impression is that the individual differences have generally mattered only a little in reactions to the organizational stressors. That is counterintuitive to most psychologists and we can take that as a challenge for future research to explain.

These studies all fit within the organizational psychology approach to occupational stress and Table 1.1 can provide some perspective on what this means. It lists and describes the nature of these four research approaches. Stressors refer to the characteristics of the person's work environment that are thought to be causal in the stress process and outcomes refer to the variables thought to be consequences of stress. Strain is a term used for aversive consequences of stress for the person. Primary targets of treatment refer to the type of variable most immediately affected by attempts to treat occupational stress; that is either some aspect of the organization or workplace or some aspect of the individual is usually the immediate focus (primary target) of the treatment process. These are discussed further in Chapter 7. The term "stressor" is not always used in these disciplines, but when it is, it is almost uniformly used to mean a theoretically causal environmental characteristic and that is how it is used in the remainder of this book. The term "strain" is used less often than stressor in these disciplines and its meaning has been a little less consistent when it is used. It usually means, however, an individual's response that could be deemed harmful to him or her and that is the way it is used here.

It may be noted that the word stress is not used to describe any variable in the table and in fact it will not be used as a name for any single variable in this book. If this seems astonishing, the reason is that stress has been defined so variously in both the scientific and popular literatures that the word itself causes more confusion than clarification when used as a variable name. One study concluded that the public tends to interpret the word stress as a combination of both stress causes and outcomes; that is, both as stressors and strains (Jex *et al.* 1992). Unfortunately, while researchers may be more precise – that is, each tends to use the word only to mean stressors or strains – they do not agree with each other.

Probably none of the researchers or practitioners in the four fields in Table 1.1 would like the narrow characterization they receive here, but it is instructive to make this characterization in order to show that these themes and approaches to occupational stress tend to proceed relatively independently of each other. It must be acknowledged, however, that people working within each of these disciplines and from each of these perspectives are not always as narrow in their pursuit of knowledge and understanding as they are painted in the following paragraphs.

Medical model approaches have historically focused on physical stressors, for example unusual temperatures or noise, and they have expected these stressors to cause physical strains or outcomes to the individual; for example, hypertension or increases in epinephrine or norepinephrine levels in the blood stream or urine (Beehr and Franz, 1987). When they treat stress, the approach tends to be individual rather than organizational. If hypertension were the strain, the treatment might be medication, which is aimed at the individual's hypertension; by contrast, the treatment is not usually to change the stressors in the organization or workplace.

Beehr and Franz (1987) argue that the clinical/counseling approach to occupational stress is similar to the medical approach, with the major exception that psychological stressors (rather than physical stressors) and psychological strains (rather than physical strains) are the outcomes of

Table 1.1 Four approaches to occupational stress (reprinted with permission from Beehr and Franz, 1987)

Approach	Typical stressor	Typical outcome	Typical primary target of treatment
Medical	Physical	Physical strain	Individual
Clinical/Counseling psychology	Psychological	Psychological strain	Individual
Engineering psychology	Physical	Job performance	Organization
Organizational psychology	Psychological	Psychological strain	Organization

interest. In this approach, direct treatment of individuals' psychological strains is common. Neither of the approaches above the dotted line in the table was developed with the workplace as the primary focus, but they are now becoming widely applied there. Most employee assistance programs seem to use one or both of these approaches.

The third approach to occupational stress in the table is labeled engineering psychology and it has a longer history of research on work-related stress (Beehr and Franz, 1987). In its work on occupational stress, engineering psychology has traditionally focused on physical stressors such as heat or noise and it has been almost unique among stress researchers in its focus on job performance as an outcome variable.

The final entry in the table is labeled organizational psychology and has always focused historically (although it has a shorter history than the disciplines in the other approaches) on psychological stressors in the workplace and on psychological strains. In this regard, it resembles the clinical/counseling psychology approach to occupational stress. For treatment strategies, however, it recommends changes in the organization or workplace more often than the clinical/counseling approach does (Beehr and Franz, 1987). As noted by Ivancevich and Matteson (1987), organizationally targeted treatments have rarely even been tried; recommendations from this approach to the topic have largely fallen on deaf ears. More attention is given to this issue in Chapter 7.

These four professional approaches to occupational stress can cause confusion and disagreements among researchers, readers of the literature, and applied professionals. Some of the disagreements are simply due to differences in the use of the words as in, for example, the situation in which one person calls an environmental stimulus stress, a second reserves the word stress for the individual's response to the stimulus, and a third person uses the word stress to mean a topic area of research or practice but not any one specific variable. All of these definitions have been used in the research literature (Ivancevich and Matteson, 1980; Mason, 1975).

If researchers and practitioners are careful to define their own use of the word in each of their projects and if others read carefully and overlook their personal preferences for the use of the word stress, this problem might be overcome. This does not always happen, however. Even if it did, there are more problems with integrating the occupational stress literature than just the definition of the word. As can be seen from the four approaches, there are fundamental differences among people regarding the nature of what is acceptable as evidence of the existence of a stressful situation. The ultimate dependent variable or typical outcome is one of the most crucial elements in occupational stress, and there is disagreement regarding what constitutes evidence for even this. It is not necessarily true, for example, that changes in Table 1.1 outcomes of physical health, psychological health, or job performance coincide with each other, are part of a single global construct, or are caused by similar organizational events or situations. The history of psychology in the workplace has taught one not to make such an assumption without great caution. A prime example is the long-held but apparently incorrect assumption that job satisfaction affects job performance (e.g. Herzberg *et al.*, 1959; Vroom, 1964). One should not assume relationships among the stress outcome variables without good evidence.

The complexity and confusion caused by different technical disciplines approaching the topic very differently is apparent, but aside from these professional definitions, there is yet another approach to operationalizing job stress that occasionally appears in the research literature. That is the practice of letting each individual research participant use their own implicit or explicit definition of stress. This happens when, for example, a questionnaire simply asks respondents to rate the amount of "stress" in their jobs or lives without defining it (for example questionnaire items using the word stress or one of its cognates can be found in Cooper *et al.*, 1988; Hendrix, 1987; Ivancevich and Matteson, 1980; Motowidlo *et al.*, 1986; Potter and Fiedler, 1981; Schaubroeck *et al.* 1989; Steffy and Jones, 1988). This results in a study in which there may be more than one lay person's definition and no technical definition at all. In this case, even the researchers themselves do not know what definition of stress was used in their own study – because the definition used depended upon the interpretation of each individual research participant. This approach lacks precision, makes it difficult to communicate results to others, and impedes comparison of results across studies. It is probably better for research at least to recognize and make explicit which general approach to occupational stress is being used.

Research implications regarding definitions of stress

Even the general definition and outline of occupational stress suggest some research needs. Occupational stress shares with other types of stress some problems arising from the fact that stress is a commonly used word among the public and researchers and workers in many professions. It has already been defined in many ways, both technical and popular, and it is too late to impose a single definition acceptable to all parties.

One important problem of the meaning of the word stress has occurred with increasing frequency in recent years. While occupational stress research has relied in part or sometimes entirely on self-reports or employee survey data almost since its inception, the word "stress" was not usually used in the survey questions themselves. Recently, however, there has been an increasing tendency to ask respondents directly about the "stress" in their work lives. If researchers who have focused their attentions on the topic have no common definition, asking the general public to rate the amount of stress they have might only be asking for information about the unknown. What do people in general – that is, those who have not studied stress – mean when they use the word?

My colleagues and I (Jex *et al.*, 1992) sought to answer this question. We located published articles in which questionnaire items had used the word stress or one of its close cognates (e.g. stressful). From these, we took sixteen such "stress" items and incorporated them into a questionnaire in random groups of four. These groups of stress items were randomly distributed among groups of other items from the literature that formed scales measuring stressors (i.e. role ambiguity, role conflict, perceived workload, and interpersonal conflict), psychological strains or potential stress outcomes (overall job dissatisfaction, anxiety, frustration, depression, and turnover intentions).

We were interested in determining whether items containing the word stress, or its cognates, would be interpreted by the survey respondents as environmental stressors, as individual strain responses, as both, or as neither. By examining the empirical relationships of the stress items with stressors and strains, this judgment could be made. Two samples of respondents were obtained, but their data were combined into one sample for analysis, because there appeared to be little difference in the correlations found in their data. The two samples consisted of 131 city and county workers and 113 hospital workers.

The sixteen stress items, formed into a composite "stress" scale, were correlated significantly (p<0.01) with every other index in the study. The highest correlations were with one strain, anxiety (r=0.72), and one stressor, role conflict (r=0.60). The correlations were interpreted to mean that questionnaire items using the word stress tend to measure or to be interpreted by the general public as both stressors and strains. Canonical analyses using the sixteen separate stress items were then used as a summary statistic and the same interpretation resulted. This was done to examine the relationship with both the strain variables and with the stressor variables. The redundancy indices indicated that about 40 percent of the variance in the stress items could be accounted for by the strain variables and that about 33 percent of the variance in the stress items could be accounted for by the stressor variables.

These results can be interpreted to mean that the word "stress" probably means both environmental stressors and individual strains to questionnaire respondents. Although it might carry more strain meaning than stressor meaning, there seem to be substantial amounts of both. The use of self-reports to measure both stressors and strains has been fairly common in the job stress research, but this practice almost automatically raises the specter of potential correlated measurement errors leading to spuriously high correlations among these two classes of variables. As noted by Jex and Beehr (1991), measures do not always correlate with each other just because they were in the same survey. If they did, there certainly would never be any problem with low internal consistency reliabilities, for example. After all, when low reliabilities are obtained, that means that even questionnaire items that are supposed to be correlated with each other for content reasons have failed to do so. Some characteristics of self-report items probably make them more or less susceptible to this measurement problem, however. One obvious item characteristic in the study of occupational stress is the use of the word stress in self-report items. This practice probably leads to contamination of the stressor items with strain and vice versa, and it is a practice that should be avoided.

Aside from the use of the word stress in questionnaire items, it has also been recommended that the word stress not be used in scientific reporting to mean any variable, but simply to refer to an area of interest and study (McGrath, 1976; Jex *et al.*, 1992) In this way, it is perhaps similar to the word leadership in industrial/organizational psychology. There are all kinds of leadership and the word itself is an umbrella concept describing a broad domain for a wide variety of types of research rather than a variable that is operationally defined, at least without an adjective such as participatory, authoritarian, etc. It is recommended that the term occupational stress can be used in organizational psychology to refer to a situation in which elements of the job, by themselves or in combination with elements of the job incumbent, lead to poor individual health and/or welfare (Beehr, 1987).

Regarding terminology, if stress is not used for a variable name, it is recommended that stressor refer to environmental stimulus variables in the workplace that are thought to be causal and that strain be the term for variables referring to the individual's aversive health or welfare reactions to stressors. The strains could be physical or psychological. When the terms stressor and strain have been used in the research literature in the past, they have usually been used in this way; therefore, usage of these terms should cause little new confusion.

With only this broad introduction to the topic, some fruitful directions for future research are apparent. It would help researchers, practitioners, policy makers, and many other interested parties to know how the different definitions of stress are consistent or inconsistent with each other. When stressors from any approach to occupational stress are present, do they have the effects that the other approaches would expect? For example, when a psychological stressor such as role overload exists, does the employee experience changes in (1) physical health, (2) psychological health and well-being, and (3) job performance? Do all the various stressors result in the same intervening variables or processes (physiological processes such as secretions of catecholamines or psychological processes such as uncertainty regarding response selection, for example)? One suspects the answer to these questions would be negative, but it may be discovered that there are broad ranges or categories of stressors that have common effects within categories of processes. If so, there may be a more interesting and useful way to categorize approaches to occupational stress than the fourfold one based on professions (Beehr and Franz, 1987). A simple non-experimental field study determining relationships among occupational stressors and strains from the various wide-ranging approaches would be a useful starting point.

It was insightful to determine the meaning of the word stress to the lay public in the study by Jex *et al.* (1992). The word has become so frequently used both publicly and professionally that it has probably come to mean something entirely different from any of the professional, technical meanings. As noted already, some researchers have taken to simply asking people to rate their own occupational stress, using the word stress. Since it appears that the word has a variety or even conglomeration of meanings to the public, studies using the word in surveys can probably not help us understand the phenomenon very much.

THE ORGANIZATIONAL PSYCHOLOGY APPROACH TO OCCUPATIONAL STRESS

This book focuses on the organizational psychology approach to occupational stress, as outlined previously. It is important to keep in mind the other approaches, however, because they will be encountered frequently in the research, popular, and practitioner literatures, and this sometimes is very confusing. In the research literature, the focus of this book, researchers are sometimes surprised to find that "standard" theories and knowledge about occupational stress do not seem to hold up under rigorous scrutiny, and one reason is that some of these standards were developed using variables and operationalizations different from the ones being examined. If stress is defined and operationalized variously as glandular secretions into the blood stream (e.g. Balick and Herd, 1987), as role ambiguity in the workplace (French and Caplan, 1973; Kahn and Quinn, 1970) or the non-specific bodily response made to any demand (e.g. Selye, 1974), it should come as no surprise that stress is not consistently related to other variables in the same way across studies.

The term occupational (or work-related or job) stress is used here to describe not a variable but a situation in which some characteristics of the work situation are thought to cause poor psychological or physical health, or to cause risk factors making poor health more likely. Health is broadly conceived so that the term well-being sometimes seems more appropriate. The core of an occupational stress experience, then, is the presumed causal relationship between characteristics of the work or workplace (stressors) and poor worker or employee health (strains). In addition to this core, however, other important related events or states are often of interest. In 1978, the Beehr–Newman model of occupational stress outlined these in a way that is general enough to encompass virtually all aspects or facets of the job stress process. It summarizes the usual ways of thinking about occupational stress and serves as a backdrop to the research program described in this book.

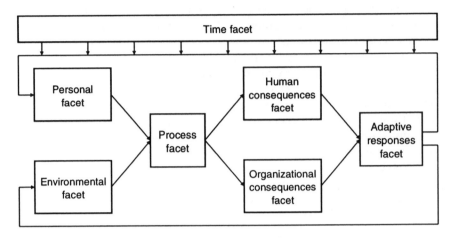

Figure 1.1 A general model of occupational stress (reprinted with permission from Beehr and Newman, 1978).

THE BEEHR–NEWMAN MODEL OF OCCUPATIONAL STRESS

The model in Figure 1.1 was designed to encompass not only all variables studied from the various approaches to occupational stress, but also virtually all theories about the topic (Beehr and Newman, 1978). The core of occupational stress, the relationship between job stressors and individual strains, is illustrated by the relationship between the environmental facet (which contains occupational stressors) and the human consequences facet (which contains individual strains), a relationship that has an intervening step through the process facet. From most organizational psychology points of view about stress, this relationship is required as all or part of the definition of work stress. In addition to this core, however, there are other sets of variables that are frequently included in the theories and research on the topic.

The Beehr–Newman model was a result of research and theory on occupational stress prior to 1978. It was not proven by prior research, since it was developed from prior research; nor, for that matter, is it the type of model that one tests and proves or disproves. It is not specific enough to be easily proven or disproven, although it can be a starting point for developing hypotheses, models and theories that can be useful for empirical testing. Instead, it lists the classes of variables in which researchers on occupational stress are usually interested and it arranges the variables in a way that shows the typical thinking used by most researchers, theoreticians, and even practitioners. Having the environmental facet precede the human consequences facet in time and presumed causality, for example, is merely reiterating the definition of occupational stress, i.e. stressors lead to strains. If occupational stress exists, then this part of the model is correct. If occupational stress does not exist, then of course the model is not correct. Any specific study usually focuses on only parts of the model and makes no attempt to be inclusive; that is, specific studies in the program of research described here – and other research, for that matter – never pretends to measure all potential stressors in the environmental facet, all potential strains in the human consequences facet, or all potential elements of any one facet. The model can serve as a basic outline for understanding the typical thinking of occupational stress workers.

While the Beehr–Newman model in Figure 1.1 encompasses all elements of occupational stress, the subsequent program of research and theory development described in this book has not yet covered all of these facets. This research program to date has addressed the more limited model in Figure 1.2. This figure shows that, in this program of research, the core relationship in job stress is truly the core of the research program, because any other variables are examined primarily to determine their relationship to the variables in this core.

The core relationship of occupational stress

The theoretical causal factor in the core relationship of occupational stress is the set of job stressors in the environmental facet. These include the well-known role stressors such as role ambiguity and role conflict (Chapter 3), but in addition, any characteristic of the work that affects health adversely would be a stressor (Chapter 4 illustrates these). Examples might include the weekly work schedule (e.g. Ivancevich, 1974) or organizational structures. These might be considered chronic stressors in the sense that they are consistent, long-term states of the job or organization that change only

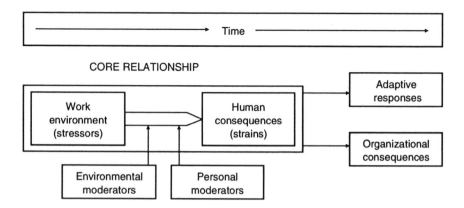

Figure 1.2 Model illustrating the research program described in this book.

slowly, if at all (Beehr and Franz, 1987). In contrast to these, however, are short-term events in the workplace that may be stressful.

Such time-limited events have been a major focus of interest and research in the so-called "life events" stress literature (e.g. Holmes and Rahe, 1967; Sarason *et al.*, 1978), but have never caught on very strongly in organizational stress research. Some examples of "acute" or time-limited stressors might include being laid off (the event of being laid off occurs quickly, although the state of being laid off could last longer; Kasl and Cobb, 1970), tax deadline dates for accountants (Friedman *et al.*, 1958), impending computer shutdowns at universities (Caplan and Jones, 1975), and the experience of beginning a new job (e.g. nursing students providing comprehensive patient care for the first time; Eden, 1982). These have all been found stressful in the few past studies of acute occupational stress. As with most research in the field, the studies reported in this book are almost all concerned with chronic stressors. It should be noted that more research on the acute stressors seems warranted, even though my own program of research has not yet addressed them.

Besides the stressors, the other element of the core relationship of occupational stress in Figure 1.2 is the human consequences facet or the individual strains. These are examined in Chapter 5. Adverse states of individual health or well-being constitute the strains. These have often been categorized into psychological, physical, and behavioral strains, but the commonality among them is the idea that the strains are basically harmful to the individual. Examples of psychological strains include anxiety (e.g. House and Rizzo, 1972), tension (e.g. Beehr *et al.*, 1976), depression (e.g. Kaufmann and Beehr, 1989), psychological fatigue (e.g. Beehr *et al.*, 1976), and burnout (e.g. Beehr *et al.*, 1990; Gaines and Jermier, 1983).

The physical strains concern actual physical illnesses or closely related risk factors such as hypertension or high serum cholesterol levels. Fewer studies have been done that searched for or found relationships between occupational stressors and physical problems than between occupational stressors and psychological problems. The most often studied of the physical problems are the risk factors in coronary heart disease (Cooper and Marshall, 1976). The program of research described in this book is consistent with the rest of the organizational psychology studies of job stress, in the sense that most of the human consequences variables have been psychological, with only a few attempts to examine the physical strains.

Physiological responses to work stress often have the aura of being more objective and therefore better measures than psychological responses, but this may be a somewhat misleading assumption. As noted previously, there are often discussed problems with commonly used occupational stress research methods that make no intervention and measure both causes (stressors) and effects (strains) with self-reports at a single point in time. The room for response tendencies to affect relationships among the variables seems great and there is a debate in the literature about just how strong such effects are likely to be (e.g. Spector, 1987b; Williams *et al.*, 1989). Some recent discussions of the potential for an individual difference variable labeled negative affectivity to account for many findings of such research methods have increased the awareness of the problem (e.g. Brief *et al.*, 1988). The other side of the coin, however, is that physiological measurements of stress responses have their own difficulties.

While most organizational stress researchers are already aware of the response bias problem regarding psychological strains, many of them are probably less aware of certain problems with measuring physiological responses. Measures of potential stress responses such as hypertension, cholesterol in the blood stream, development of peptic ulcers, and catecholamines such as adrenalin and noradrenalin in the blood stream and urine are affected by things other than stress (e.g. family or genetic factors, recent dietary intake, transitory testing conditions, smoking, and time of day of measurement; Fried *et al.*, 1984). Many physiological measures are subject to rapid fluctuation due to some of these factors. The organizational stress studies generally have not controlled enough of these confounding variables to give a great deal of confidence in their results. This is an obvious topic for more and better research in the future. Better physiological measurement in these types of field studies might lead to different results with more clear implications for theory and practice.

Behavioral strains are behaviors the stressed employee shows that are directly harmful to him or her. There can be serious disagreement about what behaviors are harmful to the individuals involved, because of the influence of our values in determining good versus bad. Therefore, it is probably safest to be quite conservative in naming such behaviors. Possibilities include, however, excessive or abusive use of all "drugs," including cigarette smoking, excessive alcohol consumption, and the use of illegal drugs. If such behaviors are caused by the work-related stressors of the environmental facet, they can be labeled behavioral strains. Contrary to what might be assumed from some of the popular literature, there is currently little evidence that these behaviors are caused or made more severe by occupational stressors. It is difficult to say whether this is because not enough good studies have been done or because studies are not getting confirming results. It is an area in need of good organizational stress research.

There is also in the theoretical literature the idea of "good" stress. This idea can take two forms. First, positively valued work situations and events might be bad for us (i.e. that positively valued things can be stressors that cause strains). For example, the frequently mentioned "opportunity" stress (opportunity *stressors*, in the language of this book) might include promotions (e.g. Beehr and Schuler, 1982; Schuler, 1980). Usually promotions are thought to be desirable opportunities, but if they cause some people to experience strains they are stressful after all. These types of good stresses are no problem for the typical stress research program. If the job characteristic or event causes strains, it is a stressor regardless of how people may value it for itself.

Although the original life stress literature assumed that life changes that required adjustments were stressful regardless of whether the change was "good" or "bad" (e.g. Holmes and Rahe, 1967), other life stress research has suggested that negative life changes such as having a spouse die may be more stressful than positively valued life changes. That is, there is some indication that negative changes are more stressful than positive changes (Sarason *et al.*, 1978). This issue has not even been addressed in the organizational psychology research on occupational stress. It is intuitively appealing that negatively valued work events such as being fired would be more stressful or harmful to people than positively valued ones such as getting promotions; research has yet to be done on this issue, however.

More complicated is the idea of good stress defined as situations wherein stressors cause good outcomes in the personal consequences facet instead of causing individual strains. If stress is defined as a situation in which some characteristics in the workplace cause strains in the individual (probably the most common working definition among organizational psychologists), then this idea of good stress is not possible. If the work situation causes only good human consequences, then by the present definition there is *no* stress in the situation. Typical non-organizational psychology definitions of stress more easily lend themselves to the examination of this type of good stress. If, for example, the secretion of catecholamines (epinephrine and norepinephrine) is considered a measure of stress (Fleming and Baum, 1987), then this stress has not been defined as either good or bad. In itself, the release of catecholamines is neither good nor bad. If catecholamines cause some good human consequences, for example, helping the person to avoid falling asleep in dangerous but boring working conditions, then this "stress" would probably be deemed good by most of us. The research program described herein, however, focuses on potential problems in organizations and therefore is typical of the organizational psychology approach of considering stress to be a harmful rather than a good phenomenon.

In summary, positively valued stressors that lead to harmful strains and stressors that result in processes or responses defined as stress by some approaches (e.g. catecholamine secretions) even though they may ultimately lead to good human consequences are the two types of good stress, but research on them has been sparse. Only the first of these two fits with the present definition of organizational stress. The catecholamine secretions would be part of the process facet of Figure 1.1, discussed next.

Processes intervening in the core relationship

One set of stress-related variables, those in the process facet, are people's reactions that are thought to intervene in the core relationship between stressors and strains. Physiologically oriented researchers often look for the essence of stress here. One of the most popular current examples of the elements of this facet that has been discussed already is the presence of catecholamines in the blood stream.

Selye (1956, 1975) long ago hypothesized that there were "first mediators" of stress, that is, responses that occur before the more observable strains such as heart disease occur. Being from the medical/physiological stress tradition, he naturally hypothesized that the first mediators were physiological or neurological. The idea was that some bodily system that reaches all parts of the body must carry a coded "message" potentially leading to strains in various parts of the body. He never seemed entirely convinced that he had found these first mediators, but toward the end of his life he leaned toward believing that they would be something carried in the circulatory system, as catecholamines are. Whether these *are* his first mediators or not, however, is unclear. Mason (1975), debating Selye, argued that the first mediators, to the extent that they exist, are more likely to be psychological or emotional arousal responses rather that physiological responses.

Some psychologically oriented researchers and theorists suggest other processes that might be inherent in job stress, including decision making and response selection (e.g. McGrath, 1976), perceptions or appraisals of the situation (e.g. Levine and Scotch, 1970; Lazarus and Folkman, 1984), or uncertainty regarding expectancies (e.g. Beehr and Bhagat, 1985a). When the Beehr–Newman model was developed, the process facet was one of the least understood facets of occupational stress and it probably still is. Its existence, however, is a recognition that the relationship between stressors and strains is probably not a simple, direct one. In fact, in the research program examined in this book, when such processes are measured, they are usually labeled either as stressors or strains in the core relationship in Figure 1.2, rather than as intervening processes.

Research issues regarding stress processes

Stress processes are obviously an area in need of research. It is not clear that all situations labeled occupational stress include the same physiological responses, such as catecholamine secretions or tension in a particular set of muscles. Similarly, it is not clear and may be improbable that there is a single psychological response common to all occupational stress situations. There may turn out to be categories of responses that vary by the nature of the job stressors, the associated strains, or some individual differences. The field is at a point at which some taxonomic research may have much to offer researchers on occupational stress. If all of the variations in theories and measures were known and could be laid out in a systematic manner, some of the more obvious inconsistencies would become apparent.

Perception of the stress situation is one immediately occurring process that could be the target of future investigation. The simple sounding idea that people are aware of their stressful environments is not necessarily simple or straightforward. Some theories contend or imply that people must be or at least usually are aware that their environments are stressful. If stressors must be appraised as stressful (e.g. as implied in the well-known theory of Folkman and Lazarus, 1984; Lazarus, 1966; Lazarus and Launier, 1978), harmful, or threatening, for example, then one is apparently aware of the stress. But it may not be necessary for people to be aware of their situation as stressful in order for work-related stress to exist, that is, for occupational stressors to lead to individual strain responses. "Is it possible, for example, for people to believe they thrive on situations that are actually stressful and even to seek out such situations (e.g. Type A people; Friedman and Rosenman, 1974)?" (Beehr and Franz, 1987: 14).

When perceptions of environmental stressors were measured in the research program described here, they were usually treated as if they were in the environmental stressor part of the core relationship in Figure 1.2 rather than as intervening variables. It must be considered that this can be a weakness of measurement, as discussed in later chapters. In addition to perceptions of the environmental stressors, other elements of the process facet that are sometimes measured in job stress studies are physiological responses that are not by themselves always viewed as true diseases. Hypertension, a so-called "risk factor" for coronary heart disease, is an example that has been studied in the research program described here. When studied, though, it was treated as and labeled as one of Figure 1.2's strains or human consequences.

Variables surrounding the core relationship

In addition to the process facet, there are facets or other sets of variables that surround the core stressor–strain relationship. One of these is the personal facet, which consists of the employees' relatively stable characteristics that affect their perceptions, appraisals, or reactions to the stressors. Figure 1.2 shows that personal characteristics have been investigated in our research program as potential moderators. That is, some individual differences are expected to moderate the core relationship between stressors and strains.

In addition, however, some personal characteristics might have direct effects on human consequences. This would mean that there are personal characteristics leading to disease states. Of course this must be true. For example, one of the best predictors of coronary heart disease is family history. Another example is found in the assumption that physical fitness helps to prevent illness. Family history and physical fitness are personal characteristics. In occupational stress, however, we are most interested in personal characteristics when they moderate the core relationship. Except as nuisance factors, they are of little interest otherwise. This is true also for other

personal characteristics, such as abilities, needs, demographic characteristics, or physical characteristics.

If such personal characteristics are the only cause of strains, then there is
no occupational stress. If, for example, type A behavior (e.g. Burke, 1984;
Friedman and Rosenman, 1974; Ganster, 1987) is the only cause of coronary
heart disease or its risk factors (potential strains) in a study, there is no reason
to consider that to be a study of occupational stress. Although some sort of
stress may be involved, without evidence of an occupational stressor being
a potential cause of individual strain, this would not fit under the topic of
work-related stress. There have not been many consistent results regarding
personal characteristics that moderate the core relationship and the research
program described here has not focused on them very closely to date.
Whereas there is an entire chapter devoted to our research program's work
on one environmental moderator, social support, there is therefore no
chapter on personal characteristics as moderators. Our work on some of
them is noted, however, in passing as other topics are explored more directly
in subsequent chapters.

Another Beehr–Newman model facet consisting of important variables
that are frequently thought to be associated with occupational stress is the
organizational consequences facet. In contrast to the process facet and the
personal facet, this *is* included in Figure 1.2 because it has been part of the
subsequent research program. Organizational consequences consist of employee behaviors accompanying the occupational stress core relationship
that are of such direct importance to the organization's functioning that they
might be considered more important to the organization than to the individual. Changes in job performance, absenteeism, and turnover are typical
examples. These are so important to the organization that they are often
considered major criteria for evaluating some of the organization's human
resources programs (e.g. selection systems).

The adaptive responses of Figure 1.2 are concerned with any and all ways
of alleviating the aversive effects of occupational stress (basically, therefore,
ways of alleviating strains). These can be categorized along two dimensions:
curative versus preventive and individual-targeted versus organizational-
targeted (Newman and Beehr, 1979).

Curative treatments of occupational stress are those attempts to treat the
stressful situation after it has already arisen (Newman and Beehr, 1979).
Logically, they would be used after an occupational stress situation has been
diagnosed. Preventive treatments are those that could be used before a
stressful situation is manifest. If a diagnosis is done, it might determine that
the situation "only" has stress potential rather than one in which harmful
stress is already present. A treatment would therefore be preventive rather
than curative. In practice, however, many stress treatment programs are used
in both situations, that is, the same treatment is used regardless of the situation.
Unfortunately, this is often because no diagnosis of the situation was done.

The target of an occupational stress treatment attempt refers to the immediate entity that is the focus of change efforts. There are two categories of such targets: personal and organizational. While a great many person-targeted approaches are attempted, extremely few organization-targeted treatments of work stress have been attempted (Ivancevich and Matteson, 1987). Person-targeted treatments include any treatment effort aiming to change the characteristics or behaviors of the person more directly than characteristics of the organization. Examples include meditation, biofeedback, relaxation training, counseling or psychotherapy, and virtually any sort of training of the employee who is experiencing the stress (Beehr and Newman, 1978; Newman and Beehr, 1979). The potential examples of organizationally targeted treatments are more hypothetical, since they have rarely been attempted, but they would include any treatment effort that attempts to change some part of the organization more directly than the individuals who are experiencing stress. Examples would be job redesign, training of the stressed employee's supervisor (or of anyone associated with the stressed employee), restructuring the organization, adding assistants during a period of overload, role clarification, and so forth (Beehr and Newman, 1978; Newman and Beehr, 1979).

The choice of the immediate target of occupational stress often has several important implications and these are discussed in Chapter 7, where research on organizational outcomes of stress is examined. The implications include the implicit assumption about responsibility for the stressful situation, the ability and/or willingness of the individual and the organization to be changed, and the likelihood that the treatment will have relatively permanent effects. Within the Beehr–Newman model of Figure 1.1, most individually targeted treatments are aimed at changing elements of the human consequences facet, but sometimes they are aimed at the person facet or even the process facet. Organizationally targeted treatments are aimed at elements of the environmental facet. They could be aimed at elements of the organizational consequences facet, but if so they would probably be misguided as stress treatments, because the organizational consequences are not very direct causes of anything in the core relationship in the stress model. Besides the complications of stress treatments coming in such widely varying categories, another complication is the element of time. My own research on adaptive responses and techniques is highlighted in Chapters 7 and 8.

Time: the forgotten facet

Job stress research specifically on time has been minimal. The time facet in Figure 1.2 recognizes explicitly that many of the events and relationships in the model occur in sequence and over shorter or longer periods of time. Obviously, the differences between chronic and acute stressors, discussed earlier, suggest that time may be an important factor in determining categorizations of stressors, but the implications of these differences are not known yet. Little organizational research has been conducted on acute stressors, but there are models for this research to follow in the stressful life events literature. A notable study by Eden (1982) is promising for future research on critical job events. Two potential stressors for nursing students were studied: their first experience with patient care and their final examination, which consisted of demonstrations as well as written materials. These two "critical job events" were followed by increases in some measures of both psychological and physiological strains. Another study by Barling *et al.*, (1987) suggests that even dramatic acute events such as an explosion in a factory do not necessarily have much stressful effect, but this is not out of line with some other research. Popular stereotypes of occupational stress, the type that make for good television excitement, often have not appeared to be the most stressful things in the workplace. Instead, more ordinary and common events or states seem to be the ones that are stressful, that is, the ones that lead to individual strains. Examples can be found in police work. The best evidence so far indicates that being shot at by bad guys is less often a stressor for police than dealing with the police administration or court system or other more mundane things (Beehr, 1981a). Acute work stressors are in need of future systematic rearch.

Research issues include the relative strengths of effects of acute versus chronic stressors and the possibility that different coping or treatment activities may be more or less effective for stressors of different time limitations. In addition, it is unknown whether acute and chronic stressors affect the individual by leading to the same types of strains or not. For example, it might take long-term stressors (chronic) to cause some of the symptoms of coronary heart disease to appear, but certain acute, short-term stressors could touch off a depressive episode. Many types of comparisons between chronic and acute stress are important topics for future research.

Beehr and Bhagat (1985b) proposed a model of occupational stress in which duration of the stressors (a continuum of the length of time the stressors exist as opposed to a dichotomy between chronic and acute stressors) is a major factor in the severity of stress outcomes or strains. Further, we propose that the underlying psychological factor in many types of social psychological occupational stress situations is uncertainty regarding what to do in decision-making or choice situations. Our hypothesis is simply that the same amount and type of uncertainty over a long period of time will be more harmful and difficult to deal with than it would be over a shorter time period. This type of thinking seems more applicable to the chronic stress situation than to the acute stressors, however, because it is usually more easy to conceive of the chronic stressors occurring over a period of time rather than being "time-limited" by definition (as defined by Beehr and Franz, 1987).

The study of time as a social psychological variable is relatively new and in an exploratory stage (McGrath and Kelly (1986) explored this subject). Several ideas regarding research issues, both methodological and conceptual, have been developed recently regarding the importance of time in stress research (McGrath and Beehr, 1990). In non-experimental field research, which has been the dominant method used in occupational stress research, the timing of measurement is an example of a particularly tricky issue. Different physical, psychological, and behavioral changes may occur at different rates in response to stressors. An implication of this is that *when* to measure might turn out to be just as important as how and what to measure in this field. If this is the case, the field may have some serious issues to consider before future research can make strong new progress.

Time takes various forms and affects the stress process at various points. The person experiencing job stress, for example, is often at a (time-related) developmental stage of his or her life and career (McGrath and Beehr, 1990). Such long-term developmental stages of life and work are still not clearly understood, but the stressors one is likely to face, the way these are appraised, and the means at one's disposal to deal with them probably vary at different developmental stages.

Besides the slower moving human developmental stages, there are also likely to be more quickly recurring or cyclical episodes in one's work and personal life that could alter the effects of stressors and the ability to deal with them effectively. These could include such diverse recurring processes as biological cycles of the person and task cycles of the job. These are somewhat predictable in time, but they are time-related events that can interfere with both application and research in the area. Therefore, they are themselves fair game for investigation within occupational stress research (McGrath and Beehr, 1990).

In addition to the effects of time-related personal variables, examples also abound of time-related environmental variables that influence occupational stress and research on it. The chronic versus acute stressor concept and the duration of stressors concept have already been noted, but there are still others possible. For example, one effect of periodic or episodic stressors is that they may be more or less predictable (McGrath and Beehr, 1990). Knowing that a stressor is coming at a certain time (e.g. the annual tax deadline time for accountants) may be quite different from knowing that a stressor will occur but not knowing when (e.g. it is common to many university campuses that one can be sure that the computer will break down, but nobody can predict when). Regularity of such episodes over time makes them more or less predictable and perhaps makes the resulting stress situation more controllable in some ways. Knowing when a stressor is likely to occur may, for example, allows one to rearrange other parts of one's life to accommodate the situation temporarily. These other parts of one's life constitute the context within which occupational stress can be viewed. Since the appearance of the Beehr–Newman model in 1978, my colleagues and I have not conducted empirical research focusing on time as an element in occupational stress. We have further elaborated the theory about it, however, as described in various chapters. Most notably, Chapter 2 examines the elaboration developed with Bhagat. In addition, some research with Gupta examined relationships among measures obtained at different points in time regarding the organizational outcomes in Chapter 6.

THE CONTEXT: WORK IN RELATION TO THE REST OF LIFE

Work does not constitute all of one's life, although most research in industrial/ organizational psychology and organizational behavior could be accused of making this assumption. Researchers usually study relationships between work-related variables without reference to employees' lives outside of the workplace. Only occasionally is it made explicit that people's non-work situations affect what happens at work and vice versa (see Zedeck, 1992).

Theories arguing that there is a spillover effect (a consistent or positive relationship between work and non-work attitudes and behaviors), a compensatory effect (a negative relationship between work and non-work attitudes and behaviors), or no effect (the segmentation hypothesis, that there is no relationship between work and non-work attitudes and behaviors) have been proposed and studied for a period of decades (e.g. Gupta and Beehr, 1981; Kabanoff, 1980; Meissner, 1971; Wilensky, 1960), with typical results suggesting that the spillover effect is the most likely. These theories have a literature of their own that is outside the job stress research domain and they have had little impact on studies of job stress – or other topics of the organizational sciences for that matter. Although classic organization theory and practices have often considered only the work-related part of the employee, it is apparent that individuals have the audacity to enter work organizations as whole people, bringing with them a host of personal characteristics, situations, strengths, and weaknesses (Katz and Kahn, 1978).

Bhagat (1983) has noted that this situation is the norm in occupational stress research in particular as well as organizational psychology research in general and he developed a model of total life stress giving non-work stressors and the strains caused by them a prominent place in the etiology of work-related outcomes such as job involvement, performance effectiveness, and job satisfaction. Some support was subsequently found in tests of the model's propositions (Bhagat et al., 1985).

It is notable that the stressful life events research has typically included work-related elements in its domain, thus appearing to integrate the domains (e.g. Holmes and Rahe, 1967; Sarason et al., 1978). For example, the scales used in this research usually ask about work-related events (as well as many non-work events) such as retirement or changing jobs as potentially stressful events. The distinction between the two domains of stress, life and work, and their possible interaction has not been addressed explicitly in most of that research, however. Thus, it is impossible to tell from the research on stressful life events what the separate, joint, and independent effects of stress from each domain on the employee are.

It would be interesting, for example, to determine whether the types of stressors encountered by individuals within one role (work or home) are similar to or different from those encountered in another. This issue could have implications for the whole field of occupational stress. If people consistently encounter or report encountering the same types of stressors (e.g. overload) across roles, it may mean that some stable personal characteristics are strongly influential in the stress process. People might tend to perceive similar characteristics in their environments somewhat independently from the actual situation, they might consistently select themselves into objective situations that are characterized by particular types of stressors, or they might act in such as way as to create certain types of stressors in most of their life roles.

Alternatively, such studies might discover that types of stressors are situation-bound; for example, that work roles tend to be characterized by overload, family roles by ambiguity, and combinations of the two by conflict. Probably neither of these two scenarios will be found cleanly by such research, however. The interplay between personal characteristics and environmental roles no doubt is quite complex, but it needs more research.

The occupational stress topic in which there has been the most explicit recognition of the non-work context of work-related stress concerns the experience of female employees experiencing the stressor called inter-role conflict. Inter-role conflict is the condition in which there are conflicting demands or expectations of someone when these expectations arise from his or her occupying more than one role. The role of family member may demand that one be home for dinner at 5.30, while the role of manager in a certain company may require that person to continue working until the boss leaves at 6.00.

Inter-role conflict was explicitly ignored by Kahn et al. (1964) in their pioneering study of role conflict and ambiguity in the US workforce; instead, they focused on role conflicts occurring entirely within the work role. Most organizational stress researchers have followed suit ever since, perhaps because of a reluctance to depart from their primary area of expertise, the work setting. Exceptions (e.g. Greenhaus and Beutell, 1985; Herman, 1977; Shamir, 1983) have appeared, however, especially in research concerned with women's work role stress. Many women are newer to the workplace or career market than are men and their traditional emphasis on home and family activities is thought to make them more prone to placing equal and strong emphasis on both arenas, thereby heightening the conflict experienced.

It is likely that inter-role conflict will be on the rise for the foreseeable future, because there are more dual-career couples in the workforce in recent years (Greenhaus and Beutell, 1985; Gupta and Jenkins, 1985; Sekaran, 1983). As long as one member of a couple stayed home and took care of most of the non-work problems, the inter-role conflict between home and work was lessened, and in the traditional family, the woman served in this role. The male, in turn, could therefore devote more of his energies to the work role. If there were conflicts for either party, their priorities were clear; they could favor one role over the other and it was clearly known and acceptable to them and to others which role that "should" be. It is likely that in dual-career families, this picture has become clouded. There are demands that could come from either role for either person. How this is worked out probably varies from couple to couple, but there are likely to be residual cultural tendencies in the value system of many people. Thus there is a common observation that males still favor work over home relative to females and that females still favor home over work relative to males if their activities are observed. These residual cultural tendencies may be conceptualized in terms of the relative salience of work and home roles to males and females (Greenhaus and Beutell, 1985). Such cultural residuals need to be addressed by research, and such research could be done in any situation wherein current pressures or opportunities for people run counter to traditional cultural expectations for them.

These tendencies may vary according to whether the couple have careers or jobs. As noted by some of my colleagues a career–job continuum has been defined in part by the work-related attitudes held by the person (Gupta and Jenkins, 1985). People in careers are typically more committed (greater salience) to their work and are typically in jobs for which there is a progression through which the person develops over time (Gupta and Jenkins, 1985; Rapoport and Rapoport, 1971).

As depicted in Figure 1.3, dual-career couples have several sources of dual-career stress, some of which are unique to them and some of which they have in common with people who are not part of dual-career couples. Some they share with anybody who is part of a couple, regardless of whether they are dual-career couples, some they share with all people who work regardless of whether they are part of a couple, and some they share only with other members of dual-career couples (Gupta and Jenkins, 1985). This is important to keep clear when conducting research on dual-career couple stress, because it helps to sort out the real psychological meaning and impact of dual careers.

Only two of the six cells in the figure are unique to dual-career couples, although the literature often does not recognize this explicitly. People who are part of couples can experience stress from their relationship regardless of whether they work (cells 2 and 5). This type of stress, by itself, is not in the typical areas of expertise of organizational researchers. Anyone who

	Work role	Family role	Inter-role
From own role(s)	1 Experienced by job/career holders	2 Experienced by couples	3 Experienced by job/career holders
From interaction with partner's role(s)	4 Experienced by two-job/career couples	5 Experienced by couples	6 Experienced by two-job/career couples

Figure 1.3 Sources of dual-career stress (reprinted with permission from Gupta and Jenkins, 1985).

works can experience stress from the job role, regardless of whether he or she is part of a couple (cells 1 and 3). This type of stress has traditionally been within the areas of expertise of organizational researchers. Only people who are part of a couple who both work in careers experience the unique dual-career stressors (cells 2 and 6). Few researchers actually have broad enough expertise to work easily in this area. The occupational stress domain includes all areas of research in the table except cells 2 and 5, the cells concerned with the stress of people who are part of couples but not necessarily part of the workforce. Regarding the stressors unique to dual-career couples (cells 4 and 6), large scale (and therefore potentially representative) studies are still rather rare, in spite of the wide-ranging publicity of the problem (Gupta and Jenkins, 1985). In addition, it has been noted that there has been frequent use of unreliable scales, of open-ended scales that may make coding difficult, and of one- or two-item scales in much of the research on work–family conflict (Greenhaus and Beutell, 1985). Although our research helped to identify the relationships among the different domains of life that can be susceptible to stress (Gupta and Beehr, 1981) and we have examined coping as it occurs at both home and work (Beehr, Johnson, and Nieva, 1989), more and better research is still needed in this domain.

SUMMARY

Occupational stress has been studied from the perspectives of a wide variety of disciplines and personal preferences and because of this, there is no universally accepted definition of the term, the topic, or the preferred mode of treatment. This state of confusion is itself a topic in need of research. Such research could tie together the different approaches or it could provide a taxonomic framework defining their similarities and differences. The Beehr and Franz (1987) categorization is offered as a modest taxonomy based on generalizations derived from the basic themes in four disciplines. A more complete taxonomy should be developed and tested, however. The taxonomy would then help define the field for future research.

The Beehr and Newman (1978) model of occupational stress summarized and allowed categorization of many of the current research issues in the field. The core idea is the general definition of occupational stress, that is, that job stressors lead to individual strains. This book discusses the research on occupational stress conducted by my colleagues and me over a couple of decades and the extent of this program of research is illustrated in Figure 1.2. Not all parts of the Beehr–Newman model have yet been examined and there is therefore much yet to do.

This process facet is still one of the most mysterious and untouched parts of the model for organizational psychology researchers. One specific direction for research is proposed in the next chapter, namely the idea that the psychological state of uncertainty underlies many of the types of occupational stress situations that have been of interest to organizational scientists. Many of the variables surrounding the core relationship in the stress model have been of interest to a broad range of industrial and organizational psychologists over the years. They include individual difference variables, work environment variables such as social support (which is examined in detail in a later chapter), job satisfaction and other work attitudes, and organizationally relevant criterion variables such as job performance, absenteeism, and turnover. In addition, the model highlights the importance of coping, treatment, and adaptation techniques specifically related to job stress. Time is the forgotten facet, but it is important for both methodological reasons (e.g. it is an obvious factor in longitudinal designs) and because it is a factor in the development of many stress reactions.

Finally, the context of work is important. Research has examined some work–non-work relationships over the years, but only a little of it has focused on occupational stress. Working women's inter-role (work–home) conflict is the occupational stress topic that has received the most work and within this topic, dual career couples have become the objects of particular interest. There is a need for more and better quality research on the context of occupational stress. This is a topic that my colleagues and I have yet to explore ourselves, but it nevertheless seems important.

The empirical research on occupational stress by my colleagues and myself has examined much but not all of the original Beehr–Newman model. Figure 1.2 illustrates the domains included by this program of research until now and the subsequent chapters delineate the research program on these stress elements. The first part of the book sets the stage by explaining how we have developed some models and theories of occupational stress. Parts II, III, and IV lay out our empirical research on the theoretical causes or stressors in the workplace, the outcomes of stress to the individual and the organization, and the means of alleviating problems of stress in the workplace, respectively. Part V, consisting of a single chapter, outlines conclusions and recommendations drawn from the research program.

Chapter 2

Models and theoretical approaches to occupational stress

The likelihood that "stress" will fade away from our vocabulary is as good as are the chances that the state will wither away in Communist Russia.

(Kasl, 1987)

In 1978, Beehr and Newman identified thirty-seven job or organizational characteristics that might be occupational stressors and these were split into four categories: job demands and task characteristics, role demands or expectations, organizational characteristics or conditions, and organizations' external demands and conditions. Although the thirty-seven potential stressor areas were not considered to be exhaustive, the list was still somewhat comprehensive and it included nearly all of the stressors that were currently in the literature as having been studied or even discussed. Most of them, in fact, had not been studied in any relatively rigorous way at all. Since then, an increasing number of studies of occupational stress have appeared in the research literature. Figure 2.1 shows this trend by plotting the entries appearing each year since 1970 in the index of *Psychological Abstracts* under the heading of occupational stress. Regarding Kasl's (1987) quote beginning this chaptaer, although the state in Russia may not be fading away in the manner predicted by communist theory, communism itself seems recently to be disappearing in Eastern Europe; Figure 2.1 indicates that occupational stress is far from fading away in psychology's research vocabulary, however.

With this rapidly increasing research interest in the topic, more stressors have been identified but there is still no clearly accepted, universally used categorization of stressors. In addition to the four categories indicated above, other examples of categorizations have included opportunity stress (opportunities to have something desirable), constraints on attaining something desirable, and demands on attaining something desirable when its attainment is uncertain (e.g. Schuler, 1980); the lack of fit between what someone desires and what the job can supply, and the lack of fit between what is demanded of the person by the job and the abilities or resources that the person has to meet those demands (e.g. Caplan *et al.*, 1975; Harrison, 1985); organizational characteristics and processes, job demands and role

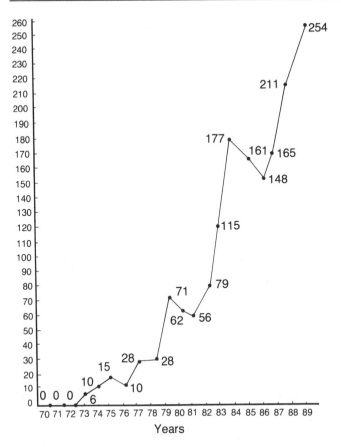

Figure 2.1 Annual entries under "occupational stress" in the indices of *Psychological Abstracts* from 1970 to 1989 (updated from Beehr, 1987, Figure 4.1).

characteristics, and individual characteristics and expectations (Beehr and Schuler, 1982; Brief *et al.*, 1981); and physical environment, individual level stressors, group level stressors, and organizational level stressors (Ivancevich and Matteson, 1980). Obviously, there are many opinions about the nature of occupational stressors and also more than one way of categorizing the same stressors. In addition, there has been more than one well-known model of occupational stress from which to choose.

MODELS OF OCCUPATIONAL STRESS

If we restrict the discussion to occupational stress, rather than general life stress models, perhaps the best known is the so-called Michigan model, emanating from the University of Michigan and its Institute for Social Research

(ISR). In fact, there is apparently not a single Michigan model of occupational stress as writers seem to believe. We have noted elsewhere (Jex and Beehr, 1991) that this social environmental model of stress, which comes from ISR research (Figure 2.2), was an early conceptualization of the occupational stress process. In this well-known model, the environment affects the person's perception of it, which in turn affects their responses, which finally influence the individual's health (French and Kahn, 1962; Katz and Kahn, 1978). Individual differences and elements of the social environment can alter these relationships. This is one of the two basic Michigan models and researchers have sometimes elaborated upon it to make it fit their particular interests (e.g. House (1974) especially added some coping processes to the model).

A second well-known Michigan model from ISR is the Person–Environment Fit model (P–E Fit; French *et al.*, 1974). It can be considered a very specific elaboration of the properties of the person and the person's environment (both subjective and objective). While many researchers sometimes use person–environment fit language quite loosely, the ISR P–E Fit model is rather constrained. There are two specific types of person–

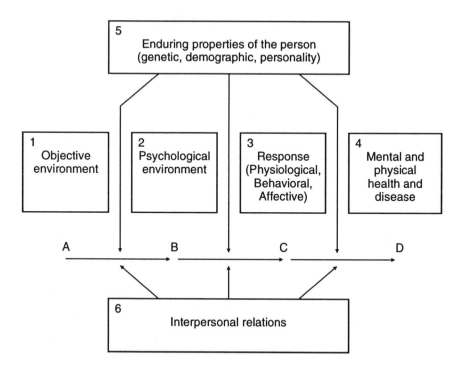

Figure 2.2 Katz and Kahn's model of work stress (reprinted with permission from Katz and Kahn, 1978).

environment misfit that are expected to lead to ill health and welfare for the employee: misfit of the individual's needs and preferences with the organization's or job's provision of rewards and supplies; and misfit of the individual's skills and abilities with the job's demands and requirements (Harrison, 1985). Furthermore, these fits are meant to be in regard to very specific domains. For example, researchers might consider the fit between a person's need or preference for something as specific as having a single yearly deadline for all work with the job's requirement for such a deadline.

The third well-known occupational stress model, not known as a Michigan model this time, comes from McGrath (1976) (Figure 2.3). In this model, an objective situation is perceived, as in the social environmental model of Figure 2.2, but there is a stronger emphasis placed on appraisal in this perception process than is found in the social environmental model. This appraisal leads to the decision making phase of the model, resulting in a decision to engage in a specific response. The response here is primarily voluntary behavior, rather than a combination of behavioral, physiological, and psychological responses as in the social environmental model. While those two models are consistent with each other, they differ in the type of outcomes that are the focus. While the social environmental model focuses more on the types of individual strains that are emphasized in this book, the decision processing model virtually ignores these aversive outcomes to the individual in favor of explaining voluntary behavior, especially task performance. The well-known decision processing model, therefore, is not directly relevant to the type of occupational stress explored in the research program explored here and its emphasis on performance behavior is somewhat unusual in the organizational psychology literature on occupational stress.

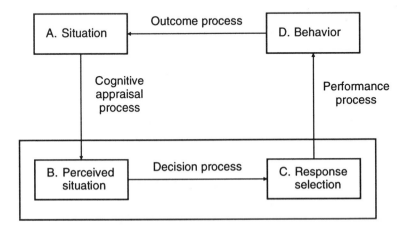

Figure 2.3 McGrath's response selection model of stress (reprinted with permission from McGrath, 1976).

THE ROLE OF UNCERTAINTY IN ORGANIZATIONAL PSYCHOLOGY

It has been argued that an experience common to many of the job stressors in the organizational psychology approach is uncertainty and another recent model of occupational stress is built upon this argument (Beehr and Bhagat, 1985a). The term uncertainty has a history of use in industrial/organizational (I/O) psychology and especially in organization theory (e.g. Galbraith, 1977; Thompson, 1967) and this makes the concept attractive as an explanatory variable in occupational stress, but one must be clear how the variable is defined conceptually and operationally each time it is used. In conjunction with occupational stress, uncertainty has been defined as the "micro" (individual level) condition in which the employee is required to or desires to make a response or take an action but is not sure about important outcomes that might follow their various actions.

In other common uses of the term in I/O psychology, uncertainty refers to one or more "macro" (organizational level) conditions. At the most general level, the concept of organization itself implies predictability and, therefore, a type of certainty. Uncertainty within an organization is often reduced by pressures toward uniformity of behaviors of organization members. Such uniformity is, after all, a part of the essence of organized human actions. It provides predictability for organization members, allowing planning and more efficient work in the organization.

Uncertainty outside the organization (i.e. in the organization's environment) is also a problem for managers and management theories often recommend a "looser" organization style to cope with such uncertainty at the organization level. Thus, for example, contingency theories have long maintained that relatively flexible, organic structures are more effective for organizations or parts of organizations dealing with uncertain or rapidly changing environments, while relatively rigid, mechanistic structures are recommended for efficiency in dealing with stable environments (e.g. Burns and Stalker, 1966; Lawrence and Lorsch, 1967).

Uncertainty has also been used at a group level, in defining types of inputs from the environment that are relevant to organizational groups such as hospital emergency units (Argote, 1982). Thus, uncertainty has been a concept of theoretical interest at all levels of organizational psychology, but especially at the more macro levels. Occupational stress is primarily a micro or individual level concept, however, and the theoretical role of uncertainty in job stress must be conceived mainly at this level.

An obvious area in need of investigation is the degree to which uncertainty at all of the conceptual levels of organizational psychology is related. Is uncertainty at the macro or organizational level related to uncertainty at the group and individual levels? If there is a relationship, is it causal? There is an intuitive argument that there could be such a relationship between uncertainty in the environment (as in Lawrence and Lorsch, 1967) and role ambiguity and uncertainty stress (defined below) at the micro or individual level, at least among those individuals in the organization who have to deal with the part of the environment that is uncertain. Uncertainty at the group level might also be affected by the environmental uncertainty if the group is close to the organizational boundary (as in Argote, 1982).

Other scenarios could be constructed, but it does appear possible that the different levels of uncertainty could be related to each other. Uncertainty at the individual level is of foremost interest here, however, and it would be especially instructive regarding occupational stress to determine how this type of uncertainty is related to other types. One could postulate a causal effect, for example, in which macro level uncertainty in the environment tends to result in uncertainty at the individual level. Perhaps high level people and/or others in the organization who deal with the environment can buffer others in the organization from experiencing the stress at their or-ganizational locations. If so, is there an especially high "cost" to the buffer person in terms of stress? Perhaps misery loves company and a trouble shared is a trouble halved; the sharing of uncertainty might make its stressful impact less. The themes of the social support literature are consistent with this idea.

UNCERTAINTY OF EXPECTATIONS AS A CRITICAL VARIABLE IN OCCUPATIONAL STRESS

It has been noted that there is a need for theory to guide more of the organizational psychology research on job stress (Schneider, 1985). In one theoretical development, it has been proposed that many of the types of stressors from the organizational psychology perspective have in common some resulting uncertainty. This uncertainty is posited as a central variable within the process facet of the Beehr–Newman model (1978) described in Chapter 1. It is, therefore, a model limited to a more specific part of the stress process than that meta-model was.

It is interesting that a review of occupational stress from an engineering psychology viewpoint also concluded that "if any one variable were to be singled out as the predominant underlying source of occupational stress it would be uncertainty" (Sharit and Salvendy, 1982: 150). Beehr and Bhagat (1985b) proposed that uncertainty, importance, and duration combine to define and determine the strength of a stressful situation at work. Of these, uncertainty is the key concept. For many stressful situations in the workplace, the individual must take action and uncertainty regarding the result of this action is proposed as the essence of job stress in many of these situations. The three elements are proposed to combine multiplicatively, so that experienced stress (S) = Uncertainty (Uc) × Importance (I) × Duration (D). The basic reasoning behind the proposal of a multiplicative function is that for most of the stressful situations studied in organizational psychology, if any of these three elements (Uc, I, D) is missing or zero, no stress is experienced.

Uncertainty is the key concept in this approach and its definition in this framework comes from expectancy theory (Beehr and Bhagat, 1985b). Many approaches to occupational stress seem to be consistent with the idea that stress is something that *happens to* people and this obscures the fact that people do tend to be proactive, so that they have goals and try to make things happen as well as waiting for things to happen to them. Expectancy theory of motivation is consistent with this assumption that people are proactive and it can be used to explain the type of uncertainty inherent in some stressful situations.

In the simplest forms of expectancy theory, motivation = expectancy × valence. Expectancy can be broken into more than one type and two of them are of relevance here: the expectancy that one's efforts will lead to performance (E→P) and the expectancy that one's performance is linked to obtaining specific outcomes (P→O; Lawler, 1973). Expectancies are basically subjective probabilities that people may have regarding the likelihood that two events are linked with each other. Expectancy theory can be thought of as a proactive theory in the sense that it assumes that people are or can be forward-looking; they consider what will occur in the future based on their actions in the present, and they act and plan to act based on such thinking. Past experience, of course, can be one of the important influences on expectancies about the future.

While expectancy theory of motivation in the workplace is concerned with the *level* or strength of subjective expectancies, it is argued that the link of expectancies to stress in the workplace concerns the person's *uncertainty* about these expectancies (Beehr and Bhagat, 1985b). If the individual has work-related goals (outcomes) that he or she seeks but is not sure what path will lead to them, there is some uncertainty regarding expectancies. The two expectancies or paths that are usually the foci when expectancy theory is used in the workplace are (1) performance as a path to rewards and (2) effort as a path to performance (e.g. Lawler, 1973; Vroom, 1964). Although there are often other possible ways to obtain important outcomes in the workplace, performance is one of the most culturally acceptable and organizationally sanctioned ways. That is, pay raises, promotions, and other such rewards (outcomes) are supposed to be provided based on job performance, according to common cultural and offical organizational values. Therefore, the uncertainty theory of motivation focuses on uncertainty related to performance, either uncertainty regarding what leads to performance (effort) or uncertainty regarding what performance leads to (outcomes such as rewards).

Expectancy theory of motivation is a general theory rather than a work-specific theory. In other words, it is suposed to be able to explain motivation to engage in any behavior, not just work-related behaviors. In the work setting, organizational psychologists have usually used the theory to explain behaviors related specifically to job performance. The uncertainty model of job stress is consistent with this tradition. This may be wise as a starting point in understanding work-related stress using this framework, but it should be recognized that behaviors other than strictly defined job performance can be important in the workplace and these could also be sources of stress. For example, instead of or in addition to job performance being a path to the outcome of a promotion, marrying the boss's daughter might result in a promotion. If so, the uncertainty that specific efforts (courtship) will lead to the behavior (marriage to the daughter) might be stressful and the uncertainty that the behavior (marriage) will lead to the outcome (promotion) might be stressful. It seems logical to focus on performance in initial statements and tests of the uncertainty theory, but a fuller understanding of this approach to occupational stress might eventually require research on other types of behaviors in the workplace.

The focus here is on stress due to uncertainty regarding the way to reach important goals. Uncertainty is the first element of the model, and it is obviously related to the expectancy theory of motivation. Importance, the second element of the stress model proposed here, is akin to valence in expectancy theory. It is the importance of the outcomes that are relevant in the work situation, that is, the importance that the outcomes have to the individual employee. It is intuitively obvious that stronger responses, including stress responses, are likely when important outcomes are at stake rather than when unimportant ones are apparent. If an employee is uncertain how to do a job in order to avoid being fired, this usually involves a more important outcome than a situation in which the employee is uncertain how to do the job in order to obtain a longer lunch break. Stress due to uncertainty is expected to be greater when the outcomes are of more importance to the individual. Expectancy theory of motivation has a close parallel to importance, namely the valence that is attached to outcomes. Importance of outcome can actually be considered an individual difference variable rather than a property of the outcomes, because the same potential outcome is valued differently by different people.

The third element of the stress model is duration (Beehr and Bhagat, 1985b). This relates to the relatively unresearched time facet of job stress from the Beehr and Newman (1978) model described in Chapter 1. It is expected that a type of uncertainty experienced over a longer period of time will be more stressful or result in more serious strains than the same uncertainty experienced for a shorter period of time. As with importance, the argument regarding the role of duration in the stress process is intuitively logical, although it has not really been tested.

Duration of uncertainty and duration as a factor in job stress in general needs more research. Pardine (1987), in a study described in more detail later in this chapter, has done some tentative analyses of job tenure as a surrogate measure of duration of uncertainty. If people have been in a specific job longer, they may have also been in their current stressful situation longer. Therefore, job tenure could be related to duration in the uncertainty model. For longer job tenured employees uncertainty tended to mediate the relationship between role stressors and strains more than it did for shorter job tenured employees, and this was taken as tentative support for the importance of the concept of duration. At this point, it seems odd that such an intuitively obvious component as duration of stress has received so little research attention. It is an area ripe for more research activity.

According to this uncertainty approach of Beehr and Bhagat (1985a), uncertainty regarding E→P and/or P→O expectancies (or both) is the common result of many environmental stressors. In the Beehr and Newman (1978) model, described in Chapter 1, such uncertainty would be a part of the process facet. It is an internal state of the person that occurs after the exposure to an occupational stressor (in the environmental facet) and before the actual strains occur (in the human consequences facet). Importance is part of the person facet, because it is a somewhat stable, individual difference characteristic of the person, and duration, of course, is part of the time facet. The uncertainty model of Beehr and Bhagat (1985b), therefore, fits within the meta-model of job stress (Beehr and Newman, 1978), just as most other job stress theories do.

The uncertainty model is also consistent with a four-stage model of occupational stress developed by McGrath (1976), in which the employee is exposed to a potentially stressful situation, perceives it, chooses a response aimed at improving the situation, acts, and is then exposed to a new situation, partially of their own making. As in that model, the Beehr and Bhagat model assumes that people are proactive and take some actions in stressful situations. The uncertainty, however, reduces the ability to make an informed decision regarding what action to take. It is interesting that McGrath's model was somewhat similar to the present one even though his outcome was performance (in the organizational consequences facet) instead of an individual strain (in the human consequences facet), the primary outcome of the present model. Besides the potential uncertainty regarding response selection, another similarity with McGrath's model is that McGrath maintained that another determinant of stress is the level of the perceived consequence of task performance. This is similar to the present model's second concept, importance of the consequences.

Uncertainty and role ambiguity

Since role ambiguity is one of the stressors in the environmental facet and uncertainty is an element in the process facet of the Beehr and Newman (1978) model, an obvious difficulty is the determination of the differences between the two. They must be different theoretically if they appear as two different variables in two different places of the same model. Their labels, uncertainty and ambiguity, give little or no clue regarding how they are inherently different and the difference is only that which is defined operationally by researchers. Role ambiguity has been used in occupational stress research, along with some other role stressors including role conflict and role overload, to mean stressors in the workplace – which are part of the environmental facet of the Beehr–Newman model. Uncertainty, on the other hand, is used by Beehr and Bhagat (1985b) as a label for an element of the process facet that results from some environmental stressors.

Role stressors are characteristics of the work role and in social psychology, roles are often defined by expectations that members of a role set have for the behaviors of the person occupying a given role (Biddle, 1979; Kahn *et al.*, 1964; Sarbin and Allen, 1969). In the workplace, members of an employee's role set typically include the supervisor, co-workers, subordinates, and any other people who interact with the role incumbent and hold expectations or make demands of them in the workplace. Role ambiguity, therefore, refers to lack of clarity of these expectations and of messages in any and all their forms sent by members of a role set to the role incumbent. It is different from uncertainty, then, which is the role incumbent's certainty regarding effort-to-performance and performance-to-outcome expectancies. Role ambiguity, as well as some other stressors, are likely to lead to uncertainty, however.

Pearce (1981) noted that role ambiguity has been operationalized differently in different research articles, but primarily in two ways: as unpredictability or information deficiency. While the Beehr and Bhagat (1985a) model agrees with this insight, they prefer to label information deficiency in the environment as role ambiguity and to label unpredictability as uncertainty. This seems more consistent with role theory's definitions, because role expectations are in the person's environment. Deficiency of information from the environment can cause people to be uncertain regarding their expectancies, however. While this distinction can be made conceptually, clearly different operationalizations of the two are more difficult to devise.

As noted by Pearce, only one study (Beehr, 1976) clearly operationalized role ambiguity as unpredictability. The Beehr and Bhagat (1985a) framework kept unpredictability as the key aspect of occupational stress, but it defined role ambiguity as information deficiency, making it more consistent with other uses of the term. According to Pearce, information deficiency may not always be stressful, but it is likely to lead to dissatisfaction. The uncertainty model of Beehr and Bhagat is consistent with Pearce's discussion conceptually, although it used the term role ambiguity differently. It argues that information deficiency (role ambiguity) is stressful *if* it leads to unpredictability (uncertainty). As with Pearce, it is the unpredictability (uncertainty) that is most clearly associated with most experiences of job stress.

EMPIRICAL STUDIES MEASURING UNCERTAINTY OF EXPECTATIONS

The task of developing measures of uncertainty will be a difficult one. An ideal uncertainty index would measure uncertainty of both E→P and P→O expectancies and would not be confused with either environmental role ambiguity or the expectancies themselves.

The first of the two sources of possible confusion is evident from Pearce's (1981) article. In addition to the similarity in labels and concepts, many of the role ambiguity indices that have been used in previous research have measured unpredictability, which seems identical to uncertainty. The second source of confusion, that is the potential confusion of uncertainty of expectations with the levels of expectancies themselves, brings to mind the difficulty of measuring expectancy levels in expectancy theory research. Perhaps one reason for the difficulty in measuring expectancies derives from the varying levels of uncertainty that people experience regarding their expectancies. If people are unsure what their E→P and P→O expectancies are, it would be very difficult to measure these subjective states. While the present focus is on uncertainty of expectancies and accompanying stress, research focusing on expectancy theory of motivation might profit from considering the degree to which people are certain about their expectancies, perhaps as a moderator of motivation predicted from levels of reported expectancies.

Measuring uncertainty of expectations is likely to be difficult, but three attempts at scale development have been undertaken.

Uncertainty among hospital nurses

The first of these attempts focused on differentiating the uncertainty of expectancies from the strength or level of those expectancies by priming respondents to be aware of the difference (Beehr, 1987; Beehr et al., 1986). The uncertainties of hospital nurses were studied. Prior to the study, however, a major task was the development of measures of uncertainty. Three samples of college students who worked at least part-time were examined in an iterative effort at scale development and the resulting instrument was administered to a sample of hospital nurses as part of the main study.

Regarding the development of the uncertainty scale, some items were taken from occupational stress literature scales and others were newly developed, all based on researchers' judgments about their face validity for measuring E→P or P→O uncertainties. Most of the items from the previous literature came from occupational stress studies, especially those using role ambiguity as a variable. In these, however, Pearce's (1981) concept of unpredictability was the focus for item selection rather than information deficiency. Four hundred and sixty two students in an introductory psychology class at a medium-sized, midwestern university then answered the questions regarding jobs in which they currently or formerly had worked. The questionnaire contained forty-nine items, twenty-five intended to measure E→P uncertainty and twenty-four intended to measure P→O uncertainty. The responses were obtained on a seven-point, agree-to-disagree Likert type scale. Based on item-total correlations, fourteen E→P and fifteen P→O items were retained and used in the second questionnaire administration. The resulting P→O scale had poor reliability in spite of this procedure. Therefore eleven more items were written that were intended to measure P→O uncertainty and these were added to the questionnaire for the second administration.

The items on the second iteration of the questionnaire were rewritten, if possible, to be answered on a seven-point Likert scale with the points labeled "very unsure," "a little unsure," "unsure," "neither sure nor unsure," " a little sure," "sure," and "very sure." For six P→O and ten E→P uncertainty items, it was not deemed possible to rewrite them for the new scale and still keep them very close to the same wording used in the original items. Therefore, they were kept on the agree–disagree scale used in the first administration. Based on the researchers' concerns that some respondents in the first administration may have answered the questions by reporting their levels of expectancies rather than the uncertainty they had about the level of expectancies, further changes were made in the second iteration. For those items answered on the "sureness" scale, respondents first were asked to answer each item true or false. That is, they were asked whether they held this expectancy or not. They then were asked to answer the same item on the second scale, which was the extent to which they were sure of their expectancy. The true–false question was intended to prime the respondents by sensitizing them to the difference between their perceptions of their expectancy levels and the certainty they have about those levels.

Two hundred and thirty three introductory psychology students at the same university answered the questionnaire during the second scale de-velopment phase. Thirty-five items were retained for a third iteration based on their item reliabilities in the E→P or P→O scale.

One hundred and seventy-three students in upper division courses in a four-year business-oriented college in the midwest comprised the sample for the third iteration. Seven new items, all designed to measure E→P uncertainty, were added to the thirty-five items remaining from the second iteration. This was because the E→P uncertainty index in the second iteration had a lower reliability than the P→O uncertainty index did. The response scales were the same as in the second iteration. One item was deleted from the E→P uncertainty index based on its item-total correlation, but its deletion had no effect on the index's reliability at the second decimal point.

Table 2.1 contains some results of the three iterations of the scale de-velopment phase of the study. The emphasis was on obtaining reliable indices for each type of uncertainty and the reliabilities of the final indices were 0.85 for the E→P uncertainty and 0.84 for the P→O uncertainty. The

Table 2.1 Results of uncertainty scale development (Beehr *et al.*, 1986)

Administration	Number of respondents	Original numbers of items	Original alphas	Final numbers of items [a]	Final alphas
		E→P P→O	E→P P→O	E→P P→O	E→P P→O
First	462	25	0.38	14	0.79
		24	0.24	15	0.63
Second	233	14	0.67	13	0.76
		26	0.74	22	0.81
Third	173	20	0.85	19	0.85
		22	0.84	22	0.84

a   After deleting items with low item-total correlations

ten best items for each uncertainty index are in appendices A and B. For the sake of parsimony, these could be used without much loss of reliability.

Because the second and third items of the E→P index were so similar, the eleventh best item replaced the third item in the main study of hospital nurses. This item read, "If I loafed at work, my work performance would suffer." The uncertainty indices developed from the college samples were administered to a random sample of registered nurses from seven hospitals in Michigan that were chosen to represent a variety of hospital sizes. Two hundred and twenty five nurses (response rate of 67.7 percent) completed the questionnaire. Ninety-three percent were females, 74.1 percent were married, 81.5 percent had at least an associate's degree or nursing diploma, their experience in nursing ranged from one to thirty-five years, and their average age was about 35.5 years.

This was part of a larger, federally funded study of nursing role conflict in seven mid-Michigan hospitals and another study focusing on social support was also derived from these data. It is described in a subsequent chapter. The hospitals were quite varied in size and types of communities, but their environments ranged from rural to small city. Two were in a city with an approximately 100,000 population, two were in cities with populations from 25,000 to 30,000, and three were in towns with populations of less than 10,000. They employed from nineteen to more than 300 staff nurses. At the larger hospitals, randomly selected nurses were chosen for participation. The questionnaires were distributed and collected on-site by the researchers themselves.

The uncertainty indices in that study had alpha reliabilities of 0.78 and 0.75 for E→P and P→O expectancies, respectively. As expected, the reliabilities were lower than they were in the samples on which they were developed, but they were deemed acceptable. The means were 59.72 and 57.11 and the standard deviations were 5.46 and 6.47 for the E→P and P→O expectancies, respectively.

The indices were part of a larger questionnaire that also included measures of job stressors and of individual strains. For stressors, there were two measures of role conflict (one specially created for the study and one from Rizzo *et al.*, 1970) and one measure of role ambiguity (Beehr, 1976). The two role conflict measures were combined because of their high intercorrelation.

For strains, there were measures of depression (Zung, 1965), job satisfaction (a combination of eight facet-specific items developed for the study based on preliminary interviews and four global satisfaction items from Quinn and Shepard, 1974), and the three subscales of the Maslach Burnout Inventory (emotional exhaustion, depersonalization, and personal accomplishment; Maslach and Jackson, 1981).

In addition, propensity to leave was measured by thirteen items asking about the nurses' desires and plans to leave their jobs or profession.

The correlations of the uncertainty scales with the two job stressors (role conflict and role ambiguity) were all significant, but weak (range was 0.12 to 0.22; Table 2.2). Seven of their ten correlations with the psychological strains were significant. Depersonalization (a form of burnout) was not related to either type of uncertainty and emotional exhaustion (another form of burnout) was not related to the P→O uncertainty. The range of the significant cor-

Table 2.2 Correlation of uncertainties with role stressors, psychological strains, and employees' intentions to quit

	Correlation with uncertainties	
	$E{\rightarrow}P$	$P{\rightarrow}O$
Role stressors		
Role conflict	0.18**	0.12*
Role ambiguity	0.22**	0.19**
Psychological strains		
Depressed mood	0.21**	0.14*
Job dissatisfaction	0.24**	0.13*
Burnout		
Emotional exhaustion	0.13*	0.05
Depersonalization	0.04	0.07
Low personal accomplishment	0.32**	0.23**
Intentions to quit	0.28**	0.13

* $p<0.05$
** $p<0.01$

relations was 0.13 to 0.32, with the strongest being between the E→P uncertainty and low personal accomplishment (the third form of burnout). The E→P uncertainty was related to propensity to leave (0.28) but the P→O uncertainty was not.

From this study, it appears that uncertainty is somewhat promising as a variable in the occupational stress process. It seems possible to develop reliable measures of uncertainty. The two measures correlated with each other quite strongly, however (0.58), bringing into question their discriminant validity. An obvious question is how strongly even perfect measures of the two types of uncertainty would correlate with each other. That is, to what extent do they tend to occur together in the actual world of work? They probably do co-vary somewhat, but there are no theories or data that clearly answer this question.

It was also obvious in the data that the E→P uncertainty correlates consistently more strongly with job stressors, psychological strains, and propensity to leave than the P→O uncertainty does. For all seven of the variables for which there were significant correlations, the correlation with the E→P uncertainty was stronger than the correlation with the P→O uncertainty. If this result is consistently replicated in other research so that it appears to be generally true, there are potential theoretical implications. E→P expectancies more clearly refer to internal or intrinsic reward expectancies than the P→O expectancies do and the P→O expectancies are more obviously external or extrinsic than the E→P expectancies (Beehr and Bhagat, 1985b). In addition, the E→P expectancy items have more of the character of uncertainty regarding very specific, work-related internal control items than the P→O uncertainty items have. Therefore, future research on this uncertainty could have implications for internal–external control theories.

The data suggest, therefore, that uncertainty regarding intrinsic expectancies might be more stressful than uncertainty regarding extrinsic expectancies. If this is the case, then some more insight into occupational stress might be gained by focusing on some intrinsic motivation theories, such as achievement motivation and self-related motivation theories (e.g. Raynor and McFarlin, 1986), uncertainty orientation (e.g. Sorrentino and Short, 1986) or job redesign theory (e.g. Hackman and Oldham, 1980).

Uncertainty among employed evening students

A second study, not one of my own, used the Beehr and Bhagat (1985a) uncertainty model and focused on uncertainty of expectancies as a critical component of occupational stress. It represents an important test of the uncertainty ideas, since there have been few such tests. It is therefore explained in some detail here even though it is not part of my own program of research. Pardine (1987) used the Beehr and Bhagat (1985a) model to develop three hypotheses: (1) that the importance workers place on specific outcomes would moderate the relationship between uncertainty and strains; (2) that role conflict would be related to E→P uncertainty while role ambiguity would be related to both E→P and P→O uncertainties; and (3) that E→P uncertainty would mediate the relationships between role conflict and strains while both E→P and P→O uncertainties would mediate the relationships between role ambiguity and strains.

The hypotheses were derived directly from the uncertainty model of stress (Beehr and Bhagat, 1985a). The first hypothesis is part of the model in which importance and uncertainty are proposed to combine multiplicatively to lead to the experience of stress. Regarding the second hypothesis, role conflict was proposed to lead to E→P uncertainty on the grounds that it may be especially difficult to know how to direct one's efforts effectively when there are conflicting demands on those efforts. That is, if different people expect conflicting things from the employee, they cannot know very clearly what the relationship is between their efforts and overall performance. To please one of the role senders makes it more difficult or impossible to please the other and, therefore, it may be uncertain how overall performance will be assessed based on efforts directed toward either set of demands (Beehr and Bhagat, 1985a).

Hypothesis two also predicted that role ambiguity, on the other hand, was expected to be related to both E→P and P→O uncertainties (Beehr and Bhagat, 1985a). It was expected to be related to certainty regarding the relationship between effort and performance because the individual will be uncertain how to direct their efforts if the demands of the job and the corresponding messages from role senders are ambiguous. If the definition of performance is ambiguous, which it is in many cases of role ambiguity, it is difficult to know what efforts will lead to performance; and if demands regarding the direction of effort are ambiguous, as can also happen with role ambiguity, again the employee can be uncertain about the probability of their efforts leading to performance. The performance-to-outcome expectancy can also be uncertain in the face of role ambiguity, because role ambiguity has been a broad enough concept to cover demands regarding expected performance, demands regarding directions of efforts or activities, and even outcomes that could be expected contingent upon satisfactory performance. Therefore, it has been hypothesized that the job stressors called role ambiguity could lead to both E→P and P→O uncertainties (Beehr and Bhagat, 1985a; Pardine, 1987).

Pardine's (1987) third hypothesis, also based directly on the uncertainty theory of Beehr and Bhagat (1985a), proposed that the relationships of the role stressors with the individual strains would be mediated by the uncertainties. Even more specifically, the relationship between role conflict and strain would be mediated or accounted for by E→P uncertainty and the relationship between role ambiguity and strain would be accounted for by the combination of both E→P and P→o uncertainties.

Pradine's (1987) role ambiguity measure was composed of two types of items: inadequate information regarding the consequences of the employee's actions and insufficient information concerning the outcomes of the employee's actions. Both of these were information inadequacy types of measures (Pearce, 1981) and therefore, they were consistent with the uncertainty model's recommendations for separating role ambiguity from uncertainty.

Pardine (1987) administered his measures to 190 evening students in management who were employed full-time. The E→P and P→O uncertainty measures were assessed by referring to a single level of effort or performance (a high level). This followed the single alternative model of expectancy theory (Lawler and Suttle, 1973). Subsets of E→P uncertainty items (five items) were written for both quantity and quality of performance. Sample items are, "I can try my best and still feel uncertain whether my boss will like the way I've done my job," and "I can try my best and still feel uncertain about whether I will be able to complete the amount of work expected of me."

There were twenty-six P→O uncertainty items, referencing a variety of potential intrinsic and extrinsic outcomes of good job performance from the literature on job motivation. Examples of items include, "If you do a good job, can you predict how much it will affect your chances of getting a promotion?" and "If you do a good job, can you predict how much it will affect your chances of being given more challenging work to do?" Both the E→P and P→O uncertainty items were answered on a four-point scale anchored by the end points, "I'm sure that I can't," and "I'm sure that I can."

Pardine (1987) used a six-point scale with end points labeled "not important at all," and "of utmost importance" to measure the importance of twenty-eight different potential outcomes in the uncertainty model.

The strains were measured with the variables from the Caplan *et al.* (1975) study: anxiety, irritability, depression, somatic complaints, and job (dis)satisfaction.

A factor analysis of both role stressor items and uncertainty items, with varimax rotation of factors with eigenvalues greater than one, resulted in seven factors explaining 57.6 percent of the common variance (Pardine, 1987). The role stressors (role ambiguity and role conflict) tended to load on factors separate from the factors on which the uncertainty measures loaded. This is important, because it suggests that uncertainty, which is theorized to result from but to be a separate variable from job stressors, can be operationalized distinctly from the stressors. The primary concern, as discussed above, is that uncertainty and role ambiguity might be indistinguishable for respondents to a questionnaire. It appears, however, that these two concepts can be measured separately, because there was very little cross-loading of items in Pardine's questionnaire.

The first two factors and the seventh (and final factor) consisted entirely of P→O uncertainty items and the fifth and sixth factors consisted entirely of

E→P uncertainty items. The third factor, however, consisted of secondary cross-loadings of two E→P uncertainty items along with strong loadings from all of the role conflict items and secondary cross-loadings from two role ambiguity items. The fourth factor consisted of the strongest loadings of all of the role ambiguity items. Overall, there was a strong tendency for E→P and P→O uncertainty items to load separately from the role stressor items and from each other. There was a breakdown into two factors for each type of uncertainty. Alpha reliabilities of the indices formed tended to be in the 0.80s and 0.90s.

Hierarchical regressions were used to test the first hypothesis, that uncertainty and importance combined multiplicatively to result in a cognitive state of stress. The interaction between uncertainty and importance (i.e. the product of uncertainty and importance) predicted four of the five strains (anxiety, irritability, depression, and somatic complaints), even after the effects of uncertainty on the strains were accounted for in a previous step. For these four strains, the average percent of variance accounted for by uncertainty alone was 10.6 percent (range from 4.8 percent to 16.8 percent) and the average additional percent of variance accounted for by the uncertainty × importance term was 9.9 percent (range from 8.7 percent to 12.1 percent). Importance apparently had not, however, been entered into the regressions and therefore this was not a test of a true interaction or moderator effect. Instead, it could be more accurately described as a test of the predictive power of uncertainty compared with the additional predictive power of uncertainty weighted by importance, which is also a meaningful test and which fits the uncertainty theory well. Taken together, the results of the zero-order correlations and the hierarchical regressions did show that both uncertainty and importance were related to the strains and that their combination provides greater predictive power than either alone.

The combination of uncertainty and importance predicted anxiety, irritability, depression, and somatic complaints greater than uncertainty alone did, but did not predict job satisfaction better. The four that were predicted better are more traditionally considered strains in the job stress literature than job satisfaction is, however, making this a very supportive finding. The effects of the P→O uncertainties appeared to be somewhat stronger than the effects of the E→P uncertainties.

As predicted in the second hypothesis, role conflict was related to the uncertainty of E→P but not to the uncertainty of P→O, while role ambiguity was related to both types of uncertainty.

The third hypothesis received some support, as the P→O uncertainty mediated the relationships between role ambiguity and some strains, but the E→P uncertainty did not, and E→P uncertainty did mediate the relationships between role conflict and most of the strains in a series of regressions. Pardine (1987) concluded that, overall, the results were generally supportive of the uncertainty model.

Uncertainty among the staff of accounting agencies

A third set of studies of uncertainty has been conducted by O'Driscoll and Beehr (1989). We administered questionnaires to personnel from one major accounting firm in New Zealand and a second major accounting firm in the United States.

In New Zealand, one hundred and twenty three employees (forty-two males and seventy-eight females) from the offices in three cities participated. On the average, they had been on their current jobs for about twenty-nine months and in their present organization for thirty-one. Most had completed or partially completed tertiary educations and their mean age was 28.8 years. About 32 percent were audit specialists and 33 percent were in business service operations. Consulting and administration offices accounted for 17 percent and 18 percent of the sample. The anonymous questionnaires were distributed via company mail but returned directly to one of the researchers at his university address in pre-paid, self-addressed envelopes.

Measures of uncertainty were developed by taking items from the two studies described previously (i.e. Beehr *et al.*, 1986; Pardine, 1987). Under the supervision of one of the principal researchers, graduate students in the US were then instructed about the concept of uncertainty and they rated the extent to which each item fit the concept. Final scales of the ten highest rated items from the pool of E→P uncertainty items and the ten highest rated items from the pool of P→O uncertainty items were developed. The scales did not include the true–false measures of absolute levels of expectancies for priming purposes, as had been done in the Beehr *et al.* study, however.

In addition to these indices of uncertainty, measures of supervisor predictability, supervisor behaviors (initiating structure, problem solving, support, and feedback), role ambiguity, role conflict, outcomes (psychological strain, somatic complaints, job satisfaction, and turnover intentions), and potential moderator variables (tolerance for uncertainty and perceived control over the environment) were used.

The uncertainty indices were both correlated with psychological strain and job satisfaction (Table 2.3). The P→O uncertainty was correlated with turnover intentions, but E→P uncertainty was not. The role stressors, particularly role ambiguity, were generally more strongly related to the strains than the uncertainty measures were. In addition, multiple regressions indicated that role ambiguity was the predictor most likely to lead to the outcomes. This would not be predicted by the uncertainty model, because the two uncertainties should be closer to the strains in a causal sequence than the role stressors are.

In addition to role ambiguity, an index labeled supervisor uncertainty was related to job satisfaction in the regressions. It consisted of items such as "How certain are you that your supervisor will have respect for you as a person?". Each item had an outcome in it (e.g. respect for you as a person)

Table 2.3 Correlation among variables in the New Zealand study of uncertainty among accountants (n=123)

	Uncertainties			Role stressors	
	E→P	P→O	Supervisor	Role ambiguity	Role conflict
Strains					
Psychological strain	0.44*	0.26*	0.34*	0.62*	0.44*
Job dissatisfaction	0.38*	0.44*	0.46*	0.61*	0.43*
Turnover intent	0.17	0.23*	0.21*	0.34*	0.34*
Supervisor behaviors					
Initiating structure	−0.09	−0.24*	−0.29*	−0.30*	−0.13
Goal setting	−0.20	−0.28*	−0.40*	−0.42*	−0.28*
Problem solving	−0.25*	−0.38*	−0.50*	−0.32*	−0.26*
Support	−0.31*	−0.44*	−0.40*	−0.40*	−0.36*
Feedback	−0.28*	−0.40*	−0.57*	−0.38*	−0.27*

*   p<0.01

and this index would clearly be a P→O uncertainty index if the items also had the concept of contingency of the outcome on performance. They did not, however, and therefore the predictive power of this index is not very strong support for the uncertainty model.

The study also examined the link between supervisor behaviors and the two types of uncertainty. Supervisors' intiating structure, goal setting, problem solving, and feedback were related to the P→O uncertainty, with support having the strongest relationship and initiating structure the weakest (Table 2.3). Only supervisor problem solving, support, and feedback were related to the E→P uncertainty, with support having the strongest relationship and problem solving the weakest. Multiple regressions of the uncertainties on the supervisor behaviors found that only supervisor support was an independent predictor.

In the United States accountants' study (Beehr and O'Driscoll, 1990), 113 employees responded to the same measures that had been used in the New Zealand study. On the average, they were about 26.4 years old, about 58 percent were females, they had been in the current positions for about 2.3 years and they had been working in their firm for about three years. Their average level of education was a bachelor's degree plus some postgraduate work. About 34.0 percent were in tax specialties, 29.2 percent in auditing, 19.8 percent in accounting, 5.7 percent in consulting, and 7.5 percent in administration.

The E→P, P→O, and supervisor uncertainties were positively related to the strains, with the exception of the correlation between E→P uncertainty and psychological strain (Table 2.4). The two role stressors were also related to the strains and supervisor behaviors were related to both sets of these variables.

In hierarchical regressions, the two role stressors, role conflict and role ambiguity, predicted some additional variance in most of the strains even after holding the uncertainties constant, however, and this did not support the theory's contention that uncertainties account for the effects of job stressors on strains. Overall in these data, there was more support for the idea that job stressors might cause uncertainty directly than that uncertainty was the primary mediating variable between job stressors and employee strains.

Overall, the three studies that have been conducted using the uncertainty model of occupational stress have led to some promises and some disappointments. The research program's attempt to investigate the inner workings of the stress process – that is, to determine the psychological contents of the process facet from the original Beehr and Newman model described in Chapter 1 – has gone in the direction of analyzing uncertainty, but only modest success has resulted as yet. We are able to examine the stressors, strains, and some moderator variables (notably social support, as explained in a later chapter) better than the internal or intrapersonal essence of occupational stress thus far.

Any research on models using variables that require developing new

Table 2.4 Correlation among variables in the US study of uncertainty among accountants (n=113)

	Uncertainties			Role stressors	
	E→P	P→O	Supervisor	Role ambiguity	Role conflict
Strains					
Psychological strain	0.20	0.22*	0.28*	0.33*	0.33*
Job dissatisfaction	0.31*	0.51*	0.52*	0.51*	0.32*
Turnover intent	0.34*	0.22*	0.27*	0.39*	0.36*
Supervisor behaviors					
Initiating structure	−0.19	−0.30*	−0.44*	−0.47*	−0.44*
Goal setting	−0.31*	−0.43*	−0.46*	−0.61*	−0.39*
Problem solving	−0.20	−0.24*	−0.34*	−0.42*	−0.40*
Support	−0.20	−0.39*	−0.41*	−0.41*	−0.49*
Feedback	−0.24*	−0.33	−0.38*	−0.36*	−0.26*

* p<0.01

measures is likely to go slowly, because when the data do not match the model perfectly one is often not sure whether the model needs revising or the measures need improvement. In the uncertainty model, the concepts of E→P and P→O uncertainties are especially troublesome to operationalize because of their complex nature. The items need to ask about the certainty of a contingency. Expectancy theory research on the contingencies themselves has been troublesome and adding the concept of uncertainty of the contingencies can only complicate things for the respondent even more. This may simply be the price of studying a complex phenomenon.

SUMMARY

An increasing amount of occupational stress research has been published over the last couple of decades, but there is currently no universally accepted model of stress being used in the field. Part of the reason for this is the multidisciplinary interest the topic enjoys. There are many different theoretical and methodological approaches to understanding occupational stress, which may be a strength and a weakness simultaneously. The strength is that with such a diverse set of researchers working on the topic no stone will long be unturned in the effort to understand it. The corresponding weakness is that such different researchers do not communicate well with each other, resulting in many different occupational stress fields rather than one.

The focus of this chapter is on a model (Beehr and Bhagat, 1985a) for studying occupational stress from an organizational psychology perspective. The model proposes that uncertainty about effort-to-performance and performance-to-outcome expectancies is a subjective experience common to many types of stress in which organizational psychologists have been interested. Future occupational stress research derived from this model might not be restricted only to uncertainty about these expectancies but could also include uncertainties related to work-related behaviors other than performance.

Uncertainties of various sorts and at all levels (individual, group, and organizational) have long been of interest to industrial and organizational psychology, but this type of uncertainty is a very specific one at the individual level. The relationship, if any, between this type of uncertainty and the others is unknown, but it is a prime topic for research.

The basic model itself, uncertainty × importance × duration, needs testing. It is related to expectancy theory of motivation and the concept of uncertainty of the expectancies might even be incorporated into that theory by future research. The current concern, however, is with the stress model rather than the expectancy motivation theory.

Little or no research has focused on duration as a variable in occupational stress and this seems to be an obvious area for future research. Intuitively, it would seem that the longer one experiences a stressful situation (uncertain expectations, in this model), the stronger the stressful outcome would be.

The measurement of this type of uncertainty is likely to be a problem. Measuring expectancies for expectancy theory of motivation is not easy, but here the task would be to measure the certainty with which these subjective expectations are held. There is a danger that the level of expectancies is likely to contaminate the measures of uncertainty of expectancies. Another difficulty is the likely tendency of uncertainty scales to be contaminated by role ambiguity, which should be a situation of information deficiency in the work environment. Previous measures of role ambiguity have included both information deficiency and unpredictability or uncertainty (Pearce, 1981). Therefore, future research needs to be alert to this possibility in order to minimize this potential contamination in the measures used. Three preliminary studies of uncertainty have been conducted and the results are promising. These studies have developed measures of uncertainty that can be used or revised to form the basis for future studies.

The uncertainty model focuses on the intrapersonal, psychological experience of stress itself. It must be concluded at present, however, that this part of occupational stress is still somewhat of a black box phenomenon. We are able to study such stress from the outside, but we see the insides only dimly. While this chapter examined the theoretically proposed, immediate, internal reactions to occupational stress, the subsequent chapters examine relatively more external parts of the stress process that are more easily inspected. This chapter examined a key work stress factor without which it is difficult to integrate all the other parts. Research continues on it.

Part II

Stressors in the workplace

This section describes the causal factors in occupational stress – the work environment stressors in Figure 1.2 from the first chapter. One chapter examines the first two stressors to receive widespread attention in the organizational psychology approach to job stress: role conflict and ambiguity. The majority of the chapter focuses on role ambiguity, because that is where my research program focused from the start. In fact, my 1974 dissertation was entitled "Role ambiguity as a role stress: some moderating and intervening variables."

Most organizational psychologists' interests in role ambiguity and role conflict, including my own, can be traced to a 1964 book by Kahn *et al*. This work described both a large-scale US study and a simultaneous, smaller, intensive study of these two stressors in a variety of organizations. When a number of other researchers began to study job stress, about a decade later, this book seemed to be resurrected as the starting point for many of them. Because of its influence on many early investigations, it can be considered a pioneer work in the field. More studies have been done on these two stressors than on any others in the organizational psychology approach to occupational stress and they are therefore given a chapter of their own. As noted earlier, however, in my own research program role ambiguity has received more attention than role conflict. This is because I believed in the beginning, and still do, that the general concept of ambiguity (and uncertainty) is central to a great many organizational problems.

It is unlikely that role conflict and role ambiguity are the entire story in occupational stress and fortunately, researchers have more recently begun to examine other types of workplace stressors. My work on these is examined in a separate chapter of this section and recommendations are made for further exploration beyond role conflict and ambiguity.

Chapter 3

Role ambiguity and role conflict in the workplace

Role ambiguity and role conflict were among the first social psychological stressors to be studied in the workplace. The theoretical and empirical description of these two stressors in *Organizational Stress: Studies in Role Conflict and Ambiguity* (Kahn *et al.*, 1964) thrust them on to center stage in this research. Furthermore, "Role conflict and ambiguity as critical variables in a model of organizational behavior" (House and Rizzo, 1972) helped keep researchers' attention on them for almost two decades. It was noted in 1981 that all studies of role conflict and ambiguity conducted after the one by Kahn and his colleagues relied upon the theoretical approach of that early study (Van Sell *et al.*, 1981). In order to understand my own research on them, it is useful to examine this approach as background.

It should also be noted that the influence of these two projects on subsequent research also may have had two negative side effects. First, many researchers probably kept their attention focused on these two stressors and a few others that are thought closely associated with them (e.g. role overload) far too long. They seem to have been emphasized when there is little reason to focus on them other than that they were early arrivals. My own research began with role ambiguity but has become broadened since then to include a wider variety of potential stressors, as can be seen in the next chapter.

Second, role conflict and role ambiguity have been studied and discussed together in the same breath so often that they are often treated as one. It is common, for example, for research to hypothesize the same relationships for each of them with third variables. Their almost constant linking in the same research projects may have at times led researchers away from thinking about their differences. My own research has not fallen prey to this tendency too often, as can be seen in this chapter.

Having said this about the dangers of mixing role conflict and role ambiguity, here they are presented together in the same chapter. They are, however, discussed in separate sections. For still more detail, readers are referred to four works reviewing them together (Fisher and Gitelson, 1983; King and King, 1990; Jackson and Schuler, 1985; Van Sell *et al.*, 1981).

Our research on role ambiguity and role conflict has examined the relationship of these two organizational stressors with a variety of individual and organizational outcomes. Much of it has been a search for moderator variables in the stressor–strain relationship, as indicated in Figure 1.2. More recently, this moderator research has focused on social support as a moderator – so much so that most of the discussion of social support has been given special attention in a separate chapter. My own research began with the exploration of role ambiguity and this interest is probably what led Bhagat and me to develop the uncertainty theory of job stress. Recently, however, my colleagues and I have turned our attentions to a special form of role conflict purported to be found in family businesses – inter-role conflict due to incompatible expectations. First, however, an overview of these two stressors is necessary.

SIMILARITY AND DIFFERENCES BETWEEN ROLE CONFLICT AND AMBIGUITY

Because of their common use and measurement together, there has also been concern, although perhaps not enough, with the degree to which role conflict and role ambiguity are similar and different. This issue has both a conceptual and an empirical version. First, how are they alike and/or different theoretically and second, how do the measures of them relate to each other?

Role conflict and role ambiguity are conceptually distinct job characteristics. Because of their roots in role theory, they are conceptualized as characteristics of the expectations or demands that people in a role set have for a person in the focal role (the one being studied) in that role set. These expectations are probably more or less efficiently communicated to the focal person in a somewhat continuous series of role episodes. Figure 3.1 illustrates the role episode process as conceived by Kahn *et al.* (1964).

The role senders consist of everyone in the focal person's role set. A role set for any focal role consists of all of the roles (positions or offices) to which the focal role is directly "attached." Formal organization charts illustrate the concept of attachment quite directly. All of the positions in any focal person's role set have lines connecting them to that focal position. Of course, the formal chart often does not faithfully represent all of the formal (let alone informal) role relationships. Anyone who (or any role that) consistently makes legitimate demands upon the focal person can be considered a member of the role set. Taken to the extreme, even non-organizational people (roles) may make legitimate demands upon some focal jobs. For example, customers may make demands of people in boundary positions such as in sales. These expectations or demands are legitimate and may function similarly to the demands of people in the organization. Therefore, it is not too farfetched in the context of role stress to consider them members

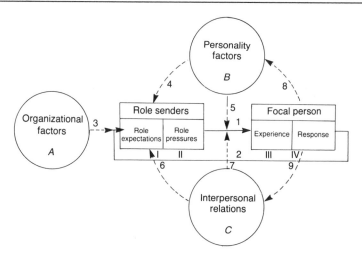

Figure 3.1 A theoretical model of factors involved in adjustment to role conflict and ambiguity (reprinted with permission from Kahn *et al.*, 1964).

of the focal person's role set, although most writers implicitly disallow this possibility.

The core of the Kahn *et al.* (1964) model is the role message(s) sent from the role sender to the focal person, although the bulk of the research, including my own, has focused on the relationships between the focal person's experiences and responses. This focus probably is related to the heavy use of self-report methods for measuring both experience and response. It should be noted, however, that Kahn *et al.* also examined the conflict of role messages as reported by the role senders themselves and found them to be related to perceived role conflict. This is often taken as evidence for the validity of the self-reports of role conflict.

A role episode, in which one or more focal people send a message containing an expectation to the focal person, is a central feature of the model. Role senders hold expectations for the focal person which they may send in the form of messages containing objective role ambiguity or role conflict. The focal person receives the message, thereby perceiving some amount of ambiguity and/or conflict, and has several different possible responses. Symptom formation is the figure's label for strains. My own research has separated the focal person's responses into strains, adaptive responses, and responses with direct organizational consequences, as illustrated in Figure 1.2.

Both the focal person's responses and the objective organizational situation can directly influence the expectations that role senders have for the focal person; in addition, it is posited that these responses can indirectly affect the role senders' experience through their impact upon interpersonal relations and even on personality factors (Figure 3.1). Finally, the interpersonal factors and personality factors may act as moderators of the relationship between role senders' responses (characteristics of role messages) and the focal person's experience of them.

Most moderator studies, however, have actually tested the model as if the vertical, broken arrows were between the focal person's experience and responses. That is, they have searched for interactions between the focal person's experience of stress (perceived stressors) and their responses to stress. This is again probably because of the use of self-reports to measure stressors. Self-reports of stressors have usually been heavily influenced by the focal person's experience. Even though self-report measures can vary in their likely objectivity and are not necessarily very different from "objective" (non self-report) measures, typical self-report measures of role conflict and role ambiguity are probably at least somewhat susceptible to contamination by respondent biases. The study of item wording by Jex *et al.* (1992), discussed in Chapter 1, focused on the use of the word "stress," but it implies that item wording in general can lead to either fewer or greater problems of measurement in using self-reports in stress research. More research on the issue of what makes self-reports more or less objective is needed and we are now in the planning stages of such research.

Role conflict and role ambiguity are alike, then, because they are embodied in role episodes, they are derived from role theory, and they frequently have been studied together. As occupational stressors, they are characteristics of the work environment that can lead to employee strains. The path followed in my own research is embodied in Chapter 1 (Figure 1.2). It distinguishes and investigates types of responses more finely than most models. Three separate types are proposed: human consequences or strains, adaptive responses or coping, and organizational consequences.

Role conflict and role ambiguity each has multiple forms, but they can be defined generally as follows. As stressors or characteristics of the work environment, role ambiguity is deficient or uncertain information in the environment regarding the role behaviors expected of the focal person, and role conflict is the existence of two or more sets of expectations on the focal person (and sent pressures) such that compliance with one makes compliance with the other more difficult.

ROLE AMBIGUITY AS A WORK-RELATED STRESSOR

Early work on role ambiguity

Two of our own early studies showed that role ambiguity is related to human consequences, as the core relationship in Figure 1.2 proposes. The focus of the first one was the environmental moderators in the figure and the second was on a potential personal moderator. The first was a study of 651 employees of five midwestern companies, with the people chosen in order to replicate closely the types of job categories found nationally (Beehr, 1976). The people in those jobs averaged about thirty-five years old, about three-quarters had finished high school, about 80 percent were white, and about two-thirds were married. The data were obtained via approximately 90-minute interviews in the employees' homes conducted by interviewers from the Survey Research Center.

The perceived stressor in the work environment, role ambiguity, was correlated with four human consequences, job dissatisfaction, life dissatisfaction, low self-esteem, and depressed mood, but the median r was only a modest 0.19. Three situational characteristics were examined for their potential moderating effects on these relationships: group cohesiveness, supervisor support, and autonomy. Group cohesiveness and supervisor support were chosen because of a theory of social support, which since then has become much more well-known, holding that social support should buffer or moderate the relationship between work-environment stressors and strains (e.g. Beehr, 1985b; Beehr and McGrath, 1992; Cohen and Wills, 1985; House, 1981; Vaux, 1988). This theory and my program of research on it are detailed in a later chapter. For now, the point is that there was little strong evidence in that study that these two potential measures of social support in the workplace moderated the relationships between role ambiguity and human consequences.

The evidence regarding moderating effects of autonomy were more clear, however. Using subgroup analyses and a median split of the sample, the correlations of role ambiguity with all four human consequences were greater for the half of the sample with high autonomy scores than for the half with low autonomy scores. Two of the differences in correlations were significant at the $p>0.01$ level and one was marginally significant ($p>0.10$). Thus, this relatively early work on role ambiguity, testing the environmental moderators of Figure 1.2, especially indicated that autonomy might be a moderator. While my colleagues and I have not done much more with autonomy, the concept, or variables measuring similar concepts, has since then been incorporated into others researchers' work on occupational stress. Perhaps the best known of these works are those of Karasek and his colleagues (e.g. Karasek, 1979; Karasek et al., 1981).

Also in 1976, my colleagues and I (Beehr, Walsh and Taber) published another study in which role ambiguity was conceived as a stressor, was measured with a questionnaire, and was correlated significantly with three psychological human consequences: job dissatisfaction ($r=0.51$), fatigue ($r=0.20$) and tension ($r=0.26$). One hundred and forty three members of a white collar union, employed by a heavy manufacturing company in the midwest in drafting, mechanical, and technical/clerical jobs were surveyed via anonymous questionnaires in groups on site, during working hours. There were seventy-nine males and sixty-four females, and they averaged thirty-four years old.

This study was one of the few in which we examined a personal moderator variable. It was hypothesized that role ambiguity would be more strongly correlated with the human consequences for people with stronger higher order needs than for people with weaker higher order needs. Subgroup analyses, comparing the top and bottom thirds of the sample on their higher order need strength scores, were computed. The differences between all three pairs of correlations were in the expected direction, but none of the differences was significant. This result did not encourage us to concentrate our future work in personal moderators of the work stressor–strain relationship, although we have looked at this part of Figure 1.2 occasionally in subsequent research.

These early studies on role ambiguity showed that it was related in expected ways to human consequences. The relationships were modest, however, and much of our subsequent empirical research has followed theories advocating moderators in the relationship; if moderators exist, then there might be some individuals or situations for whom the relationships would be stronger. Our work on social support, examined in a separate chapter, represents the single most frequently investigated dimension of this search for moderators. In addition, a second direction has been more theoretical. My colleagues and I have pondered the nature of role ambiguity in the workplace. This thinking is explored next.

Information deficiency versus unpredictability

Based on a reading of questionnaire items from several studies, Pearce (1981) noted that role ambiguity had been operationalized both as information deficiency in the employee's environment and as the employee's resulting inability to predict. The former is closer to role ambiguity and the latter is closer to the type of uncertainty of expectancies that the Beehr and Bhagat (1985a) uncertainty theory proposed as a key to many types of job stress. To reiterate from a previous chapter, an obvious issue for future research is the operational separation of role ambiguity from uncertainty and the subsequent determination of their relationships with each other and with third variables.

Pearce concluded that, among the studies reviewed, only one role ambiguity index clearly referred solely to unpredictability; most of the others implicitly or explicitly included both environmental information deficiency and the person's perception of unpredictability. The one index singled out was from a study of mine (Beehr, 1976) and the items are in appendix C. My own thinking has evolved since the 1976 research cited by Pearce, however. Since then, and as argued most explicitly in Beehr and Bhagat (1985a), I have come to believe that role ambiguity should be a term reserved for information deficiency. Unpredictability (i.e. uncertainty, or specific forms of unpredictability) should continue to be studied alongside role ambiguity, however.

Information deficiency should be easier to measure objectively or by reports other than self-reports, because it is conceived as an element of the work environment. Predictability, however, is a subjective state of the focal person and therefore could only be measured by self-reports. In some of its forms, Pearce's unpredictability would be the same as uncertainty in the uncertainty theory framework of Beehr and Bhagat. Close examination shows that this does not differ greatly from Pearce's arguments in substance. The main difference is in the use of the word ambiguity. Now that the issue has been sharpened (in Pearce and in Beehr and Bhagat), research on this issue should be able to proceed more quickly.

The call for measurement of almost anything from more than one source, especially from sources other than the "self-reports," or focal person in role stress, has been widespread in recent years in industrial and organizational psychology. Kahn *et al.* (1964) took this approach with role conflict by asking role senders as well as focal people to describe the expectations for the focal people's work roles, but it has not been done with role ambiguity. In part, this may be because role ambiguity has been conceived more as a person variable than role conflict has. That is, role ambiguity has been considered to be especially in the eyes of the beholder. That is a position Beehr and Bhagat's (1985a) uncertainty model advocates against, however. Instead, we argued that role ambiguity, like role conflict and all other stressors, must be considered part of the environment (information deficiency). While the resulting personal uncertainty is very important in the stress process (in fact it is central, according to the uncertainty model), it is not considered an environmental stressor in their model. By definition, the word stressor is reserved for variables that may be considered environmental situations, although reactions closely aligned to these are of obvious importance.

A relevant research question is whether role ambiguity, as an environmental stressor, can be measured in any way other than through self-reports. An observational study has tried to do that, but with little apparent success. Some of my colleagues, when we worked at the Institute for Social Research, asked trained observers to report the degree of certainty (low role ambiguity) on items looking like a mixture of environmental role ambiguity and resulting personal uncertainty (Jenkins *et al.*, 1975). Different observers generally were able to agree with each other in rating certainty when observing the focal person simultaneously, but not when observing them at different times. The index had moderate internal consistency reliability, but was only very weakly related to self-reports of certainty obtained during interviews with the focal person ($r=0.14$).

This uncertainty index was, however, composed of both uncertainty and role ambiguity items as defined in the present framework. It might logically be argued that role ambiguity, being more environmentally based, could be observed better than uncertainty, which is a personal reaction. Enough data were reported in the study to judge the agreement among raters for separate items. Examination of the study's inter-rater reliability of individual items, however, does not reveal a clear pattern of differences between the two types of items. Research aimed at developing measures for role ambiguity other than with self-reports is needed. Based on my colleagues' work, however, these may or may not be observations.

Forms of role ambiguity

While some serious attention has been paid to different types of role conflict, little has been done regarding differentiating types of role ambiguity. As noted earlier, there has been some attempt to note the difference between information deficiency in the environment and the resulting feelings of unpredictability in the person. It is preferred here, however, only to label information deficiency "role ambiguity" because it is in the environment and to label the resulting personal reaction of unpredictability "uncertainty." Therefore, in the current scheme, these are not two categories of role ambiguity.

Kahn *et al.* noted that two types of ambiguity may exist and labeled them task and socioemotional ambiguity (1964: 94). It is interesting that these labels sound similar to the two most commonly cited leadership or group behaviors, one focusing on task and one on emotions. Task ambiguity appears to be the same as information deficiency, while socioemotional ambiguity is described as "the person's concern about his standing in the eyes of others and about the consequences of his actions for the attainment of his personal goals" (ibid.). Lack of clarity about the consequences of one's actions sounds similar to uncertainty rather than ambiguity in the current conceptualization; furthermore, this part of the quote does not seem necessarily *socio*emotional. Concern or ambiguity about one's standing in the eyes of others, on the other hand, does seem *socio*emotional, but is not clearly and directly *role* ambiguity because it does not directly refer to the expectations or demands on a person's role behavior. Instead, it is ambiguity about a sort of outcome (evaluation by others). By inference, however, this evaluation can give focal people information about expectations for their role – if people are certain that the evaluation is related to their role behavior. Therefore, this can be a form of role ambiguity in the present sense, albeit an indirect one. Kahn *et al.*'s socioemotional ambiguity, therefore, does not completely fit into the refined concept of role ambiguity as defined here.

If socioemotional and task ambiguities are not clearly different types of environmentally based role ambiguity, then what are the different types of ambiguities, if there are any? One potential dimension for differentiating types of ambiguity is by the source of role message. Perhaps the most basic distinction is between personal and impersonal sources of messages regarding role expectations. Most literally, it would seem that role theory demands that the source of role messages must be personal (human). That is, a member of the role set can tell the focal person what they expect the focal person to do. Impersonal sources, for example documents or written instructions, would not fit into this rigid role theory definition of role messages. For the example of documents and many other examples, however, it must be remembered that some person did write the documents and someone probably instructed the focal person to read them. They can still fit into the role theory definition, therefore. Furthermore, regardless of their origin, they do pose demands or expectations on the person and these demands can be more or less ambiguous (i.e. can be characterized by more or less information deficiency). Therefore, it is proposed here that a basic division in the taxonomy of role ambiguity is personal versus impersonal sources of role messages.

As Table 3.1 indicates, after the break between personal and impersonal sources of ambiguity, the personal sources can be further divided into role senders who are organizational members and people who are not members of the organization in which the focal person is embedded. Among role senders who are members of the organization, a distinction can be made based on the hierarchical level of the role sender in the organization relative to the focal person. That is, the role pressures can come from superiors, peers, or subordinates.

Among the non-organization members, role messages can originate from people who, although they are not organization members, do nevertheless interact in important ways with the organization or they can originate from people who do not or rarely interact with the organization. In the former category, for example, are frequent customers, suppliers, and even many "faceless" people with whom an employee may interact frequently on the phone in order to get the job done well. Some sources of role expectations that are not people who interact with the organization in any consistent or apparent way (except that they interact with at least one organization member – the focal person) include ambiguous or deficient information embedded in "messages" about the employee's work role behavior stemming from society

Table 3.1 A taxonomy of role ambiguity by source

S O U R C E		Impersonal		I	
	Personal	Organization members		II	Superiors
				III	Peers
				IV	Subordinates
		Non-members of organizations		V	Interacting with organization
				VI	Not interacting with organization

at large (e.g. cultural values regarding how one should work), specific people who are well-known and important to the focal person (e.g. friends and relatives), and specific people with whom the focal people come into contact, but about whom they know little (e.g. the stranger walking down the street who asks a storekeeper for directions).

These sources can send messages to the focal person regarding what they think they should do in the conduct of the focal job, even if they are strangers to the person and the employing organization. Role conflict theory and research has gone far in the direction of the non-organizational member as a role sender in its treatment of inter-role (usually work–home roles) conflict, but thought and research on role ambiguity has not dealt with this type of role sender very much. Their role messages can be ambiguous in addition to or instead of being in conflict with messages from role senders inside the organization. Future research can help to illuminate the frequency of this type of role ambiguity and the severity of its consequences *vis-à-vis* ambiguous role messages from inside the organization.

These types of "external" role senders can be important to the focal person, even though some of them would not have been considered members of the focal person's role set in the narrowest sense. In the context of role stress, it is important to recognize that many people send messages to and have expectations for employees of work organizations, and any of these can therefore contribute to the environmental ambiguity of the employee.

Currently used measures of role ambiguity seem to encompass a mixture of a few of the sources in Table 3.1. Kahn *et al.* (1964) asked employees to name the people in their role sets and included them all in their subsequent questions about role ambiguity. It is doubtful that non-members of the organization were named often, however, because this was not mentioned in the study. Many measures of role ambiguity have employed some items regarding the supervisor, including those of Dougherty and Pritchard (1985; performance evaluation ambiguity) and Beehr *et al.* (1976); most have at least some items referring to anonymous people (e.g. using the word "others" Beehr, 1976; Caplan *et al.*, 1975) and most also include items that refer to situations such as having ambiguous goals or expectations (e.g. Beehr and Drexler, 1986; Rizzo *et al.*, 1970).

Having thus divided role ambiguity into five parts, it can then be asked whether these parts act or react in different ways. The division by source seems more closely linked to causes of role ambiguity than to consequences and therefore a logical question is which of the different sources are more and which are less likely to lead to role ambiguity. Does this stressor usually stem from one or a few of the sources and rarely from the others? It might be hypothesized, for example, that most role ambiguity originates from within the organization, simply because that is where most of the research has focused in the past. One might also ask, however, whether certain types of jobs, such as boundary-spanning jobs, exhibit more external role ambiguity than other jobs. A boundary-spanning job would be one in which the person works on the boundary of the organization, that is, both with people inside and outside of the organization. Salespeople are obvious examples.

The question of how much of a problem is caused by each type of role ambiguity is also a legitimate one and its answer may also vary with the type of job. In other words, the strength of association between role ambiguity from the different sources and outcomes such as strains may vary depending on whether the job is embedded strongly in the organization, whether there are more frequent and accurate performance appraisals by some sources than others, and so forth. A source of role ambiguity who is monitoring focal people's behavior and rewarding or punishing them for it probably is a relatively important source of role messages, and importance of outcomes is a key element of the Beehr and Bhagat (1985a) uncertainty theory of occupational stress. Being unable to comply with role expectations due to their ambiguous nature might have more serious stress-related consequences when the source of the ambiguous message has such powerful characteristics.

Classifying role ambiguity according to source and developing separate measures for each source has yet to be done, but it may prove to be fruitful for future research. Such measures could then be examined for their potential to illuminate issues regarding role ambiguity as a role stressor. Some laboratory experiments may even be possible in which the different sources are manipulated to provide strong causal inference regarding their effects. As with much job stress research, however, this will probably require some creative and innovative work. The laboratory does not automatically resemble a job and purposely manipulating presumably stressful stimuli, that is stimuli that could be harmful to people, may be unethical.

Causes of role ambiguity

It has been proposed indirectly above, while outlining the types of role ambiguity, that each of the six sources in Table 3.1 can be a cause of role ambiguity. Beyond that, however, one can ask why and under what circumstances each of those sources provides the focal person with ambiguous role messages. Kahn *et al.* (1964), of course, proposed a model (Figure 3.1) in which some types of antecedents to role stressors (certain role messages) were suggested, but little has been done to examine them empirically. These antecedents were organizational factors, personality factors, and interpersonal factors. In addition, the focal person's responses to the role messages influence the role expectations reciprocally.

The proposed organizational antecedents include organizational structure (including size, shape, division of labor), the products, the financial base, and the reward system (Kahn *et al.*, 1964). The individual's situation in relation to these is, of course, especially important. In relation to role ambiguity, little research has actually been conducted on these, but two meta-analyses provide a summary of the results. Fisher and Gitelson (1983) and Jackson and Schuler (1985) both reported that role ambiguity was typically related to formalization and participative decision making negatively, but that the variations in the correlations suggest that there may be moderators of these relationships. Jackson and Schuler also reported that the organizational level of the focal person's position and role ambiguity were positively related, but that moderator variables were likely. Finally, Fisher and Gitelson concluded that having a boundary-spanning role was weakly and negatively related to role ambiguity and that no moderator variables are likely to be affecting this relationship. Positive conclusions about moderators are always intriguing and pose a challenge to theory developers.

These organizational factors are somewhat macro level determinants of role ambiguity, but at the job level some work also has been done to explicate the determinants of role ambiguity. Shaw and Riskind (1983), in a creative study using archival data from the Position Analysis Questionnaire (PAQ) data bank, the Dictionary of Occupational Titles (DOT), and the job stress data from Caplan *et al.* (1975), found relationships between role ambiguity in the Caplan data and four divisional job dimensions of the PAQ: "interpreting what is sensed" was related negatively to role ambiguity, "performing handling and/or related manual activities" was related positively, "working nontypical versus day schedule" was related positively, and "performing unstructured versus structured work" was related negatively. Jackson (1983, 1984), studying role ambiguity as part of a larger causal model, found that increases in the frequency of staff meetings instituted to randomly selected groups in a unit of a university hospital (the intervention was conceived as an increase in participative decision making) led to slightly less role ambiguity both six ($r=0.19$) and nine months ($r=0.29$) after the intervention began.

In our own work (Walsh *et al.*, 1980) we performed path analysis of non-experimental data on three samples (shop, management, and office employees in a single company) in which role clarity (the reverse of role ambiguity) was one of the critical ingredients leading to job satisfaction. Based on previous research and theory (e.g. Greller and Herold, 1975; Hanser and Muchinsky, 1978; House and Rizzo, 1972; Kahn *et al.*, 1964; Sieber, 1974) we expected that supervisor feedback and task feedback would lead to role clarity. Although the strength of the relationships varied across samples, these relationships were found in all three. Therefore, there is some evidence that feedback can reduce role ambiguity and this certainly is logical.

Consequences of role ambiguity

Consequences of stressors, such as role ambiguity, have often been divided into three categories: psychological, physical or physiological, and behavioral (e.g. Beehr and Newman, 1978; Brief *et al.*, 1981). Another way to divide the consequences is individual and organizational, that is, whether the consequence is one that is primarily valued by the individual or by the organization. Usually the employee's behavioral consequences are examined for this type of analysis. For example, an employee's job performance is a potential behavioral consequence that is particularly valued by the organization. The present discussion will use the three-way division of psychological, physical, and behavioral consequences, but the other division (individual versus organizational) is also important for some purposes and should be kept in mind. Our own work, as exemplified in Figure 1.2, uses this distinction.

The two meta-analysis studies (Fisher and Gitelson, 1983; Jackson and Schuler, 1985) provide summary statistics on the relationships between role ambiguity and its potential consequences. There apparently have not been enough studies of physical or physiological outcomes in relation to role conflict and role ambiguity to conduct a meaningful meta-analysis, but these studies have provided results and conclusions about psychological and behavioral consequences.

Regarding psychological consequences (strains) linked to role ambiguity, both meta-analyses concluded that organizational commitment, job involvement, and satisfaction with promotions were negatively related to role ambiguity and that future research on moderators for these relationships were not likely to be successful. They also agreed that tension/anxiety was positively related to role ambiguity, while overall job satisfaction and satisfaction with pay were negatively related to role ambiguity, but that all of these relationships are likely to be moderated by third variables. Their recommendations disagreed for three psychological variables, however. Fisher and Gitelson (1983) concluded that the relationship of satisfaction with co-workers to role ambiguity was not likely to be moderated by third variables, while Jackson and Schuler (1985) thought that further research into such moderators could be fruitful. They came to the opposite conclusions regarding satisfaction with the supervisor and satisfaction with the work itself, however, with Fisher and Gitelson suggesting that there would be moderators for these relationships and Jackson and Schuler not recommending a search for moderators in future research.

Regarding the behavioral consequences, results regarding turnover were not reported, but both meta-analyses concluded that the positive relationship between role ambiguity and turnover intentions was likely to be moderated by other variables, given the unexplainable variation of results across studies. Absenteeism was examined in the Jackson and Schuler (1985) study, but not in the Fisher and Gitelson (1983) study, and it was concluded that there were not likely to be moderators of the role ambiguity-absence relationship. Both studies concluded that there were likely to be moderators of the weak (on the average) but negative relationship between role ambiguity and job performance as measured by either self-reports or other reports (usually the supervisor). Only Jackson and Schuler's analysis included studies of objective job performance and they also concluded that there were likely to be moderators of the relationship of role ambiguity and this type of job performance measure.

The authors of these two meta-analyses did not come to the same conclusions with regard to the probability of existence of moderator variables, with the study done later (Jackson and Schuler, 1985) pointing out the differences. The disagreement could have been for several reasons. First, they used slightly different sets of studies, with Jackson and Schuler including all of the studies reviewed by the earlier study by Fisher and Gitelson (1983) and adding others. Second, they used different types of meta-analyses with different criteria for making conclusions. Third, in these meta-analyses, the second study (Jackson and Schuler, 1983) attempted to control more statistical artifacts (sample size, range restriction in the predictor, reliability of predictor and criterion, and variations in range restriction and reliability across studies) than the first study (which controlled only sample size).

The differences in conclusions and recommendations about moderators, however, may not be reflected in clear, strong differences in the results of the two meta-analyses. A more recent review of the potential for moderators provides evidence that both of these meta-analyses may have overestimated the likelihood of moderator effects due to both studies' probable overestimation of reliabilities of the measures (King and King, 1990). In a conservative statement, the King and King review concluded that it would be best not to make conclusions one way or the other about moderators based on these meta-analyses.

Jackson and Schuler (1985) had recommended that for some variables *theoretically based* moderator research could be pursued. Given the difficulty of interpreting the meta-analyses that have been done thus far, one should probably recommend that this strategy be used for the relationships between role ambiguity and *all* outcome variables. Multiple variable research (as opposed to the continued study of simple bivariate relationships) is needed in the area and theoretically driven moderator variable research is one way to implement this. The chapter on social support reports the results of our attempts to examine one of these theoretically based moderator variables. Another, autonomy, was suggested by my 1976 study, reported earlier in this chapter, on role ambiguity. As noted earlier, variables similar to autonomy have since become major factors in some theories of job stress (e.g. Karasek, 1979).

ROLE CONFLICT AS A WORK-RELATED STRESSOR

Role conflict is usually defined as the existence of two or more sets of demands or expectations on the focal person such that compliance with one would make it more difficult or impossible to comply with the other(s) (e.g. Kahn *et al.*, 1964). Definitions and operationalizations have varied a bit regarding whether role conflict is an environmental variable, a person variable, or both, but the present treatment of role conflict as an occupational stressor requires it to be environmentally based (rather than a part of the person). That is, all stressors must be clearly based in the work environment. If they are not, then it is argued here that one is not dealing with an industrial/ organizational psychology topic. Instead, this may be a province of clinical psychology. Fortunately, with role conflict it is easier to conceptualize and perhaps easier to operationalize as environmentally based than it is with role ambiguity.

Even if role conflict is environmentally based, that does not mean that self-report measures are inherently wrong as measures of it. Such measures have a problem of perceptual bias and furthermore, the bias can lead to the finding of spurious relationships if other variables (e.g. strains) are also measured from the same source. The amount of bias in such measures, however, should logically vary with the nature of the measure itself. If a focal person is simply asked the extent to which they think that other people are always expecting conflicting things of them, there is probably more likelihood of a strong response bias effect than if asked whether they report directly to two supervisors (an indication of the likelihood of role conflict occurring). The second question seems likely to evoke a more objectively accurate response than the former. If so, it would be because the second question asks about a situation or event that is more concretely described and observable and it requires less judgment and interpretation on the part of the employee. It is argued here that survey items with such characteristics reduce the likelihood of serious response bias affecting the research data. My colleagues and I are now beginning a project to study this issue.

Regarding the nature of such questions, however, there is probably a paradox about what is being measured. First, it could be argued that the more objective items (e.g. the number of direct supervisors) tend to measure precursors or causes of role conflict rather than the existence of conflicting role messages themselves. Second, to the extent that the more objective style of question can be used for concepts such as role conflict, it must be recognized that role conflict as usually measured may be a somewhat summary judgment by the respondent. That is, it is the respondents' overall impression of the nature of their role messages over a period of time and over a number of sources of role messages. By asking the incumbent to make this summary judgment, fewer questions are needed. If, on the other hand, more objective and specific questions were asked, far more questions would be needed in order to summarize role conflict over a long period of time and over many sources. There may be no perfect solution to this dilemma and therefore it is probably wise at this point for research to use different approaches. While one approach may be able to measure some specific things more accurately and objectively, the other can claim to measure a global concept better. This paradox is reminiscent of Kaplan's comment "If you can measure it, that ain't it" (1964: 206).

Forms of role conflict

Although different forms of role ambiguity have not been the subject of investigation or even of much speculation, the division of role conflict into types has been somewhat common from the very beginning of organizational role stress research, if Kahn, *et al.*'s (1964) pioneering study can be taken as the beginning. Table 3.2 shows a list of types of role conflict, based on a combination of who sends the role messages to the focal person and what role the focal message is about. The core of the table contains three basic types of role conflict (intra-sender, inter-sender, and person-role conflict) that, based on their labels, focus on who sends the role messages. These three, along with inter-role conflict, have been listed as the four types of role conflict (role overload has also been added as a special form of role conflict, but it is being saved here for discussion as a separate form of job stressor). The arrangement in the table shows that there are really two divisions or dimensions inherent in these labels, however: division by type of sender and by type of role.

Type of role

Regarding type of role, intra-role conflict refers to conflicting messages about the expectations for a single role, usually a job or work role in the context of I/O psychology. Inter-role conflict refers to conflicting messages about expectations for more than one role, one of which (in I/O psychology) is

Table 3.2 Forms of role conflict

	Division by role	
Division by sender	*Intra-role conflict*	*Inter-role conflict*
Intra-sender conflict	A	B
Inter-sender conflict	C	D
Person-role conflict	E	F

usually the job. Everybody has more than one role in life, although the job is usually the one to which I/O psychologists give the most attention. The mere existence of multiple roles may not guarantee this type of conflict, but it probably does increase the chances for it. Expectations accompanying one's roles as a patriotic citizen of a nation, a member of a religion, an incumbent of a work role, a member of a family, and so forth, can easily be in conflict from time to time.

Type of sender and the special case of family business

Regarding the person who sends the messages, demands from two or more people can obviously conflict (inter-sender conflict), but even demands from the same person can be in conflict with each other. Such intra-sender conflict refers to a situation in which the expectations or demands that one role sender has for the focal person are in conflict with each other. An example can occur with the expectation that the focal person does a large quantity of work while following an organization's safety procedures to the letter. If the quantity demanded is especially great, the employee may be tempted to cut any corners that will speed up production – including ignoring safety procedures. In this example, one role sender (perhaps the supervisor) may be sending two messages that conflict with each other. That is, compliance with one expectation reduces the likelihood of compliance with the other.

It is obvious that intra-sender conflict can and usually is a form of intra-role conflict and Kahn *et al.* (1964) have been interpreted as classifying it this way (King and King, 1990). It is also possible, however, as indicated in Table 3.2, for intra-sender conflict to occur between two or more roles. This is possible when the same person is a member of two or more of the focal person's role sets. It occurs, for example, in situations where members of one's church are also co-workers or customers of one's workplace, or where people in a family-run business are members of both the family and the business. In this situation, the same person is a sender for more than one role set and can provide conflicting expectations based on the different roles of the focal person.

Family businesses pose a particularly intriguing set of possibilities for such research. There is a relatively new but rapidly growing literature about them, often focusing on conflicts that occur in these businesses, but little of it seems to be informed by the type of occupational stress literature we are interested in here. In fact, perhaps due to the relative newness of the field of family business, the knowledge about these businesses seems to come largely from case studies and observations by consultants rather than from empirical research. My colleagues and I have recently tried to study role conflict in family-owned businesses from an organizational psychology point of view (Beehr *et al.*, 1993).

As an example of the potential causes of a type of conflict thought to be typical in family business, we can consider businesses and families to have different subcultures. In general, people are accepted in a family based on who they are, but in business people are accepted based on what they do. It is common to "reward" family members simply because they are related to us (e.g. the concept of an allowance for children), while in business it is more common that people are rewarded for something they do, such as productivity or at least putting in a certain number of hours at work. Immediately, we can begin to see that expectations could be different in the two roles of family member versus organizational member (Danco, 1980). Furthermore, in general, the cultures of families are based on emotion, while the cultures of businesses are intended to be more rational.

Because the previous literature on family businesses was largely unsystematic and non-empirical, we conducted preliminary interviews to help guide our main project. Two graduate research assistants were trained to interview members of four retail and two machine shop family businesses in northern Michigan. Eleven family members and nine non-family members were interviewed from these family businesses. The interview was short (about fourteen minutes on average) but structured and the respondents were considered "informants" – that is, they were asked about many things and people in their organizations, and not just about themselves. The interviews focused on three potential types of conflict: intra-role conflict between demands from within the organization, inter-role conflict between demands from within and outside the organization, and interpersonal conflict or arguing. Respondents were also asked their opinion about whether they thought these types of conflict occurred more or less often in family businesses than in other businesses.

We especially expected to hear reports about inter-role conflict and the interviews indicated that this did occur. Interpersonal conflict was also reported, but intra-role conflict was not. Because of this, our main study did not investigate intra-role conflict. Also, even though we asked specifically about conflicts in the interviews, many respondents went out of their way to mention other, sometimes positive things about working in the family businesses. They talked about professional advantages that people had if they worked in their families' businesses. They also reported special pressure for good performance, which might be considered a stressor – although it would not necessarily be a form of conflict.

Based upon the previous non-empirical literature on family businesses and on the preliminary interviews, we hypothesized differences between family versus non-family businesses and family members versus non-family members of family businesses. In terms of Figure 1.2, we expected that people in family businesses would experience both more aversive human consequences (job dissatisfaction, career dissatisfaction, and psychological strain) and more conflict of each type than people in non-family businesses and that family members would experience more of these stressors and strains than non-family members in these family businesses.

In addition to the human consequences or strains, two organizational consequences from Figure 1.2 were also examined: turnover intentions and organizational commitment. Again based on the previous literature emphasizing problems in family businesses, we examined these for differences between family businesses and non-family businesses and between family members and non-family members of family businesses.

Finding comparable groups of family and non-family businesses was important, and we focused on size (number of employees) and type of industry. We tried to control size by studying only small businesses, usually employing less than twenty people. In order to control type of industry, we used two strategies. Because of the availability of knowledgeable informants about family retail businesses in Maine and about family machining businesses in northern Michigan, we sampled businesses only from these industries and these locations (Beehr *et al.*, 1993) Furthermore, within the general category of retail businesses in Maine, we matched businesses by type of retail business; for example, if we obtained the participation of a family-owned pharmacy, we also obtained the participation of a non-family-owned pharmacy. It was thus a matched sample of pairs of family and non-family businesses.

In order to avoid sensitizing people to the precise nature of the study, people were told only that it was a study of small businesses, not that it was specifically a study of family businesses. Of the twenty-one pairs of Maine retail businesses identified, seventeen complete pairs agreed to participate. When owners of only one of a pair of businesses agreed to participate, their data could not be used due to lack of a match. In Michigan, all businesses in machining and light manufacturing were considered to be matched by industry type with each other and eleven of the fourteen businesses identified agreed to participate (six non-family and eight family businesses).

Sampling of individuals within the businesses was also a consideration. First, the owners and all members of the owners' families who worked in the family businesses were included. We wanted to increase the probability that the different comparison groups would have at least the same number of people. Therefore, two was added to the number of family members and we included that number of non-family members of the family business (if the business was large enough to have that many people). Two was then also added to the total sample size of the family business and that number was sampled in the matching non-family business. Thus, even with the possibility of non-responses, we anticipated obtaining at least as many non-family members as family members of family businesses and at least as many members of non-family businesses as of family businesses. The strategy was generally successful. Of the 372 people sampled in the forty-five businesses,

255 participated, for a 69 percent response rate. Due to missing information on some questionnaires, however, for most analyses the number of usable questionnaires was about 220. Of these, there were fifty family members, seventy-three non-family members in the family businesses, and ninety-seven people in non-family businesses.

There was one other complex issue in sampling. Since the owner is one of the family members and their relatives are probably likely to have higher than the average status in the family businesses, family and non-family members of family businesses are likely to vary in hierarchical rank as well as in their family–non-family status. To control this somewhat, we tried to sample non-family members in family businesses who were of relatively high rank, when possible. Nevertheless, there can be little doubt that there was a difference in rank among these groups, although we did not measure rank to determine this. This is a complex issue, in part because rank differences may be an inherent part of working in family businesses. If so, it can be argued that no attempt should be made to control for it. Instead, rank is tied into the whole nature of family membership and is a necessary part of it. Respondents averaged thirty-nine years of age, their organizational tenure was about nine years, and they had "some" college education. About 57 percent were married and 40 percent were females.

The previous empirical literature on inter-role conflict focused on time-based conflict, that is conflict between roles due to having too little time to meet both sets of demands. In the present situation, however, neither previous literature nor the preliminary interviews suggested that this type of inter-role conflict was the pivotal one. Instead, inter-role conflict due to incompatible expectations from two different roles was identified as the likely problem. Seven new items were written based on phrases and contents of responses to the preliminary interview questions about inter-role conflict, and they can be found in appendix D.

Principle components and reliability analyses, however, suggested the formation of two indices from them rather than only one. Two items were therefore combined separately to form an index of high family expectations (alpha=0.73), while the others were combined and interpreted as work–family conflict (alpha=0.68). In addition, we measured interpersonal conflict with the index from Spector *et al.* (1988) and personal advantages with items created from preliminary interview information. In this chapter, however, we are mainly concerned with the conflict measures, role and interpersonal conflict.

In these small business settings, work–family inter-role conflict was indeed correlated with all three human consequences (median r=0.34), as was interpersonal conflict (median r=0.44). They were also correlated with the two organizational outcomes (mean r=0.27 for work–family conflict and 0.34 for interpersonal conflict). Based on analyses of variance, they were not, however, related to being members of families in business. Thus, although the results were consistent with the model followed in our program of research as represented in Figure 1.2, no real clue was provided regarding where conflict comes from. We had hoped that multiple roles in the workplace, as in family business roles, might provide the answer, but they did not.

This family business study was aimed at examining the special case in which intra-sender conflict can be a form of inter-role conflict. Also regarding the person who sends the messages, the focal people can be interpreted as senders in their own role set and this opens up the possibility of the person-role conflict in the table. Kahn *et al.* (1964) had used this term primarily to mean conflicts between the role messages focal people received from others and their own internal, psychological needs and values. It is argued here, however, that person-role conflict is more likely to be a broader phenomenon than that. People have expectations for their own role behavior and these expectations can be quite strong determinants of their actions. An example is employees who expect their own work role behavior to include job performance up to their own strong capabilities, while the co-workers expect nobody to be "rate buster." In this case, person-role conflict can be interpreted as a form of intra-role conflict and in fact Kahn *et al.* (1964) have been interpreted as classifying person-role conflict as a form of intra-role conflict (King and King, 1990).

As indicated in Table 3.2, however, this may not be entirely correct. Person-role conflict probably can occur as a form of inter-role conflict as well. Because people are likely to be role senders for all of their own roles, theoretically they can hold expectations for their behavior in one role that conflict with their own expectations for their behavior in a second role. Thus, focal people can expect themselves to work a great many hours at their profession and also expect themselves to "work" many of the same hours at their family roles, setting up potential inter-role conflict.

Some of these forms of role conflict have been entirely overlooked in the past in both theory and empirical research, while others have been the focus of a large amount of research. Future research could be aimed at the further development of the forms of role conflict, operationalizations of them, examination of the extent of each, and determination of their causes and consequences.

Inter-Role conflict as a special case

Inter-role conflict is probably the type that has been the subject of the most research to date and it is one of the types of conflict examined in the family business study described previously in this chapter. The focus of inter-role conflict research has usually been on women's adjustment to their widespread entry into the workforce in general, but especially into jobs and occupations that were previously almost closed to them. Since women were often seen as the primary "worker" in the home (the homemaker role), their increasing entry into professions and jobs thought to typically require high amounts of involvement, dedication, and commitment probably signalled the potential for greater work–non-work conflict than the average male had experienced in these types of occupations.

Even the "traditional" women's roles of wife, homemaker, and mother may not blend into one nearly as well as stereotypes and tradition suggest (Baruch *et al.*, 1987). In this case, there appears to be a need for research examining role conflict among these roles of women as well as role conflict between work and home roles. The former, however, is usually considered to be outside the domain of I/O psychology, while the latter is not or should not be.

A series of intriguing and important questions naturally occur with societal changes in women's workforce participation, and some of these are related to the potential for inter-role conflict. If males' reactions to work-role expectations in these occupations had been to become more involved in work roles and less involved in non-work roles, what would women's reactions be? If men had previously been expected to become more committed to work and women had not been, would these expectations change for women in a job market that had become more open to them? For that matter, would work and non-work role expectations for both men and women change, for example to become more similar? While there are advocates for all types of changes and stability regarding these role expectations, it is not clear what has happened. Just as importantly, it is not clear what *will* happen regarding these role expectations, because the history of these changes has probably not yet become stable. There are certainly many opportunities for research in this area, including very basic research such as the documentation of changing (or stable) attitudes and expectations for women (and men).

It makes sense that the more roles people have, the more opportunity there will be for different roles to have conflicting expectations. This is probably part of the logic behind the study of women's work–home role conflict, that is, there is an assumption that for women the work role is an "additional" role and an important and demanding one. Baruch *et al.* (1987), however, noted a study in sociology concluding that occupancy of more roles, up to seven, was related to positive mental health rather than to individual strain. Furthermore, it has often been noted that women employed for pay tend to be healthier than those not so employed (e.g. Gupta and Jenkins, 1985). These results argue that the addition of the work role for women might not be very stressful. Of course, selection may act to help achieve this result. That is, healthier people are better able to hold down jobs. Research is still needed to untangle the likely causal variables in this area.

Work and non-work environments can each have their own stressors as well as combining into stress due to their impinging on each other in the work–non-work interface. This work and non-work stress research is preceded by a more general research literature on relationships between all forms of work and non-work states, events, and activities. This older research topic, which has seen a recent revival, has traditionally been concerned with ascertaining whether non-work experiences affect the job, vice versa, neither, or both (e.g. Crouter, 1984; Gupta and Beehr, 1981; Kabanoff, 1980; Meissner, 1971; Wilensky, 1960; Zedeck, 1992).

In Chapter 1, a brief discussion of dual-career stress was offered. Table 1.2 there (Gupta and Jenkins, 1985) illustrates one of the specific paths for future inter-role conflict researchers to take, namely, the investigation of the stresses of dual-career couples. In their situations, each member of the dual-career couple is eligible to experience work stressors, home stressors, and inter-role stressors. This is a case of inter-role stress that may be special enough to require research all by itself. That is, other types of inter-role conflict research might not necessarily apply to this type. It should be noted that Gupta and Jenkins make a distinction between jobs and careers. In large part, the distinction is concerned with the amount of commitment (generally defined) required of a career versus the commitment required of "just" a job. Overall, in spite of the existence of relatively more literature on inter-role conflict than on other forms of role conflict, it seems that there is even more to be done on the topic.

One variable in need of research in this area is commitment to work (to the job, the organization, or the occupation) versus commitment to the non-work role(s). It may turn out be a powerful explanatory variable. If there is little commitment to one of the roles, the amount of serious conflict may be less than if both roles are the objects of strong commitment. Dubin's (1956; Dubin and Champoux, 1975) central life interest concept may provide a theoretic basis for such research. Within the specific domain of stress research, Beehr and Bhagat's (1985a) uncertainty theory provides a basis for directing this type of research with its concept of importance. Roles providing more important outcomes may turn out to be the roles to which the individual is more committed.

Causes of role conflict

Intra-sender, inter-sender, and person-role conflict may have different causes, although this possibility has not been investigated. Rarely do studies look at all of these forms simultaneously, but as advocated by Jackson and Schuler (1985), future research might benefit by this approach. For example, having multiple roles has sometimes been proposed as a cause of role conflict, but this is usually expected to be a cause of inter-role conflict. Having boundary roles in the organization is thought to be a cause of role conflict, but this probably refers to inter-sender conflict that is within the work role (therefore it is inter-sender, intra-role conflict, in Table 3.2). Other causes proposed for role conflict may also be based on the consideration of specific forms of it. This should be kept in mind in designing future research and testing hypotheses. If research examines such situations for their ability to predict conflict, the "correct" type of conflict must be measured for an adequate test of the hypotheses. Too frequently, researchers have been tempted to use the most readily available measure of role conflict rather than choosing or developing the one that fits their purpose best.

As with role ambiguity, the two meta-analyses (i.e. Fisher and Gitelson, 1983; Jackson and Schuler, 1985) provide some insight into likely causes of role conflict, although they do little to illuminate the precursors of specific forms of conflict. Fisher and Gitelson concluded that participative decision making was negatively related to role conflict and that boundary spanning was positively related to it. Among other potential causes of role conflict, Jackson and Schuler concluded that organization level was negatively related to role conflict. At a more individual (less structural) level, Jackson and Schuler concluded that supervisors' consideration and initiating structure, and feedback from the task and task identity were negatively related to it. Finally, Jackson and Schuler concluded that two person-type variables could be (positive) causes of role conflict: internal locus of control orientation and tenure.

As with role ambiguity, each meta-analysis also offered conclusions about the potential causal variables whose relationships with role conflict were most likely to be moderated by third variables. Both studies recommended future research on moderators for relationships between role conflict and three of its potential causes: formalization; employees' education; and employees' age. In addition, Fisher and Gitelson proposed moderator analyses for the relationships of the following with role conflict: tenure, skill variety, autonomy, feedback from others, and participative decision making.

Shaw and Riskind (1983) found, in the PAQ and the Caplan *et al.* (1975) data, that more job dimensions (potential causes of role stressors) were correlated with role conflict than with role ambiguity. "Using various sources of information," "using various senses," "making decisions," "performing skilled and technical activities," "engaging in general personal contact," "engaging in personally demanding situations," and "working under demanding circumstances" were negatively related to role conflict in the 0.35 to 0.55 range. "Communicating judgments" and "working non-typical versus day schedule" were related positively to role conflict in this range.

Jackson's (1983, 1984) experimental study found that an increase in participative decision making was not related to role conflict six months after the change, but was correlated with role conflict nine months after the implementation of participation through required staff meetings (r= −0.49). These types of studies, in which potential causes of role stressors are either measured via methods other than self-reports or in which the potential causes are manipulated, are particularly valuable in lending credence to results from studies using non-experimental, cross-sectional, self-report data.

Consequences of role conflict

Regarding the potential consequences of role conflict, the meta-analyses (i.e. Fisher and Gitelson, 1983; Jackson and Schuler, 1985) agreed that four psychological outcomes, namely involvement in the job and satisfaction with pay, with supervisors, and with co-workers, were negatively correlated with role conflict. In addition, Fisher and Gitelson concluded that organizational commitment was negatively related to role conflict and the Jackson and Schuler study concluded that satisfaction with the work itself was negatively related to job performance. They also concluded that a few relatively behavioral outcomes were related to role conflict: supervisor ratings of job performance (negatively) and propensity to leave (positively).

Aside from these likely main effects of role conflict, these studies also came to conclusions regarding which potential outcomes of role conflict were most appropriate for future research on moderators. They agreed that some psychological outcomes, namely tension/anxiety, overall job satisfaction, and satisfaction with promotions, were outcomes with potential moderators in their relationships with role conflict. They also agreed that the relationship of one behavior with role conflict was a good bet for future research using moderators: self-rated job performance. Fisher and Gitelson (1983) also recommended moderator research for the relationship between role conflict and supervisor ratings of job performance, while Jackson and Schuler (1985) recommended it for the relationships between role conflict and absenteeism and role conflict and organizational commitment. As already noted in the discussion of moderators in regard to role ambiguity, there are enough problems in these two meta-analyses to question the results and recommendations of either or both. In this context, it is important to note that moderators have been found only occasionally and have rarely been replicated for either role conflict or role ambiguity (King and King, 1990). It is probably best to regard all the recommendations about moderator analyses as very tentative and to proceed with moderator analyses that make the most theoretical sense, as recommended by Jackson and Schuler (1985). Our future research on moderators, both the environmental and personal moderators illustrated in Figure 1.2, can follow those recommendations.

RELATIONSHIPS BETWEEN ROLE CONFLICT AND AMBIGUITY

As noted in the beginning of the chapter, there are conceptual similarities and differences between role conflict and role ambiguity. In spite of this, many studies have treated them essentially as the same construct, for example by proposing the same relationships for each with other variables (noted by King and King, 1990). One example of a model making differential predictions for role conflict and role ambiguity is the uncertainty model of occupational stress (Beehr and Bhagat, 1985b), described in a previous chapter. Role ambiguity was predicted to be related approximately equally to both E→P (effort to performance) and P→O (performance to outcome) uncertainties, while role conflict was expected to be related to E→P uncertainty more than to P→O uncertainty. As reported in Chapter 2, a study by Pardine (1987) has supported this proposition. In addition, two preliminary studies have reported data on this proposition. Beehr and O'Driscoll (1990) found strong support for this proposition in a survey study of 106 accountants of a "big eight" accounting firm. Role ambiguity was correlated approximately equally with the E→P and P→O uncertainties (0.61 and 0.52, respectively; difference ns), while role conflict was correlated more strongly with the E→P than with the P→O uncertainty (0.45 and 0.27, respectively; different at p<.01). A second study (Beehr et al., 1986), among 225 registered nurses of seven hospitals, found weak but significant correlations between the role variables and the uncertainties (role ambiguity 0.22 and 0.19 and role conflict 0.18 and 0.12 with E→P and P→O uncertainties, respectively). In that study, although the directions of the differences were consistent with the uncertainty theory, the difference between 0.18 and 0.12 was not significant. That study is described in more detail in the chapter on social support, which was the focus of the study.

There is more reason to believe that there should be more conceptual and theoretical distinction between the two role constructs if one considers the previous discussion of subtypes of each. One might expect the subtypes of role conflict and ambiguity to be related differently to other variables; if so, there is even more reason to expect the two more global concepts of role conflict and role ambiguity to be related to third variables differently.

Even if these two role stressors are related to individual strains about equally (which could be true if they are both occupational stressors), three particular recommendations for future research on their differential correlates appear especially appropriate. First, some intervening variables might be different for the two; that is, elements of Beehr and Newman's (1978) process facet might differ for the two. As already mentioned, the potential differential effects on the types of uncertainty created by the role stressors have already been proposed (Beehr, 1985a; Beehr and Bhagat, 1985b).

Second, more moderator research might be called for, especially theoretically based moderator research. Individual differences may exist, for example in susceptibility to the noxious effects of different stressors such as role conflict and role ambiguity.

Third, precursors or causes of the two role variables are likely to be different. Going all the way back to Kahn et al. (1964), and following the theoretical comments in the literature, it is obvious that there are supposed to be some differential causes of the two. Any situation that represents information deficiency should lead to role ambiguity, while inconsistent information is more likely to cause role conflict. These types of propositions could be tested either in the laboratory or field.

Aside from their conceptual and theoretical differences, the research on role conflict and ambiguity has provided information about empirical relationships between the two. Role ambiguity and role conflict indices used within the same study have tended to be moderately correlated with each other (on the average, 0.37 in Fisher and Gitelson's and 0.27 in Jackson and Schuler's meta-analyses). A related question in separating them, mentioned previously, is the extent to which they are related differently to third variables. King and King (1990) found that the relationships of the correlations of role conflict and role ambiguity with third variables as reported in the two meta-analyses were very strong. That is, for Fisher and Gitelson, the correlations of role conflict with third variables correlated with the correlations of role ambiguity with the same third variables 0.82 (n=18 correlations), and for Jackson and Schuler the correlation was 0.86 (n=27 correlations). Even if role ambiguity and role conflict are only moderately correlated with each other, in practice they do not seem to relate very differently to third variables.

The literature on role conflict and ambiguity has been dominated by research using Rizzo *et al.* (1970) scales and therefore, much of what is known about the empirical relationship between the two constructs is based on one set of measures. One study (McGee *et al.*, 1989) employed confirmatory factor analysis of Rizzo *et al.*'s (1970) role conflict and ambiguity questionnaire to determine whether the two role constructs are independent (as Rizzo *et al.* suggested), whether they are really only part of a single construct (as suggested by Tracy and Johnson, 1981), or whether they are likely to be affected by wording confounds (because all role conflict items describe negative situations and all role ambiguity items describe positive situations, as noted first by Tracy and Johnson). The third alternative, represented by the appearance of one general factor (composed of all items) and one second-order factor on which only the negatively worded items loaded, had the most support in a test of competing factor structures. This could mean that the positive or negative wording of the items determines the factors, but because the wording is related to the item content, one cannot be sure. Therefore, it is impossible to know what the two scales measure.

The extensive use of the Rizzo *et al.* (1970) scales is unfortunate, because their relatively unquestioned acceptance for so long a period of time has probably retarded the development of other, potentially better measures (Beehr, 1985a). It has now become obvious that there is no reason to continue automatically using the scales as they now stand (King and King, 1990; McGee *et al.*, 1989). Regarding the constructs (rather than the measures) of role conflict and ambiguity, they may still be valuable in understanding role stress, however. Future research needs to develop new measures of them. The new measures should obviously avoid using negatively worded items for one construct and positively worded items for the other; in addition, it would be a significant step forward if future research used measures that divided role ambiguity and conflict into their subtypes.

Chapter 4

Beyond role conflict and ambiguity
Other social psychological stressors in the workplace

Although role conflict and ambiguity have been the subject of both early and frequent research in the social psychological approach to occupational stress, other types of job stressors have also been studied. First, there are other *role* stressors. Role overload is the most obvious of these, given its "role" family name, but some others also fit the definition that they are characterized by types of demands or expectations of the people in one's role set.

Several researchers have categorized types of job stressors. For example, Glowinkowski and Cooper (1987) named six: stress in the job itself, role based stress, relationships, career development factors, organizational structure and climate, and the work–family interface. Five categories were suggested by Ivancevich and Matteson (1980), three of which focused on social psychological stressors in the workplace. They employed the frequently used organizational psychology categorization by level of thought and inquiry: individual level, group level, and organizational level. While these approaches have taken a fairly broad view, trying to develop categories into which many specific stressors could be placed, Osipow and Spokane (1984) have settled for a much narrower set of categories: role overload, role insufficiency, role ambiguity, role boundary (role conflict), and responsibility. These are categories that can almost fit within a single category from Table 4.1 (role demands and expectations from Beehr and Newman, 1978). Thus, it is apparent that one can categorize stressors fairly broadly or more narrowly. What is the right categorization is probably unanswerable, but some ways of categorizing may prove more useful as research guides than others. At present, it is probably more useful to try to be more exhaustive in categorization of stressors in order to keep an open mind regarding what is stressful in the workplace.

An approach for broadening the list of potential social psychological stressors would be to rely on theories other than role theory for understanding and studying occupational stress (Love and Beehr, 1981). Over a decade ago, a comprehensive review attempted to list all such stressors,

Table 4.1 Contents of the environmental facet (reprinted with permission from Beehr and Newman, 1978)

a. role demands or expectations
    – role overload
    – role conflict
    – role ambiguity
    – formal and informal relationships among role set members
    – psychological contract perceived by the employee
b. Job demands and task characteristics
    – weekly work schedule
    – over- and underutilization of skills
    – variance in workload
    – pace of work
    – responsibility (for people and things)
    – travel as part of the job
    – job characteristics thought to be intrinsically motivating
c. Organizational characteristics and conditions
    – company size
    – job security
    – hours of work (both total and time of day)
    – duration of work tasks
    – sociotechnical changes
    – organizational structure (and job's position within hierarchy)
    – communication system (and job's position within system)
    – subsystem relations
    – staffing policies and procedures
    – management style (philosophical and operational)
    – evaluation, control and reward systems
    – training programs
    – organizational climate
    – opportunity for advancement
    – required relocation
    – local union constraints
d. Organization's external demands and conditions
    – route to and from work
    – number and nature of customers or clients
    – national or international unions
    – governmental laws and regulations
    – suppliers; providers of needed services
    – weather
    – technological and scientific developments
    – consumer movements
    – geographic location of organization

even those that might have been only mentioned in popular press literature, rather than examined in rigorous research (Beehr and Newman, 1978). Table 4.1 contains this list of potential occupational stressors and its categories.

Beehr and Newman (1978) noted that research actually existed only on a very few of the stressors in the table. It was not always easy to determine whether research had been done on a stressor or not at that time, for two reasons. First, some of the articles purported to have done research, but the methodological rigor of the project was so weak that we were reluctant to call it research at all. Fortunately, this has changed dramatically, with a great deal of good research now having been conducted, as illustrated in this volume. Second, we were using the Beehr–Newman model (1978), which placed job stressors in the environmental facet of the stress process, but most of the literature at that time did not convincingly measure the stressors in a way that clearly separated them from the process facet (which contains the focal person's perceptions). The discussion of role conflict and ambiguity in the previous chapter illustrates that perceptual measures of stressors still dominate the literature on role conflict and ambiguity. This is less of a problem now, however, for two reasons. First, many of the strains and other outcomes have been measured with non-self-reports in some of the studies, reducing the probability of common method variance accounting for the resulting relationships. Second, moderator research has become much more common and it is more difficult for simple method variance effects to account for moderator results.

In fact, at that time (1978), no studies of role ambiguity were uncovered that measured role ambiguity in any way except through perceptions. A major problem with role ambiguity is that it is not only often measured as a perception, but it is also sometimes conceived as a perception. That is, it is implied that role ambiguity can only be a perception. The previously discussed article by Pearce (1981) illustrates this. It was noted there that there is some discrepancy among the questionnaire measures of role ambiguity regarding whether it is conceived as information deficiency in the environment or as unpredictability by the person. The uncertainty model (Beehr and Bhagat 1985a) clearly associates role ambiguity with environmental information deficiency (in Beehr and Newman's environmental facet; 1978) and labels the person's inability to predict as uncertainty (in the process facet).

In addition to role ambiguity, research literature could be found in 1978 on several of the other stressors, although the research had often not operationalized the stressors independently from the focal person's perceptions. The table is, however, quite inclusive and it also organizes the stressors into four categories for better understanding: role demands or expectations, job demands and task characteristics, organizational characteristics and conditions, and organization's external demands and conditions. These can be used to examine stressors other than role ambiguity and conflict. The following discussion examines selected stressors within each of the four categories of Table 4.1 and subsequent studies of them. Our work has now included several specific stressors from that table, including role overload, role conflict, role ambiguity, relationships among role set members, underutilization of skills, intrinsically motivating job characteristics, organization size, and management style. Our emphasis has been on micro rather than macro organizational psychology variables as stressors. In the language of Figure 1.2, these are the work environment stressors that have been the focus of our work.

ROLE DEMANDS OR EXPECTATIONS

While the table's first category of occupational stressors, role demands or expectations includes role ambiguity and conflict, it covers more than that. Role theory could provide more insight into occupational stress than just contributing these two stressors. More of the studies in my own program of research on occupational stress examine stressors that fall into this category than any other category in the table.

Role overload is one of these and it was originally included as a subtype of role conflict by Kahn *et al.* (1964). The Beehr *et al.* (1976) study described earlier measured role overload via self-reports and found it was related to job dissatisfaction, fatigue, and tension (median r=0.32) among white collar employees. Similarly, Beehr and Drexler (1986), in another study of white collar workers, found it was related to several facet dissatisfaction measures (median r=0.19). The focus of this study, however, was on social support and the study is described in more detail in the chapter on that topic.

In the family business study described earlier (Beehr *et al.*, 1993), we also measured expectations that family members felt were strong for their performance in these businesses. This can be conceived as pressure for heavy workload and therefore as similar to role overload. It was related to job satisfaction and career satisfaction, but not to self-reported physical and mental strains. Furthermore, its relationships with the satisfaction indices were positive. Although these expectations measures were derived based on preliminary interviews aimed at uncovering responses about role stressors, the expectations for high performance from the family members acted in very different ways from typical role stressors. This suggests that something else was operating in the family business situation. Future research might use this result to look for insights into some types of overload that do not seem to have stressful effects. Under what conditions, for example, do people work hard in response to external demands and not suffer any apparent negative consequences?

In addition, the table lists two other types of potential stressors that could be derived from role theory: formal and informal relationships among the members of the role set and the psychological contract of the employee.

Role theory can be used to categorize the contents of jobs, which, as with other roles, are defined by the activities expected of the role incumbent by members of the role set. Role ambiguity and conflict, therefore, are the results of conflicting and ambiguous expectations. Role overload, on the other hand, is the result of a sum of expectations of activities that exceeds what is reasonable or possible. A closely related concept is workload, which is often operationalized by quantity of work expected of the focal person. The more workload one has, of course, the more likely it is that the person will be overloaded.

Relationships among members of the role set

Aside from these three, the table lists relationships among members of the role set. This was also one of the major categories of Glowinkowski and Cooper (1987) and was included in the group level category of Ivancevich and Matteson (1980). While this has received little attention from I/O psychologists, it is often one of the first things that the public intuitively thinks of as stressful in the workplace. That is, extremely poor interpersonal relationships at work resulting in conflict, arguing, fighting, and so forth seem likely to evoke strong stress reactions. Since they have not been the subject of much study, we must ask why.

First, such overt problems usually demand action in organizations. There are often sanctions against physical fighting in particular, which would reduce its occurrence and might result in the dismissal of participants, further reducing the problem. Second, many studies of occupational stress in recent years have come from an interest in management and the use of management samples probably reduces the likelihood of focusing on either outright fighting or arguments. In most organizations, managerial level people must suppress these activities to have a successful career and they know it. Therefore, temptations to engage in these activities may be stressful, though suppressed.

Third, these relationships may have actually been studied in conjunction with occupational stress somewhat frequently, but under a different name and often for different reasons. Social support has received a great deal of research in the general life stress area and increasingly in the job stress area as well. Supportive people in the workplace are likely to help reduce strains. In this sense, the *lack of* social support could be considered a stressor. It has, instead, usually been considered as a treatment or adaptive activity for coping with stress. Consistent with that approach, a chapter on social support is included in this book under the section on alleviating the aversive effects of occupational stress. The literature on social support in conjunction with occupational stress is full of empirical results consistent with the idea that lack of social support is related to increased employee strains. Since interpersonal conflict seems to be an extreme example of lack of social support, this adds to the likelihood that such conflict can be a stressor in the workplace. It does seem, however, that the study of social support in occupational stress combined with the lack of studying interpersonal conflict is like a coat with one sleeve – the extreme of support has been studied, but the other extreme of conflict has not been addressed very often.

One of the few studies to include interpersonal conflict as a potential job stressor found that it was weakly to moderately related to some strains such as anxiety, frustration, satisfaction with supervisors and subordinates, physical symptoms, and intentions to quit one's job among a sample of university secretaries (Spector *et al.*, 1988). We examined interpersonal conflict in our family business study and found that it was related to job dissatisfaction, career satisfaction, and psychological strain (median r=0.44). More research on interpersonal conflict in relation to occupational stress seems to be an obvious need.

The psychological contract

The other specific potential stressor listed in the category of role demands or expectations in Table 4.1 is the perceived psychological contract (Beehr and Newman, 1978). The psychological contract is a type of social contract between the employee and the employing organization. Basically, it is characterized by an exchange concept; that is, the employee exchanges things such as efforts and skills for some of the organization's resources such as money and fringe benefits. A complete examination of a psychological contract usually finds many things exchanged besides these basic employment exchanges, however.

The theory of the psychological contract usually focuses on the so-called implicit contract between the person and the organization, emphasizing the fact that there are expectations beyond those in the written contract. The contract is psychological or perceived and both the individual and the representatives of the organization probably have perceptions of the contract, which may or may not match. In the employment situation, no doubt many of the expectations come from what is in the written contract, the formal job description and so forth, but there is always more. It should be noted that, since the psychological contract is a perception, it more correctly belongs in the process facet rather than in the environmental facet where Beehr and Newman had placed it.

Person–Environment Fit

Closely related to this contract, conceptually, is a well-developed theory of occupational stress known as the Person–Environment (P–E) Fit theory (Caplan, 1987; Harrison, 1985). P–E Fit theory maintains that there are two types of (mis)fit between the person and the environment that could lead to strains. Therefore, the poor fits are stressful. Although almost every psychological stress theory allows for the combination of characteristics of the person and the environment leading to strains, P–E Fit theory has narrowed the potentially infinite range of P–E Fits into the following categories: the fit of the job's or organization's supplies and rewards with the individual's needs or preferences, and the fit of the individual's skills and abilities with the job's demands or requirements (e.g. Caplan *et al.*, 1975; Harrison, 1985). The relationship of P–E Fit theory to the psychological contract is thus obvious. What is not so obvious is that P–E Fit theory is related to the role stressor category of occupational stress. The two approaches to occupational stress are often considered to be very different, but when it is recognized that one element of P–E Fit theory is the demand ("expectation" in role theory) that the role incumbent experiences to do certain things, the link can be identified.

A final word is in order about P–E Fit theory of occupational stress. It has sometimes not been recognized that the theory is more detailed than simply an unspecified combination of person and environmental characteristics. As noted earlier, there are two specific kinds of misfits leading to stress: the fit of the organization's supplies or rewards with the individual's needs or preferences, and the fit of the individual's skills and abilities with the organization's or job's demands and requirements. Furthermore, the theory maintains that the fits in these two areas are fits of very specific parallel elements (Harrison, 1985). For example, potential sources of occupational stress would be the lack of fit between the amount of workload the employees have and the amount of workload they desire, or the amount of quantitative ability the job requires and the amount of quantitative ability the individual has. Simply using any person variable to moderate the relation-

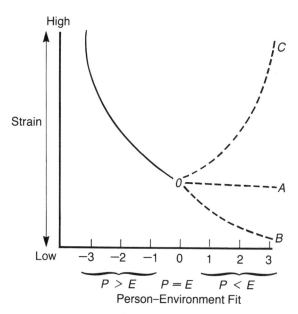

Figure 4.1 The hypothetical shapes of P–E Fit relationships with strain (reprinted with permission from Harrison, 1985).

ship between any stressor and strain does not necessarily constitute a test of the P–E Fit theory, although some researchers have not understood this. Furthermore, the specific relationship between fit and strain may vary according to the specific type of fit being examined (Caplan *et al.*, 1975). Figure 4.1 above illustrates the three most often occurring shapes of the relationships.

Regarding the Beehr–Newman (1978) model of occupational stress and its four categories of stressors, the E part of the P–E Fit approach falls into the environmental facet, and the demands part of the E can be placed into the role demands or expectations category. The supplies and resources part of the E, however, would probably fall into the job demands and characteristics category as a job characteristic. Furthermore, the P part of the P–E Fit theory belongs in Beehr and Newman's personal facet rather than their environmental facet. The key distinguishing factor of P–E Fit theory is that it is very explicit in maintaining that very specific elements of the person are a necessary part of the stress process.

JOB DEMANDS AND TASK CHARACTERISTICS

Job demands and task characteristics, under the environmental facet in Table 4.1, include demands that emanate from others in the workplace less clearly than the demands known as role demands. Although any work-related demand can ultimately be linked to others (e.g. time-and-motion experts, top management, inventors of machines who originally created some of the current working conditions and demands), the following are examples of job demands that probably are less directly attributable to members of one's work role set: weekly work schedule, over- and underutilization of skills, variance in workload, pace of work, responsibility (for people and things), travel as part of the job, and job characteristics thought to be intrinsically motivating. These are potentially stressful and are often rightly or wrongly seen as a given that are inherent in a job, that is, seen as not due to specific demands from others in one's role set. Some studies in the research program described in this book have examined stressors in this category, most notably underutilization of skills and job characteristics.

The work schedule

Work schedule has been a topic of research interest lately, although most of the interest has not been in the context of occupational stress. Both shiftwork and alternative work schedules have been studied with increasing interest. On the surface, one might surmise that shiftwork is bad (stress-inducing) and the freedom to use alternative work schedules is good (stress-relieving).

Non-standard working schedules (almost anything but regular, daytime, weekday work) in general seem to be correlated with some indicators of poor adjustment in family roles. They especially are related to role conflict between the work and home (e.g. a national survey by Staines and Pleck, 1984). The effects of flextime (in which employees are usually allowed some discretion regarding arrival and departure times) on employee attitudes seems to be positive or nil (e.g. Hicks and Klimoski, 1981; Orpen, 1981). Compressed work schedules seem to have some positive effects on attitudes (e.g. Dunham *et al.*, 1987; Latack and Foster, 1985).

Regarding one of the oldest "non-standard" schedules, shiftwork, Dunham's (1977) review concluded in part that shiftwork is related to many kinds of physical and psychological problems. Frese and Okonek (1984) have shown that many people say they have left shiftwork to get away from the negative health effects that shiftwork had on them, while Zedeck *et al.* (1983) found evidence suggesting that those who remain very long on a shift may have at least a slight tendency to adapt to its difficulties. A recent study of coal miners found that changing to a twelve-hour, four-day shift had no apparent effect on physiological measures (Cunningham, 1989). It also has been found to be related to disturbances in sleep quality and quantity (e.g. unpublished research summarized by Hurrell and Colligan, 1987), psychosomatic complaints (e.g. Frese and Okonek, 1984), and disruption of family roles (e.g. Staines and Pleck, 1984).

Recent work, however, has indicated that the relationships between shiftwork and many strain-type variables are quite complicated and could be due to the association of shiftwork with other variables, such as age of the employee (Frese and Okonek, 1984; Peterson, 1985; Zedeck *et al.*, 1983).

A basic methodological problem is the inability to assign randomly which employees get on a certain shift. This is likely to remain a thorny problem and it muddies the meaning of most of the studies so far. At a minimum, however, it indicates that future research would be well advised to control statistically some potentially confounding variables while analyzing the relationships between shiftwork and strains (or other stress-related variables, for that matter). Exactly which variables ought to be controlled, however, is difficult to determine with finality at this point. Some possibilities include age, gender, family status (marital and parental), type of job (e.g. physical labor, mental vigilance, decision making), the voluntariness of the assignment to non-standard schedules, and the specific type of non-standard schedule. These may very well turn out to be moderators of the shiftwork–outcome connection. There is a common belief that certain people can adapt to non-standard schedules more easily than others. If such people could be identified a priori, there are potential benefits to both practice and theory. Other people, who might be labeled shiftwork-reactive, might be hypersensitive to non-standard schedules. They would suffer more than the average person under such conditions. Separating the adaptives from the reactives on the basis of individual difference variables, both demographic and psychological, is a task remaining to be accomplished.

Skill utilization

Overutilization of skills (sometimes labeled qualitative role overload) and underutilization of skills have been related to strains in past research, including studies that have attempted to operationalize these stressors objectively (e.g. Coburn, 1975). More often, however, underutilization has been measured somewhat subjectively (e.g. differences between self-reports of education and education needed for the job were part of the operationalization of underutilization in Gupta and Beehr, 1979). In the few studies done on underutilization, it has been related to a variety of psychological strains and to somatic complaints (Caplan *et al.*, 1975), and to absenteeism and turnover (Gupta and Beehr, 1979; described in detail in the chapter on organizational outcomes).

Pace of work and machine pacing

Machine pacing of work, which is often studied by human factors specialists but rarely by organizational psychologists, characterizes the jobs of those whose rate of work must keep pace with some sort of external, non-human controller. Machine pacing has been found related to elevated heart rate (e.g. MacKay *et al.*, 1979), to elevated noradrenaline (e.g. Frankenhaeuser and Gardell, 1976), and for some people, to psychological strains (e.g. Caplan, *et al.*, 1975; Broadbent, 1985).

Machine pacing and workload

Pace of work is logically related to workload and therefore to overload, especially quantitative overload. Studies of machine pacing need to control the effects of the pace itself while determining the effects of the source of the pacing (machines). If machines set a fast pace, one would expect overload to result and the overload could be stressful. The overload might be due to the pace itself rather than to the fact that the pace was set by a machine, however.

In addition to the actual pace of the work, it is also logical to control variability of pace. That is, industrial machines usually allow little or no variability in the pace demanded of the employees. Again, the question is, what is machine pacing? If machines allow some variability, the results may be different from machines that do not have variable paces.

Studies have indicated that there may be physiological effects of machine pacing, but the results are not entirely consistent (Hurrell and Colligan, 1987). Very few studies have been conducted regarding machine pacing and psychological strains, but there is some evidence that these are affected by machine pacing as well. Investigation of the factors that might make machine pacing stressful is recommended. Two examples provided here are workload and lack of variability. A third factor is control.

Machine pacing and control

Hurrell and Colligan (1987) noted that, while taxonomies of the important elements of machine pacing have not been universally accepted, the issue of control is central to the concept of machine pacing. Machine pacing is likely to be related to control of the work in general and therefore to job autonomy. There is of course a large quantity of published research on autonomy, usually in conjunction with other job characteristics. In addition, Karasek (1979) has developed a model of occupational stress focusing on lack of job decision latitude (this is, perhaps, control or autonomy in common job characteristics parlance) as one of two main work characteristics likely to combine to create stress in the workplace (the other is high demand for productivity).

Machine pacing of work as a potential stressor is a topic needing more research, especially research investigating the psychological nature of machine pacing such as perceived workload, variability, and control. Such pacing is probably much more complex than research has usually acknowledged. Machine pacing in industry probably involves more variables relevant to organizational psychologists than those discussed above. Machine-paced jobs often involve repetition (low cycle time), impersonal treatment of workers, and so forth. None of these are necessarily inherent in the concept of machine pacing, and they vary in the extent to which they are present from one machine-paced job to another. A taxonomy of machine-paced work has been suggested by Hurrell and Colligan (1987) based on the amount of time the machine is available during a cycle, the amount of time the operator uses the machine, and the amount of time the operator waits before using it again.

Research using this or other taxonomies might improve the knowledge about machine pacing and job stress. Another approach that seems likely to produce meaningful new information would be to break machine-paced work into its variable parts as they affect the overall job (e.g. degree of impersonality on job, speed or cycle time, degree of control over machine or job overall). As indicated in Figure 4.2, the effects of machine pacing could be partly due to its effect on these variables, but that is not known as of now. Some of the inconsistent research results regarding stress due to machine pacing could be due to the likelihood that machine pacing in one study has a very different character from machine pacing in another study. Overall, the various effects of machine pacing have not been studied enough from the organizational stress point of view followed in this book.

Responsibility

Responsibility for people and responsibility for things have been studied as occupational stressors, although usually with self-reports of these variables

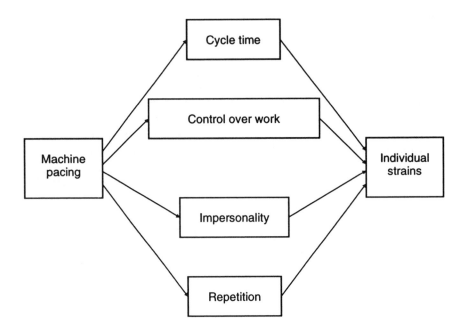

Figure 4.2 Possible intervening variables in the relationships between machine pacing and strains.

(e.g. House *et al.*, 1979; Osipow and Davis, 1988; Osipow and Spokane, 1984). There may be an opportunity for creative research to operationalize these in somewhat objective ways, however. Responsibility for things could be operationalized in terms of budgets over which people have control or the value of machines over which they are responsible. Obviously, in non-experimental field research, care would have to be taken to anticipate naturally occurring relationships between these operationalizations and other important variables such as level of pay, prestige, autonomy, and so forth. It may, however, be possible to control these either statistically or by choosing samples that are matched on such characteristics once they are recognized as potential contaminants of the relationships under scrutiny.

Intrinsically motivating job characteristics

Job characteristics thought to be intrinsically motivating are some other potential stressors. The best known of these are probably the set of auton-omy, variety, task feedback, task significance, and task identity from the *Job Diagnostic Survey* (Hackman and Oldham, 1980). In combination, these are sometimes labeled the motivating potential of the job.

Autonomy, participation, and perceived control

Autonomy was previously discussed above under the heading machine pacing and it is also theoretically related to the psychological state of experienced responsibility for the outcomes of one's work (Hackman and Oldham, 1980). This is a different type of responsibility from the responsibility for others and for things noted above. It refers instead to a feeling of control over the outcomes of one's work. In expectancy theory terms, this means that the person can expect that their own efforts will be closely related to their own productivity or job performance.

Perceived control (actually the lack of control) has been found related to potential job strains such as perceived stressfulness (Hendrix *et al.*, 1985) and happiness and self-confidence (Adelmann, 1987). Participative decision making could also be related to autonomy and control and it may lead to less emotional strain (Jackson, 1983, 1984) and be related to perceived stress and job-related tension (Ivancevich, 1979). Results regarding relationships of perceived control, autonomy, and participation with physical symptoms, however, are inconsistent (Ivancevich finding some relationships and Hendrix *et al.* not).

A theoretical approach for expecting perceived control to be related to occupational stress argues that control (sometimes called job decision latitude) interacts with job demands to produce psychological strains. One early study had found some evidence for such a relationship (Beehr, 1976), and the argument is that job demands arouse or motivate people but that with low control over the work, people cannot release this arousal through work performance (Karasek, 1979). While intriguing, there is presently little evidence that supports this interaction concept and there is some that does not (e.g. Payne and Fletcher, 1983; Spector, 1987a).

One intuitive reason to expect intrinsically motivating job characteristics to be stressors is that strong motivation might lead to people to work so hard they would be in danger of the popularized "workaholism." If people worked "too" hard, they would then experience overload. Type A behavior is supposed to make people more susceptible to coronary heart disease (Friedman and Rosenman, 1974) and people who exhibit heavy work schedules and time urgency also have some of the symptoms of Type A behavior.

Type A has usually been studied and described as a fairly stable behavior, similar to a personality trait. If this assumption were entirely true, then job characteristics could not very strongly affect it. Type A, however, was explicitly theorized to be a behavior (Friedman and Rosenman, 1974) and most psychologists believe in the general idea that behavior is a function of both the person and environment. If that is the case, then an obvious question is, what environmental situations are most likely to affect Type A behavior? If some job characteristics lead to Type A behavior and if Type A behavior in turn leads to heart disease, then those job characteristics could be deemed stressors. Ganster (1987) summarized the job stress and Type A research to conclude that, while laboratory experiments might find consistent relationships between work (laboratory) environments and Type A, field research has not. Future job stress research needs to be done to determine whether and which job characteristics are likely to have the effect of increasing Type A behavior. This seems an intriguing area for future research.

While intrinsically motivating job characteristics might lead to strains through their influence on Type A behavior, they might also have such effects without affecting Type A. This is a largely unexplored area for research. It seems more intuitive that intrinsically motivating job characteristics would be inversely related to strains. In this case, their relative absence would be the stressors. The reason for this probability is that some "positive" attitudes and behaviors are often positively correlated with these job characteristics, and strains, or at least the psychological strains, are more likely to be related negatively to outcomes such as job satisfaction and attendance. By extension, therefore, one would expect that the intrinsically motivating job characteristics would be negatively related to strains.

There is some evidence from previous studies that this may be true. Autonomy is one of the primary intrinsically motivating characteristics of jobs and Beehr (1976) found that it was negatively correlated with such strains as depression (r=–0.32) and low self esteem (r=–0.27); Beehr and Drexler (1986) reported autonomy to be correlated with three facet satisfactions (median r=0.34); and Beehr *et al.* (1976) found *non*-participation related to job dissatisfaction r=0.34) and to fatigue (r=0.23), but not to a tension index.

Furthermore, Karasek's (1979) theroy of occupational stress proposes job decision latitude to be a favorable factor in occupational stress and this is very similar to job autonomy. Abdel-Halim (1978) found that the MPS (motivating potential score; Hackman and Oldham, 1975, 1976) was apparently negatively related to one psychological strain, job anxiety. This can be interpreted based on a figure of an interaction presented in that study. These studies do not focus on main effects of motivating job characteristics on individuals' strains. In fact, all three studies primarily were interested in the potential for job characteristics to moderate relationships between more traditional and intuitive job stressors and strains. The interpretations offered here can only be considered suggestive. Again, more research is needed to determine the validity of the assumption that intrinsically motivating job characteristics would be negatively related to strains.

ORGANIZATIONAL CHARACTERISTICS AND CONDITIONS

The third category of occupational stressors in Table 4.1, organizational characteristics and conditions, refers to potential job stressors at the so-called organizational or macro level of organizational psychology. The list of potential stressors suggested in the table at this level is very long, but there has been relatively little research on them by organizational psychologists.

Organizational size

While there is not a lot of research on company size as a stressor, there is some related research on size and attitudes such as job satisfaction. While size of company can be interpreted in a number of ways, such as the number of employees, amount of annual sales, and net worth, consistent with the present focus on social psychological stress, size is defined here as the number of employees. Size has generally been correlated with potential strain-related variables such as absenteeism, turnover, and grievances (Payne and Pugh, 1976), although it is difficult to say exactly why this happens. In sociology and at the macro level of organizational psychology, size is also thought to be a partial determinant of many structural facets of organizations (Payne and Pugh, 1976) and because of this, it could have an indirect effect on any number of outcomes.

In extra analyses of the data from O'Driscoll and Beehr (1989), in three "offices" of a big eight accounting firm in the US, there were only small and mostly non-significant differences in amounts of strains between people employed in the large office (about 200 people) and the two smaller offices (less than 100 people each). These offices were similar in industry, type of jobs and professional credentials of employees, and region of the country, which helped to control many potential extraneous variables. They differed, however, in the size of the cities in which they were located (the large office was in a city of over one million people, while the others were located in cities in the 200–300,000 range).

Although only a few of the differences in that study between the different-sized offices were significant, there was some consistency in that four of the five "outcomes" in the study were in the direction indicating that people were worse off in the large office. Strains, i.e. physical symptoms and psychological symptoms, were greater in the large office, and turnover intentions and global job satisfaction were more negative in the large office. The other outcome, however, was a sum of satisfaction with several facets of the jobs, which was higher in the large office. If these potential occupational stress outcomes are due to differences in occupational stress, however, then the stressors shoud also be greater in the large office. There were, however, no consistent differences between the offices on two role stressors, role ambiguity and role conflict, and on uncertainty about effort-to-performance and performance-to-outcome expectancies (theorized in Chapter 2 to be intermediate elements of many stressor–strain relationships). It is, of course, possible that these are not the crucial stressors that are most likely to be affected by organization size and the study was not designed as one intended to examine size of organization as a potential stressor. Future research could help to illuminate this issue. It would start with a thorough theoretical and conceptual exploration of the potential reasons why organizational size could influence occupational stress.

Occupational position within the organizational structure

One interesting potential stressor at this level is the location of one's office in organizational space. For example, organizational boundary positions have often been proposed as stressful because of the likelihood of experiencing role conflict, with messages from people on different sides of the boundary having conflicting values and expectations for the person (e.g. Kahn *et al.*, 1964; Osipow and Spokane, 1984). In some sales jobs, for example, the salesperson experiences conflicting demands from inside the organization (pressure for production or sales) and from outside the organization (the development of mutual trust between salesperson and customer may make it difficult for the salesperson to sell if they know the product is not the best available for the customer).

A second characteristic regarding one's position in the organization that has been suggested to be stressful is the vertical location of a job in the organization. Specifically, much speculation and popular press reports would have us believe that there is more stress at the tops of organizations than at lower levels. The term executive stress is frequently used, for example. If the assumption is that the executive suite is more stress-laden than other locations in the organization, however, there is little evidence that this is true (Caplan *et al.*, 1975; Brief *et al.*, 1981; Payne, 1980). In my study with Drexler (Beehr and Drexler, 1976), of bank employees, vertical hierarchical level was moderately positively correlated with three facet satisfactions (median r=0.20). It was also positively but weakly correlated, however with three standard role stressors (role overload, r=0.06; role ambiguity, r=0.04; role conflict, r=0.13).

Overall, in spite of the popular notion of executive stress, the reverse seems more likely based on the evidence. For example, white collar American males enjoy better mental health than blue collar males (e.g. Caplan *et al.*, 1975). It is easy to see why there could be evidence for more stress at the bottom of organizations than at the top if one steps back and takes a sociological/demographic view of society. It is very logical that people in the upper classes would tend to have lower death rates and better health, probably for more than one reason. With more wealth, they can afford better medical care and better insurance, for example. In addition, poor health can effectively prevent people from reaching the top of many organizations. Thus, people at the top of organizations are not likely to evidence strain-type reactions, but it is unknown whether this is because there is less stress there or because they are better able to handle it.

Required relocation

It makes sense that changing one's living quarters could involve some stress and some jobs virtually require changing locations, at least if one wishes to be upwardly mobile. There is an intuitive link between such moves and uncertainty about a wide variety of things, both work and non-work related. Some of one's old, customary ways of behaving may still bring desirable results, while others may not. The new bosses of someone who has transferred to another location may act the same as one's former boss, but they may not. The principal in one's children's new school may or may not respond to the same requests, and so forth. There is a potential for uncertainty between one's behaviors and performance or outcomes, and this has been proposed as stressful (e.g. P→O uncertainty in Beehr and Bhagat, 1985b).

Figure 4.3 (Brett, 1980) is a proposed model of potential effects of job transfer. Consistent with the uncertainty approach to occupational stress, the model is based on the assumption that transfers result in uncertainties about behavior–outcome contingencies (P→O uncertainties, in the terms of uncertainty theory of occupational stress). This uncertainty results in the loss of a sense of control and coping behaviors are aimed at regaining this. Failure to regain such control results in illness (strains).

Conceiving geographic mobility as stressful fits into the larger literature on stressful life events, which often considers change of many sorts to be stressful. Brett's review concluded that mobility did not seem to be related to poor psychological health, but perhaps it was related to coronary heart disease. She proposed that transfers to similar work and non-work situations were likely to result in fewer or less severe strains than transfers to situations that are different. Also, apparently extrapolating from social support theories, Brett proposed that those who have families accompanying them are likely to have fewer stressful difficulties than others. Much still needs to be done to examine the validity and usefulness of occupational geographic transfer models such as that in Figure 4.3, however.

Job security

One condition that has strong intuitive appeal as a stressor and that has received some research work is job security, or lack of it. Kahn *et al.* (1964) addressed this in their study of role ambiguity under the label of job future ambiguity, which was related to role ambiguity. It is not, however, a pure form of role ambiguity, because it does not depend solely or even primarily on the expectations or demands of others in the role set. It has been only weakly related to role ambiguity (e.g. r=0.19 with Caplan *et al.*'s environmenal role ambiguity; 1975). In their national study of twenty-three occupations, Caplan *et al.* reported that job future ambiguity was one of the many

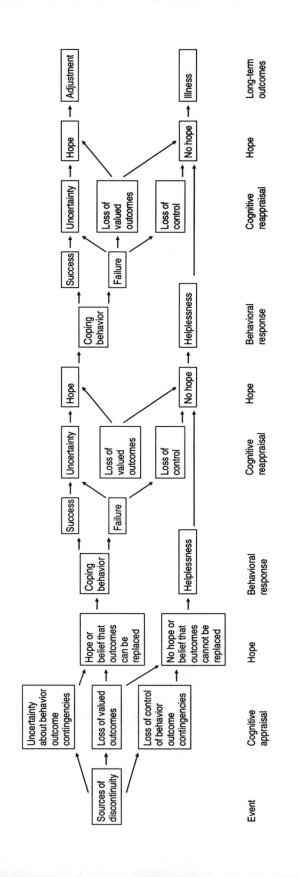

Figure 4.3 A cyclical theoretical model of the effect of job transfer (reprinted with permission from Brett, 1980)

stressors that were related to workload dissatisfaction and boredom, which were proposed as intervening variables leading to psychological and somatic complaints. While it was related to some psychological strains, its zero-order relationship with somatic complaints was negligible.

One factor likely to result in job future ambiguity is employer workforce cutbacks due to budget cuts (which are often, in turn, due to lack of demand for the company's products or services at current prices). Table 4.2 illustrates a way of classifying budget cuts that can be used to examine their stressful qualities. Two dimensions, time pressure (the relative speed with which cuts must be made) and severity (the relative size of the cuts), are proposed to be important in putting stressful pressure on those in the organization (Jick, 1985). Placed in a two-by-two table, they result in four types of situations: unanticipated major cuts, anticipated major cuts, unanticipated minor cuts, and anticipated minor cuts.

As would be expected, Jick (1985) has proposed that the unanticipated major cuts would be especially stressful, because they are high on both dimensions (lack of time to deal with the cut and severity). These occurrences of cutbacks in employing organizations may be very stressful. A study from the 1970s (Cobb and Kasl, 1972) found that there were both physiological and psychological effects on male employees when an entire plant shut down. Related to job future ambiguity or security, these strains began to occur before the shutdown happened but after word had gotten out that it was imminent. The anticipation of job loss, an obvious threat to job security, was apparently stressful as well as the actual job loss being stressful. Some of these effects included increases in serum uric acid and blood pressure, and decreases in self-esteem.

There are still other potential stressors among the organizational characteristics and conditions, including those in Table 4.1 and probably still more not listed there. Organizational characteristics and conditions have not been the favorite stressor category for organizational psychology researchers

Table 4.2 A typology of cutback situations (reprinted with permission from Jick, 1985)

		Time pressure	
		High	Low
Severity Level	High	Unanticipated major cuts ("The big bomb") High stress	Anticipated major cuts ("The time bomb") Moderate stress
	Low	Unanticipated minor cuts ("The short-fused firecracker") Moderate stress	Anticipated minor cuts ("The long-fused firecracker") Low stress

and it is probably because these are at the so-called organizational (macro) level of conceptualizing the workplace. Most psychologists, including industrial/organizational psychologists, are more comfortable thinking at the individual level, which looks at individual differences among employees or their jobs. An organizational stress study at the organizational level that uses the types of methods psychologists are comfortable with would call for a sample of organizations to be studied for differences among them. This would constitute a far more difficult task than looking for differences among a sample of individuals in the same organization.

ORGANIZATION'S EXTERNAL DEMANDS AND CONDITIONS

If one goes to an even more macro level, the organization's environment could be conceived as a determinant of occupational stress. Table 4.1 lists this category as its fourth and final potential location of stressors in Beehr and Newman's (1978) environmental facet. Budget cuts, discussed in the previous section, are often due ultimately to external demands on the organization, such as decreased demand for the organization's products or services. The table lists several other potential illustrative items that could be stressful to people in the organization. While some of these have been studied from other perspectives, there has been little or no research to date on these as they relate to occupational stress. This section discusses the potential for future occupational stress research on demands and conditions external to employing organizations.

Travel to and from work

The table suggests that simply getting to work may be stressful in itself. Using the uncertainty model of Beehr and Bhagat (1985a), big city traffic problems might be stressful if they result in uncertainty regarding one's efforts at arriving at work on time, if getting to work on time is important, and if this problem is chronic (i.e. it occurs every day over a long duration). Variables that could affect such uncertainty might include the distance that one lives from the workplace, typical amount of traffic, unpredictability of traffic problems, reliability of public transportation, reliability of one's own personal vehicle, and predictability of weather problems that could interfere with travel. These might have main effects on the uncertainty of arriving at work on time and they also seem to be logical predictors of the duration of the uncertainty, because many of them are relatively permanent factors in the work surroundings.

Importance of arriving at work on time and in a predictable manner will probably be affected by the nature of the job, the employing organization, and in some cases the immediate supervisor. Some jobs do not have a firm concept of promptness, such as some university professor jobs and some

managerial jobs. Similarly, some organizations are more concerned about
work getting done on time and well than about employees being at their
work stations during certain hours. Supervisors in such organizations may
also vary in their own predilection for their subordinates to be present during
a certain time period. Thus, while the organization may or may not officially
be very rigid regarding its members being present during certain hours,
specific supervisors may run counter to that theme with impunity.

Consistent with the nature of importance in the Beehr and Bhagat model
(1985a), these factors are more likely to have moderating effects than main
effects in the stress process. That is, if these factors lead to a situation in
which on-time arrival is not very important, then the uncertainty regarding
arriving on time is likely to be less stressful. Hypotheses for future research,
therefore, would include analyzing work situations to determine their
standing on such variables in order to classify them on factors likely to affect
the importance of arriving at a specific time. Related hypotheses could also
be deduced regarding companies that use flexitime. In general, it would
seem that such organizations place less emphasis on being "on time," although the exact nature of the flexitime program would have to be examined
before hypothesizing this for any individual site.

Just as the work situations may differ in the importance placed on promptness, it also needs to be considered that the focal person may have individual
preferences for arriving on time (as defined personally). Thus, some
employees may simply value being "on time" as a personal preference
regardless of the presence of organizational sanctions regarding tardiness. If
the person places importance on promptness either because of organizational sanctions or personal preference, the effect would probably be the
same in the model. That is, the importance to the person of being on time
would be increased and the seriousness of the potential stress would be
increased.

Presence of unions

The presence of unions has always been of interest to management and
usually this interest has been negative. That is, the presence of unions often
makes management fear that their hands will be tied when it comes to
making decisions about the unionized workforce and the nature of their
work. From the unionized workers' viewpoint, on the other hand, if they saw
fit to unionize, then they must have seen some advantages to unionization.
On the surface of it, therefore, these two reactions might suggest that the
presence of unions might tend to be stressful for managers who have to deal
with unionized workers and that the presence of unions might result in less
stress for those employees who are unionized.

Obviously, these generalizations are likely to be wrong in many cases.
Their opposites could even conceivably be true, at least in some unusual

situations, and of course, the presence of unions might be unrelated to stress at all. If unions lead to more clear working conditions and regulations (less role ambiguity), both management and unionized workers might have less occupational stress. If unions result in better job security, less stress might result for their members. If unions lead to abnormally higher wages, however, job security could be threatened during economically troubled times for the employer, leading to more stress. Obviously, there are a lot of ifs and there can be a great deal of speculation regarding the likely effects of unions on organizational stress, but only future research can really determine these effects. The mere fact of unionization is likely to have inconsistent effects on stress, because unions may have many different effects in different organizations and situations. Currently, little is really known about it because of a lack of research in the area.

Furthermore, if unions are usually formed to promote workers' self-interest, then it is logical for them to advocate improvements in their members' stressful work situations. The traditional focus of American unions on economic issues and the fact that many stressful situations are not obvious without thoughtful study of the situation has probably kept many unions from advocating this approach, however.

In summary, as noted earlier, there has been little research on extra-organizational conditions and occupational stress. This does seem to be a research area with potential for uncovering new information about occupational stress.

FUTURE DIRECTIONS

The stressors discussed in this chapter were categorized and taken from the Beehr–Newman (1978) occupational stress model. There have been calls, however, to expand the knowledge about potential stressors by exploring stressors from various theoretical and conceptual approaches (Beehr and Franz, 1987; Beehr and Newman, 1978; Love and Beehr, 1981). It has been recommended, for example, that researchers explore the idea from some life stress literature that both positive and negative changes in life can be equally stressful (e.g. Beehr and Franz, 1987). Translated to occupational stress, this might include considering whether or not such things as promotions and recognition are stressful.

Also the potential of acute occupational stressors has not been examined enough. Most of the job stressors discussed in literature could be considered chronic in the sense that they are ongoing, seemingly permanent characteristics of the work or workplace. Life stress research has paid more attention to the acute stressors, that is, events in one's life that are time-limited. An example of an acute work-related stressor is the first encounter of nursing students with responsibility for providing comprehensive patient care (Eden, 1982). Initial encounters with new jobs, organizations, and responsibilities in general may be a likely area for future research on acute stressors. After some experience, the stress should subside if it is due to the initial encounter and if it is indeed acute. This has not yet been studied much from the stress perspective. Clues regarding stressful things to study among new employees might be gleaned from the organizational socialization literature (e.g. Buchanan, 1974; Feldman, 1976; Wanous, 1980) or the career stage literature (e.g. Colarelli *et al.*, 1987; Schein, 1987; Super, 1980). While people entering new jobs or organizations may experience more of the well-known stressors, there may also be some that are unique to the entry situation.

Site-specific or local stressor measures

Aside from the general categories of stressors reviewed here, there is also the less often used tactic of devising job- and situation-specific measures of stressors based on local conditions. That is, most of the stressor measures reviewed here have been devised to be generic, to be used in as many settings and across as many jobs as possible. In-depth examination of local work situations may result in the development of more specific stressor measures to be used in research in a particular setting.

This can occur in two ways. First, totally new stressors might be discovered that had simply been overlooked by researchers who are focusing on looking for stressors that are more generally relevant to a wide variety of jobs. A second possibility, however, is that relatively general stressors might take specific, different forms in specific jobs and organizations. Thus, the exact nature of responsibility for others may be different in different organizations or jobs, as might the natures of job security or organizational position. Beehr *et al.* (1990; described in the chapter on social support), for example, examined role conflict among hospital nurses by asking them about specific sources of conflicting role messages such as doctors, patients and their families, head nurses, and so forth.

Items that ask more directly about the specific work environment of the focal employees might have some advantages such as being more precise measures of the local situation and in making more sense to survey respondents. If so, they might be more powerful predictors in stress models. In some cases, they might help define and predict the more generic stressor measures (e.g. they could indicate what responsibility for others is in a given setting). A model in which specific stressor measures lead to generic stressor measures, which then lead to strains, might prove viable.

All of this could have the effect of clarifying the nature of stressors, although it might indicate the need to make stressor measures different for different settings. If so, the research process might become more cumbersome while becoming more accurate. Research addressing such job specificity of stressors has not been done.

Part III

Outcomes of stress in the workplace

One of the necessary parts of the definition of occupational stress offered here consists of aversive outcomes to the individual – the strains. Organizational stressors lead to individuals' strains and the first chapter of this section examines three types of strains: psychological strains, physical or physiological strains, and behavioral strains. These have not been studied and documented in equal proportion to each other in research from the organizational psychology point of view of job stress. The psychological strains have dominated research from this approach, probably because of a combination of researchers' interests, researchers' expertise, and the variables' ease of measurement. The common thread in the fabric of these three strains is that they are deleterious to the individual experiencing them.

The second chapter in this section of the book focuses on outcomes to the organization. These are not strains in the language used here and they are not by definition a necessary part of job stress. If they occur, however, they are important, albeit more so to the organization than to the individual. Outcomes of individuals' stress to the organization could be either positive or negative, but past discussions in the literature have often either assumed or noted only the negative ones. Compared with the individual outcomes or strains, even less is known very clearly about the organizational outcomes of individuals' occupational stress.

Chapter 5

Individuals' strains
Psychological, physiological, and behavioral effects of workplace stress

> The direct measurement of activation level will be difficult since students and employees alike will not be eager to have electrodes implanted in their brainstems.
>
> (Scott, 1966: 25)

By definition, occupational stressors lead to strains, at least for most people and under most conditions (Kahn and Byosiere, 1992). Strains are states that are harmful and usually aversive to the individuals experiencing them. In the present language, the strains to individuals are the outcomes that define stress in the workplace and they are usually states associated with ill health, broadly defined. These outcomes can be divided into three categories: psychological, physical or physiological, and behavioral. These correspond roughly to (poor) mental health, (poor) physical health, and behaviors likely to be deleterious to one's own health and well-being.

Beehr and Newman (1978) named several psychological health consequences or psychological strains that had been studied in conjunction with the kind of occupational stress of interest here, but they were able to cite very few instances of published empirical relationships between occupational stressors and physical health consequences and behavioral strains. Much research has been done since that time, but the pattern of emphasis on psychological strains in relation to social psychological stress in the workplace has persisted. No doubt many I/O psychologists think of the difficulty of measuring physical reactions to work in terms similar to Scott's (1966) quote at the beginning of the chapter.

PSYCHOLOGICAL STRAINS

A meta-analysis focusing on the two classic role stressors, role conflict and role ambiguity, illustrates the emphasis of workplace stress researchers on psychological strains very well. Eleven of the fifteen outcomes examined were psychological or emotional strains (Jackson and Schuler, 1985). In addition, as noted by Jex and Beehr (1991), the relationships between the types of work stressors that organizational psychologists study and psychological strains are stronger than the relationships between these stressors and other types of strains.

Individual outcomes such as anxiety, depression, and dissatisfaction are often associated with occupational stressors (Beehr, 1985a). Somatic complaints could be considered a physical or physiological strain, but even they are often measured by self-reports of aches and pains rather than anything more objective and concrete (Jex and Beehr, 1991). Furthermore, similar items are often found in anxiety scales (e.g. Taylor Manifest Anxiety Scale; Taylor, 1953). Therefore, this "borderline" physical ailment is included here in the section on psychological strains rather than with the physiological strains.

Problems in measurement of psychological strains

Self-reports

The assessment of stress-related variables by self-reports in research can be a problem. For example, negative affectivity has been proposed as a stable individual difference variable that could be responsible for some of the covariation between self-reported stressors and strains (e.g. Brief *et al.*, 1988). Psychological strains are nearly always self-reported, although they do not necessarily have to be. They can be diagnosed by a psychiatrist, a clinical psychologist, or other health worker, or focal people could simply be judged on psychological strains by others who are in a position to observe them closely (friends, family, co-workers, etc.). This has not been the norm in previous research, however. Whether due to negative affectivity or not, many sorts of response sets that vary among individual respondents could conceivably lead to inflated relationships between self-reported stressors and psychological strains.

Contamination of strain measures with stressors

A second problem noted earlier with the measurement of psychological strains is the occasional practice of asking about both stressors and strains not only in the same questionnaire, but in the same *items*. Kahn *et al.* (1964) may have started this with their early and influential book on role conflict and ambiguity, in which they asked people the extent to which they were "bothered" by the stressors, role ambiguity and role conflict. Since this approach assesses both stressors and strains to some extent in the same questions, correlating the questions with others that only ask about stressors or about strains is likely to result in spuriously strong correlations. Future research should avoid this practice.

Use of the word "stress"

A third problem, noted earlier, is that some research has used the word stress (or stressor, distress, or stressful, etc.) as a key word in some questionnaire items (e.g. Motowidlo *et al.*, 1986). As discussed in an earlier chapter and elsewhere (e.g. Beehr and Franz, 1987; Ivancevich and Matteson, 1980; Mason, 1975), the term is not always used consistently even by researchers themselves. Sometimes it has been used to mean what is labeled "stressor" in this book (e.g. Beehr *et al.*, 1976; Caplan *et al.*, 1975; Frese, 1985; Lazarus, 1966; Kahn and Quinn, 1970). At other times, it has been used to mean an individual's reactions, or something closer to what is labeled "strain" here (e.g. Selye's non-specific bodily response, 1956; 1974). Still other research has argued that it should be used to mean an area of study focusing on the basic stressor–strain relationship (e.g. Beehr and Newman, 1978; Beehr and Franz, 1987). If the job stress "experts" have trouble agreeing what the term means, expecting respondents to interpret it in a consistent way also seems unlikely. At any rate, it certainly is not known what this term means to respondents. The recent study of public sector employees noted in an earlier chapter (Jex *et al.*, 1992) showed that stress may mean strain to some respondents, but might be interpreted as stressors in addition. More research is needed on this issue.

Depending on how the items are phrased, it can be unknown whether this is interpreted by the respondents as referring to a stressor or a strain. It could even mean different things to different people. In order to interpret past research using such items, research is necessary to determine the meaning of the word stress to the public (rather than to researchers), since the public comprised the respondents in such studies.

As noted at the beginning of Chapter 2, Kasl (1987) predicted that "the likelihood that 'stress' will fade away from our vocabulary is as good as are the chances that the state will wither away in Communist Russia" (p. 310). While the state is not withering away in Russia in the manner predicted by communist theory, most of the communist governments in eastern Europe, including Russia, are disappearing. It does not seem likely, however, that job stress research will benefit from a similar revolutionary trend by experiencing a decline in the confusion due to the use of this word.

Use of job (dis)satisfaction as a psychological strain

A fourth problem with the use of psychological strains in occupational stress research is that there is a temptation, perhaps especially strong among I/O psychologists, to use job satisfaction as one psychological strain. While this variable is a familiar friend to I/O psychologists and is often related to many potential stressors, by itself it probably does not indicate the presence of stress. A long history of research on job satisfaction existed before very much serious occupational stress research became public. If strain were not different from job satisfaction, there would have been no reason for job stress to emerge in theory and research. Strain is not old wine in new bottles. Even the psychological strains are not simply job dissatisfaction.

Dissatisfaction is in most ways a milder reaction to work than true strains are. Strains are likely to be experienced as actual illnesses, mental or physical. If dissatisfaction is the only or the most severe negative reaction job characteristic, then researchers have only uncovered a job factor leading to satisfaction, not a stressor. This is not to say that job satisfaction should not be measured in stress studies. In fact, if it is an outcome separate from strains, it provides additional information that many scientists and practitioners would find interesting. Job satisfaction should not, however, be relied on as the sole indicator of the presence of job stress.

Even if job (dis)satisfaction is not truly a strain, it is still valuable to include it as a potential outcome in job stress studies, just as it is valuable to include job performance, absenteeism, turnover, and other organizationally relevant outcomes even though they are not technically strains. Although the relationship between stressors and strains is the indicator of the existence of job stress, one also wants to know what other important things are influenced in the stress process. The next chapter examines more of these.

Job satisfaction, or at least its facets, can even be employed in job stress studies in ways that would help to illustrate the nature of some stressors. For example, in the data from a wide variety of people and jobs from the five work organizations described in an earlier chapter, it was hypothesized and found that role stressors were correlated with satisfaction with the social facets of the job (co-workers and supervisors) more strongly than they were with satisfaction with other (non-social) job facets (Beehr, 1981). It remains to be seen whether this would also be the case for stressors other than role stressors, which are explicitly derived from expectations of other people in the workplace (the role senders). That study hypothesized this relationship specifically because of the social nature of role stressors; therefore, it would be hypothesized that this type of relationship would not hold as strongly for stressors that were clearly not social in nature. Inspection of a correlation matrix in a study focusing on social support on the job, however, does not provide further support for this view. In Beehr and Drexler's (1986) study of over 2,000 employees of a major banking system in a western state, social satisfaction appeared to be related to one stressor, role ambiguity, more strongly than two other types of satisfaction were (resources satisfaction and higher order need satisfaction), but this pattern did not appear to hold for two other stressors (role conflict and role overload) in that study. Thus role theory is a social, interpersonal type of theory and it might be expected to be related especially to dissatisfaction with the social part of the job (e.g. role senders). Research results have been mixed on this issue thus far, however.

Interpersonal conflict at work, a job stressor studied by Spector *et al.*,

(1988) but seldom studied rigorously elsewhere, would also seem to be especially related to satisfaction with the social aspects of jobs. This type of investigation of various types of job stressors' relationships with various types of job satisfaction facets has not been done much and might be a fruitful area for future research.

Job satisfaction could also be important in stress if it leads to other outcomes. It has been proposed that job satisfaction, or lack of it, could lead to coronary heart disease (e.g. Cooper and Marshall, 1976; Howard *et al.*, 1986) or even to death (e.g. Palmore, 1971). While there are problems with the measurement of job satisfaction in the mortality studies (see Kasl, 1980; Beehr, 1986) the idea that job satisfaction could be an intervening variable between stressors and strains (psychological or otherwise) appears periodically, but it has not been studied intensively yet.

Somatic complaints

Complaints about aches and pains, sleeping difficulties, and general discomfort have been used as strain measures, but it is difficult to advocate many of these measures as being clear indicators of actual physiological problems. As noted earlier, some scales of anxiety, depression, or other psychological strains have incorporated these into items on the grounds that they are indicators of psychological problems (e.g. Taylor, 1953), while other scales consisting only or primarily of such items are simply labeled as physical strain (e.g. Osipow and Davis, 1988), somatic complaints (e.g. Caplan *et al.*, 1975; Ganster *et al.*, 1986) or psychosomatic complaints (e.g. Eden, 1982; Frese, 1985), leaving it to the reader to judge whether it is psychological or physiological. The likely tendency of people with psychological problems to experience and report such complaints makes it difficult to ascertain the "true" problem accurately. In any case, these self-reports are usually positively correlated with anxiety.

Further muddying the issue, some self-report scales may actually be somewhat better than this suggests at measuring physiological illness or symptoms, because they ask the questions that are more oriented toward actual illness or that focus on an external diagnosis. For example, items that ask people whether they have been diagnosed by a physician or hospitalized for certain illnesses seem likely to get more accurate information about physiological responses, even though they are self-reported. In this section, self-reports that are somatic complaints are discussed; under the physiological section, some self-reports are also discussed, but only those that are likely to have been more objectively diagnosed.

Somatic complaints do tend to be correlated with job stressors (at least with self-reported, social psychological types of job stressors) more weakly than the more clearly psychological strains. They have occasionally been correlated with role overload (e.g. Osipow and Davis, 1988), role ambiguity (e.g. Caplan *et al.*, 1975; Ganster, *et al.*, 1986), time spent on rotating shiftwork (e.g. Zedeck *et al.*, 1983), and several other stressors. These relationships are often weak, however, and in some studies they are not significant at all. This is an area in need of more research and possibly better conceptualization. There might be moderators that have been thus far unnoticed, the relationships found might be instances of Type I error, or measurement could be a problem.

Regarding measurement, these somatic complaints indices are often a conglomerate of barely interrelated or even unrelated aches and pains, behaviors, and so forth. It may be that some more refined and unidimensional somatic criteria would be related more consistently to job stressors. This approach in future research should start with better identification of the different themes or categories of somatic complaints, followed by the consideration of which of them are most likely to be affected psychosomatically, and ending with studies that could confirm or deny these hypotheses.

Burnout

In recent years, the term burnout has emerged in the literature related to occupational stress. Originating in the human services research literature, burnout was most often defined as a syndrome of psychological reactions to work, including exhaustion, cynicism, loss of enthusiasm, and professional disengagement and basically seems to be a psychological strain (Shinn, 1981). Psychological strains often intercorrelate fairly strongly with each other and depression often has a major empirical overlap with burnout (e.g. Sweeney, 1981).

The Maslach Burnout Inventory (MBI; Maslach and Jackson, 1981) is the most frequently used measure of burnout and it has three subscales: emotional exhaustion, depersonalization, and personal achievement (reverse scored). Several writers have concluded emotional exhaustion is the central or core dimension of burnout (e.g. Beehr *et al.*, 1990; Gaines and Jermier, 1983; Maslach, 1982), and it has sometimes been used as the sole burnout measure in occupational stress studies.

One study of emotional exhaustion (Gaines and Jermier, 1983) among 208 members of a police organization found that it appeared to be a function of several things, including primarily supervisor support, job motivating potential, work group cohesiveness, pay equity, and promotion opportunity. That study used MBI which assesses emotional exhaustion, depersonalization, and personal achievement on two response scales: one asking about frequency and one about intensity of these burnout experiences. They found more and stronger relationships between the frequency scales and other variables than between the intensity scales and other variables. Because of such experiences, some subsequent research measuring burnout, including my own, has used only the frequency response format (e.g. Beehr and King, 1986; Beehr *et al.*, 1990).

The study of a random sample of 225 registered nurses from seven different hospitals employed both depersonalization and emotional exhaustion measured with the frequency format (Beehr *et al.*, 1990). The results in these data regarding uncertainty were noted in an earlier chapter. The primary purpose of the Beehr *et al.* (1990) study, however, was to examine social support in a new and innovative way and therefore it is described in more detail in the chapter on social support. The study's three stressors, role ambiguity and two measures of role conflict, were related to both subscales of burnout (r's ranged from 0.21 to 0.50), although they were consistently related a little more strongly to emotional exhaustion (only one of the three differences was significant, however), reinforcing the notion that emotional exhaustion is probably the most central stress-related subscale of burnout.

Another study of burnout in relation to occupational stress measured emotional exhaustion of mental health center therapists' desires to abandon their profession (Beehr and King, 1986). Turnover, which is considered an organizational consequence in our model (Figure 1.2), was studied in a more extreme form – occupational turnover rather than organizational turnover. After the commitment necessary in terms of time, effort, and money that is necessary to obtain a graduate degree in a professional area, leaving the profession entirely seemed to be an extreme form of turnover. Community mental health center therapists were chosen for study because burnout was originally conceived to be a problem in human services types of jobs and because, like nursing, this profession is supposed to be known for high rates of turnover. From both a literature review and preliminary interviews with a small sample of therapists, a causal model was developed that would be specific to this occupation. In terms of the model in Figure 1.2, work environment stressors that are specific to this profession (underutilization of skills and role overload) would lead to human consequences (job dissatisfaction and emotional exhaustion, respectively), which would lead to the organizational outcome of desire for occupational abandonment. Based on the interviews and literature review, supervisor's consideration and job feedback would combine with underutilization of skills to lead to dissatisfaction, while being on call and the size of the caseload would lead to role overload.

We measured caseload and being on call from the organization's records, while the other variables were measured via a questionnaire developed after analyzing the preliminary interviews. The questionnaire consisted of standard, well-used scales except for the criterion, the desire to abandon one's profession. We wrote three of these items ourselves, based on phrases and information gathered in the preliminary interviews, and the fourth item was from Caplan *et al.* (1975). The items, which can be adapted for use with any occupation, are in appendix E.

In order to increase the response rate, we secured the support of the local administrators down to the first-line supervisory level in community mental health centers in nine rural counties, gave advance notice to participants, arrived in person on the day of survey administration and handed out the survey individually to each therapist, and remained there or returned in person at the end of the day to collect the questionnaires from each therapist. The questionnaires were completed in private, however, in the therapists' own offices at whatever time during the day they could work on them. Probably because of this personalized approach, 92 percent of the sample completed questionnaires. Furthermore, some of those who did not participate were those who were ill and absent on the day of the administration.

It has often been assumed that burnout would lead people to leave not just their current employer, but their entire profession, because the same problems would occur in any employment situation involving the same type of work. In the study, emotional exhaustion was related primarily to role overload and the desire to abandon the profession (zero-order correlations in the 0.30s). In a path analysis testing an a priori model, however, the path from emotional exhaustion to desire for occupational abandonment was reduced to non-significance. A better fitting model was proposed in which emotional exhaustion was an intermediate link between role overload and boredom-dissatisfaction and it was likely to influence occupational abandonment only indirectly through its effect on boredom-dissatisfaction (Figure 5.1).

The literature on burnout strongly suggested that it should lead to turnover and so it had been proposed that it would be a very direct precursor of abandoning one's occupation. This link was the only one in the proposed model, however, that was not supported and was subsequently changed in the revised model in Figure 5.1. In the present context, this study does provide some evidence for burnout as a strain, because emotional exhaustion did fit in the model as a consequence of a traditional stressor – role overload. It was encouraging also that role overload, although measured with self-reports, was predicted by more objective information from the organization's records, namely the size of the caseload and the frequency of being on call.

Further job stress research on burnout as a psychological strain appears to be potentially fruitful. Burnout may or may not be a very different strain from the other psychological strains, however. As noted next, they do tend to be related to each other.

Relationships among psychological strains

The relationships among the psychological strains tend to be positive and

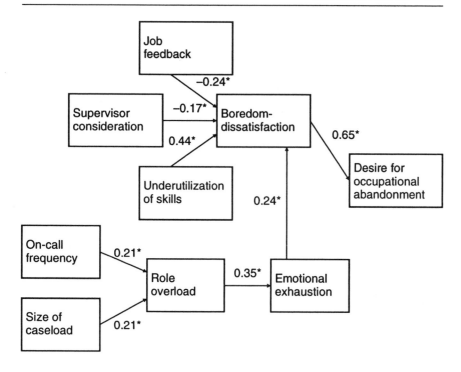

Figure 5.1 Revised model of occupational abandonment (Beehr and King, 1986).

they might even represent a single construct. Eliminating job satisfaction and its facets from consideration on the grounds that they are not clearly strains (as argued previously here), Table 5.1 shows the median correlation among the psychological strains used in several studies that measured more than one psychological strain other than satisfaction, and that reported correlations between the psychological strains. The median of these correlations is 0.456. The strongest correlation in the table, 0.62, was between depression and one of the burnout indices of the MBI – depersonalization. This provides some support for Sweeney's (1981) comment that burnout may overlap with depression. Overall, it is quite clear that the psychological strains in occupational stress research tend to be correlated with each other, although the magnitude of the correlations indicates that they are probably not identical with each other.

Another indication of the empirical overlap of the psychological strain indices typically used in occupational stress research is results from factor analyses. Kaufmann and Beehr (1986, 1989) twice factored several psychological strain indices in studies of social support's role in the stress process. These studies are described further in the chapter on social support. For present purposes regarding the relationships among strain measures, however,

Table 5.1 Relationships among psychological strains

Study	Psychological strains[a]	Median correlation
Beehr (1976)	(Low) self-esteem Depression	0.31
Beehr *et al.* (1990)	Depersonalization Depression Emotional exhaustion	0.62
Beehr *et al.* (1976)	Fatigue Tension	0.44
Caplan *et al.* (1975)	Depression Anxiety Irritation	0.47
Martin and Wall (1989)	Anxiety Depression Pressure Worry Mental health	0.42
Spector *et al.* (1988)	Anxiety Frustration	0.51

a   Job satisfaction not included

the results of our factor analyses are instructive. In our sample of 102 hospital nurses, we conducted factor analyses of a number of potential stress outcome indices: job dissatisfaction, workload dissatisfaction, job boredom, depression, pulse rate, systolic blood pressure, and diastolic blood pressure. All of the psychological indices and pulse rate loaded on the first of two factors, and the two blood pressure variables loaded on the second factor. In another study, of 121 police officers, we factor analyzed four psychological outcome indices: depression, job dissatisfaction, boredom, and workload dissatisfaction (Kaufmann and Beehr, 1989). We found one factor. Even though these two articles had the problem, from the present point of view, of including types of job dissatisfaction in their outcomes, taken together with the correlations summarized in Table 5.1, they indicate that there is probably substantial overlap among psychological types of outcomes (i.e. psychological strains) in job stress studies.

Future research needs to address the differentiability of different psychological reactions to job stressors, such as depression, anxiety, burnout, frustration, tension, fatigue, and so forth. Depression and anxiety appear to be the most central variables among the psychological strains in that (1) they seem to be used the most in research (with burnout rapidly approaching their breadth of use), and (2) they seem to correlate most strongly with the other psychological strains when they are used together in the same study.

To the extent that they tend to be part of the same whole, it is possible that their overlapping part could be negative affectivity, discussed in a previous chapter. If so, that would mean that a stable individual difference variable is part of psychological strain and negative affectivity would be part of the personal facet of the Beehr–Newman (1978) model presented in a previous chapter. If negative affectivity is part of what is measured in a psychological strain cluster, there are several potential implications for research. For example, if negative affectivity is also a strong influence on perceptual measures of stressors, then the relationships of these perceptual measures of stressors with psychological strain measures will be due largely to method variance. As discussed in an earlier chapter, this does not at present seem likely, but the final word is probably not in. If negative affectivity's effect on perceptual measures of stressors is nil or weak, however, then another problem arises. That is, the strain measures will be relatively stable within each person, so that they will not be able to vary with purported stressors. In that case, it will be difficult to discover any effect of stressors on psychological strains. Given the results of previous research, however, that does not seem likely either.

More investigation of the potential differential meanings of psychological strains is warranted within the domain of occupational stress research.

Summary of relationships among strains

Although there are several potential outcomes of job stressors, research in organizational psychology has focused on psychological reactions in occupational stress. More research probably needs to be done on the other, less studied types of reactions to the types of stressors of interest in organizational psychology.

These organizational psychology stressors tend to be social psychological in nature (Beehr, 1987). Typical of field research in this area, the measurement of stressors has employed self-reports (usually questionnaires); furthermore, the history of measurement of psychological ill health and welfare has also tended to focus on self-reports. Because of this, there are specific threats to the validity of the research and several of these were discussed here.

A relatively new psychological strain measure is burnout. For quite a while, it was not linked to the rest of the job stress literature, probably because of its development by people interested primarily in the human services professions. It is now argued that it probably is quite similar to other psychological strains. As with any occupation, however, the specific stressors in the human services occupations have, in part, their own characteristics. When the psychological strain called burnout occurs in the human services areas, it probably also has some unique characteristics such as depersonalization of those people receiving the services. Depersonalization of clients can only be a strain in occupations wherein one has clients, of course, and therefore it is occupation-specific. Other facets of burnout, however, seem to fit quite closely with psychological strains such as depression.

Not only burnout but other psychological strains tend to be related to each other, and depression (or perhaps anxiety) may be their central construct. A close examination of the similarities and differences among the psychological strains needs to be done in the context of occupational stress. This is a good area for future research.

PHYSIOLOGICAL STRAINS

It was noted in the mid-1960s that the word stress had, in much of psychology, come to be used in the research of a number of negative psychological states that had previously been studied without using the term (Cofer and Appley, 1964). In other words, there was a potential that stress research was simply a set of old concepts with a new label. In industrial and organizational psychology in particular, stress had barely arrived on the scene in the mid-1960s. Many job stress studies, however, could also be old stuff relabeled. The previously mentioned tendency to use job satisfaction as a stress outcome leans in that direction and that is why job dissatisfaction should not be considered, by itself, an indicator of job stress. Contrary to many other areas of psychology, however, strains had not been studied much in industrial and organizational psychology and therefore research using these variables in industry as "new" outcomes of old job characteristics still seemed like new wine to this old field in the 1970s.

In 1970 (McGrath), it was observed that there had been far more research in the stress literature in general (again, not specifically in occupational or job stress) on physiological strains than on psychological ones. It is likely that much of this earlier research, as well as more current research on job stress that employs physiological strains as criteria, comes from human factors, physiological, medical, experimental, and engineering psychology (Beehr and Franz, 1987), rather than from organizational psychology, which is the focus of this volume. Contrary to McGrath's 1970 observation about stress in general, twenty years later it is easy to observe that most of the stress outcomes studied from the organizational psychology perspective have been psychological. A further observation is that when both psychological and physiological measures have been used in the same study, the organizational (social psychological) stressors of the study tend to be more strongly related to psychological outcomes than to the physiological outcomes.

Partly because of the lack of studies of organizational psychology stressors related to physiological strains, the word physiological (or sometimes, physical) will be used very broadly here. As discussed earlier in this chapter, some self-reports of physical complaints appear to be at least as much psychological as they are physical and these were discussed earlier under the rubric somatic complaints. Although it has been found that such self-reported "symptoms" can correlate with physicians' diagnoses of medical problems and the taking of medication (e.g. Caplan *et al.*, 1975), this is still not in the same category of objectivity as actual diagnosis of disease by physicians.

Some self-reports of illnesses will be discussed here, however. They will be ones about which some judgment can be made that the complaint is more serious than an ache or pain and that it is more likely to have been diagnosed by a professional rather than only by the people themselves.

First mediators

Scott (1966), in his quote at the beginning of this chapter, refers to measurement of immediate neurological activity that could occur in response to a job. One of the more theoretically based physiological responses to occupational stress is the first mediator, a quick physical change occurring in an organism experiencing stress. Proposed by Selye (1956), first mediators could be the essence of stress, that is, they are common responses to all stressors and stimulate internal events that eventually culminate in the strains. Selye characterized these as internal messages that were probably carried through either the circulatory or nervous system to various parts of the body in order to stimulate further changes that would be recognized as physical strains. In decades of investigation, Selye never convincingly found the nature of these first mediators, but other researchers have sometimes used physiological indicators of stress that are seemingly conceptualized in this way. That is, they are immediate results of stressors but are not in themselves aversive enough to be labeled strains. Examples are galvanic skin response, muscular responses such as EMG readings, and especially the secretion of catecholamines (epinephrine and norepinephrine) into the blood stream. In a journal debate with Mason (1975), Selye (1975) argued that there may not be a single first mediator; instead, the nature of the first mediator may vary from one stressful incident to another. Mason, on the other hand, suggested that emotional arousal (rather than physical changes) accompanying stressful events might be the first mediator. Regardless of the nature of the first mediator, it would be part of the process facet of the Beehr–Newman (1978) model. Furthermore, if there is a single, common first mediator in all stress experiences, it could actually lay claim to the label "stress," which it has been argued here should not be the name of any one variable.

This debate is not likely to be concluded soon. The existence of one common physiological response to occupational stress seems even more unlikely today than it did in the past, given the widely proliferating list of organizational situations and events accepted as occupational stressors. The field is likely to go on considering any apparent "illness" response to organizational life to be a sign of stress, without feeling the need to tie it to an intervening physiological mechanism.

Cardiovascular diseases and symptoms

The most frequently cited physical illness thought to be due to occupational stress is cardiovascular diseases and symptoms, including blood pressure and heart rate, catecholamine and cortisol secretions, cholesterol, and actual heart attacks and strokes. The infrequency of heart attacks in the working population means that it is difficult to study them rigorously. Doing a longitudinal study of heart attacks among employed people would require a very long period of time and a very large sample. Only a few such research programs exist, and they do not usually focus on occupational stress as a cause. Therefore, there has been a tendency to rely on symptoms or risk factors in these coronary heart diseases as criteria. The symptoms occur with much more frequency and therefore are easier to study.

Reviews (e.g. Beehr and Newman, 1978; Cooper and Marshall, 1976; House, 1974; Ironson, 1992) of occupational stress and coronary heart disease (and especially symptoms) have reported that the symptoms are often related both to the types of jobs that people hold (that is, differences in job titles) and also to more specific job characteristics (stressors) inherent in a number of different jobs, including responsibility for others, overload, deadlines, social relations at work, lack of control or influence, role ambiguity, and role conflict. This is a thriving research area and is likely to continue to be. For the typical I/O psychologist, however, an interdisciplinary team approach to this research might be advisable, because most I/O researchers are probably not strong in content and measurement relevant to cardiovascular medicine.

Howard *et al.* (1986), found that blood pressure was related to role ambiguity, especially among Type A managers; Eden (1982) showed that systolic blood pressure, pulse rate, and serum uric acid were related to acute critical job events among first year nursing students; Friedman, Rosenman, and Carroll (1958) found that cholesterol levels of tax accountants varied with nearness to tax deadlines; and Caplan *et al.* (1975) reported that scientists and especially administrators were less likely to be able to quit smoking under conditions of high quantity of workload. This last outcome (smoking behavior) is, of course, thought to be a risk factor in both heart disease and cancer.

Another example of a study including cardiovascular risk factors looked at nurses in a single hospital (Kaufmann and Beehr, 1986). In this study, nurses measured each other's pulse rates, and diastolic and systolic blood pressures. The researchers also measured, with questionnaires, some potential psychological strains, including depression, boredom, and satisfaction with workload and with the job overall. As noted earlier, a factor analysis of all the strains resulted in two factors, one consisting of the two blood pressure measures and the other consisting of all the psychological strains plus pulse rate (Kaufmann and Beehr, 1986).

A factor analysis including both psychological and physiological measures is quite rare in the job stress literature and so this result is interesting in itself. The most interesting thing is the loading of pulse rate with the psychological strains instead of with the other physiological ones. Its loading on the psychological strain factor was the smallest loading on that factor (0.35, compared to a median loading of the psychological strains of about 0.50). Nevertheless, this loading pattern was somewhat surprising. Pulse rate and blood pressure are particularly susceptible to variations due to immediate and long-term environmental events of many kinds, however (Fried et al., 1984). Therefore, they could have been expected to load similarly. Understanding the meaning of this pattern of loadings is difficult.

Kaufmann and Beehr (1986) found that the blood pressure index was not related to the stressors, which were workload P–E Fit, job future ambiguity, and underutilization of skills. The other strain index, composed mostly of psychological strains but also including pulse rate, was related to the stressors. Caplan et al. (1975), in their large-scale study of people in a wide variety of occupations, found only a few relationships between these cardiovascular measures and measures of stressors. This is consistent with the earlier observation that physical strains tend to be correlated with organizational stressors much more weakly than psychological strains are. Measurement is likely to sometimes play a role in this, however (Fried et al., 1984).

Self-reports of other physical illness symptoms

Physical strains other than cardiovascular ones have been studied much less frequently in conjunction with occupational stress. Many times, the best or only indications of other physical strains in occupational stress studies are self-reports of somatic symptoms or other indicators of poor general health. For example, Caplan et al. (1975) found that dispensary visits of employees were related very weakly or not at all to self-reports of stressors and Spector et al. (1988) found that doctor visits were somewhat weakly related to a few such stressors. In another study, when holding potential work-related physical environmental causes constant, some self-reported stressors were related to self-reports of ulcers among a group of blue collar rubber industry workers (House et al., 1979).

A review by Quick et al. (1987) indicated that several physical illness symptoms could be related to stressors (although often not work-related stressors), including cancer, chronic lung disease, pneumonia and influenza, and diabetes. Most of the studies in this area can be criticized on methodological grounds. Even so, they usually suggest that the relationships between physical illness or physiological responses and the kinds of organizational stressors of interest here tend to be few and weak. In addition to the obvious emphasis on the cardiovascular system, future research could be used to illuminate the possibility of the effects of job stress on other major bodily systems, especially the respiratory system, the alimentary system, and even the nervous system.

Problems of measurement of physiological strains

Researchers in the organizational sciences have often recommended (but usually not done) measurement of physiological strains partially on the grounds that these types of measures are more objective – or at least they are not subjective from the same point of view as the individual who reports the stressors. While this seems to be the ultimate in objectivity to social scientists who are concerned with problems with perceptual measures, it may not be as simple as this.

Physical and physiological measures are also subject to error, a fact that sounds obvious once it is stated, but one that is often overlooked by organizational stress researchers. As noted by Caplan *et al.* (1975), for example, measures of blood pressure are notorious for their volatility. Job stress researchers would like to use blood pressure as a measure of a cardiovascular illness or at least as a risk factor because it is thought to be affected by the stressors in the environment. This reactivity to the environment is a major reason why it is thought to be a good idea to examine it as a strain, but its reactivity is also a problem. It can be affected by fairly momentary and otherwise innocuous personal and environmental states and events as well as by diet, age, genetics, gender, time of day, medication, etc. (Fried *et al.*, 1984).

Caplan *et al.* (1975) and Kaufmann and Beehr (1986) tried to control some of the momentary fluctuation in blood pressure by measuring it twice, both before and after completing a questionnaire in a sitting position. Systolic pressure measures at the two time periods were related to each other; r=0.84 in the Caplan *et al.* study and r=0.66 in our study. The two diastolic pressure measures were related; r=0.78 in Caplan *et al.* and r=0.80 in our study. Since loud noises, physical exertion, and so forth have the potential to affect these measures, this was better than a single measurement. Still better, of course, would be periodic measurements over a longer span of time in a resting situation.

The many problems of measurement of physiological responses to work stress were examined for perhaps the first time in a journal widely available to I/O researchers by Fried *et al.* (1984). They argue that the procedures typically used to measure physiological responses in occupational stress studies have been inadequate. Three major categories of measurement problems can affect physiological measures: stable or permanent factors, transitory factors, and procedural factors.

Stable or permanent factors

The stable factors are basically individual differences among study participants in their susceptibility to or typical levels of certain physiological symptoms. These could be related to genetic history or at least a familial tendency, race, sex, age, and dietary habits (although this last one is theoretically more alterable). A major problem, of course, is that the people with typically (i.e. stable) high levels of strains due to these factors are not likely to be randomly distributed across jobs' potential stressor levels. If these stable factors are associated with certain job conditions, for whatever reason, cross-sectional, non-experimental field studies (the kind most often done in job stress research) will reach misleading conclusions regarding the tendency for job conditions (stressors) to lead to physiological strains.

According to Fried *et al.* (1984), familial or genetic tendencies affect blood pressure and cardiac activity, are probably related to serum cholesterol, and might be related to the incidence of peptic ulcer. Gender is related to blood pressure and cardiac activity, is probably related to adult serum cholesterol, and may be related to catecholamine secretions. Race also appears to affect blood pressure and cardiac activity. Age is often correlated with blood pressure and cardiac activity and adult cholesterol levels. Diet appears to affect cholesterol levels and duodenal ulcers.

Some studies have almost unwittingly controlled a few of these factors, for example, by the selection of samples of a single sex. One of our own studies involving blood pressure, for example, was of all nurses – all of whom happened to be female (Kaufmann and Beehr, 1986). There are obvious ways to control some of these during statistical analysis or selection of participants, but most studies of work stress have not done so. Future studies can greatly improve upon past practices if researchers are aware of these potential contaminants.

Transitory factors

Transitory factors are immediate factors that affect measurement and include time of day, room temperature and humidity, posture of subjects (standing, sitting, etc.), and recent physical exertion and consumption of stimulants or some other dietary elements. As with the stable factors, these may not be randomly distributed among all levels of physiological strains and could therefore cause problems.

Temperature and humidity can affect blood pressure and cardiovascular responses (Fried *et al.*, 1984). Research participants' posture, immediate or recent diet, recent exercise or physical exertion, and even the time of day have been shown to be possible influences on blood pressure and cardiovascular responses, and they might also affect catecholamine levels. Furthermore, there have sometimes appeared to be seasonal differences in levels of serum cholesterol, with the lowest levels in the autumn or winter and the highest in the spring or summer.

As with the stable factors, the transitory factors have often gone un-addressed in work stress studies, although they are sometimes controlled accidentally (e.g. taking all measurements during the same season). Simple knowledge about their effects can help future researchers design studies that will control more of these transitory factors and will at least allow organiz-ational researchers to be more aware of the limitations of their data. When enough studies have been reported, meta-analysis of the effects of some of these factors could also be undertaken if enough detail is reported in the published results.

Procedural factors

Procedural measurement problems refer to the potential for the method of measurement to result in inaccuracy. As previously discussed, blood pres-sure is known to be quite variable and therefore a single measurement is not usually sufficient to get a good reading. When physiological measures are not accurate because of the method of measurement, obvious problems arise in interpreting research results. In this case, even well-known research methods such as randomization of participants will not affect what is basic-ally a measurement problem. Examples of such procedural factors include the number of times a variable is measured, the precise type of instrument used to measure the variables, the varying definitions of a single physio-logical condition, and the criteria accepted as evidence of a physiological condition. These are often interrelated with each other.

Fried *et al.* (1984) note that the number of times a variable is measured can affect blood pressure and cardiovascular measures and catecholamine secretions. With blood pressure, for example, even the techniques used by Kaufmann and Beehr (1986), that is, measurements both before and after questionnaire administration, are not totally accurate. More measurement events with longer time intervals are often recommended. In addition to time intervals between measurements, the length of time during which the measure is taken can influence the accuracy. With pulse rate, for example, it is common among some medical personnel to take the measurements for only fifteen seconds and to report one-minute rates by multiplying by four (and often not to report that it was done this way). The appropriate time interval even varies with the variable being measured. Aside from cardio-vascular measures, fluctuations in catecholamine levels can be fast due a very short half-life in the blood stream.

Type of measuring instrument can affect accuracy of measurement of blood pressure, depending, for example, on whether it is taken with a sphygmomanometer (the most usual way, using a pressure cuff) or direct measurement through a catheter inserted into a blood vessel (usually thought to be a more accurate measure). Related to this, catecholamines can be measured in either blood or urine samples (where the half-life is longer).

Fried *et al.* (1984) note that the problems of definition and criteria occur in relation to the measurement of peptic ulcer. As with some other diseases, peptic ulcer can actually be defined as a group of heterogeneous diseases (e.g. gastric and duodenal ulcers) of varied origins. Furthermore, the criteria for diagnosis has varied in research studies, including patient symptoms, doctor diagnosis, radiological evidence, and surgical evidence. The use of some of these is likely to overestimate its incidence, while others might underestimate it. At any rate, they often will not agree with each other.

While I/O psychologists are generally aware of the potential problems with the measurement of psychological variables, a belief that physiological measures of strains might be the solution is probably an oversimplification. The various threats to accurate measurement are serious if they are not understood and attended to. Because of the relative disregard for these threats, much of the past organizational psychology research on job stress and physiological responses can be said to be only suggestive. Future research, however, can benefit from increased awareness of the problems, many of which can be reduced once they are known to researchers.

BEHAVIORAL STRAINS

While the physical and psychological strains clearly fit the definition of ill health, behavioral strains are more difficult to define. Strain, in the context of job stress, means some type of deleterious condition of the individual that is due to job stressors. Therefore a behavioral strain would be a behavior that is in itself harmful to the individual. It is important to note that this means that poor performance in the job is therefore not necessarily an instance of a strain. While performance decrements are likely to be harmful to the organization, it is often not harmful to the person unless it is very extreme (and causes them to be fired, for example). Similarly, high rates of absenteeism are not necessarily instances of behavioral strain. Absenteeism, while it usually is harmful to the organization, is not necessarily harmful to the individual. These types of behaviors, while potentially due in part to job stress, are not, by definition, strains. Their existence as responses to the workplace does not necessarily indicate job stress; strains in response to job conditions, by definition, do indicate the existence of job stress. Performance and absenteeism may be influenced by stressors at work, but they are classified as organizational consequences of stress and not as individual strains (Beehr and Newman, 1978).

Examples of behavioral strains could include alcohol, tobacco, and drug abuse, over- or under-eating, suicide, risky behavior (e.g. reckless driving), and behaviors leading to poor interpersonal relations (e.g. with family or friends). The keys to whether these are strains are (1) whether they are due to job stressors and (2) whether they are deleterious to the individual personally. The issue of whether or not any behaviors are deleterious to the person is partially in the eye of the beholder. The examples cited above are judged as being deleterious to the person by this author and probably would be judged that way by most people. Other examples might be more controversial, however.

The issue of whether such behaviors are linked to job stressors is an empirical one. There is some evidence that smoking behaviors are linked to job stressors or at least to occupations (as noted by Beehr and Newman, 1978). Smoking behaviors, as strains, include being a smoker, amount of smoking, and difficulty in quitting smoking.

Research on most of the behavioral strains in relation to job stressors is sparse. Studies of behavioral strains other than smoking have been even more rare and the results are often inconsistent. One does see, however, much speculation in the popular press about stress leading to these types of behaviors. Furthermore, given the national interest in recent years regarding drug and alcohol abuse, it seems likely that researchers have thought of doing this research and that there is interest among federal funding agencies regarding such research. In such circumstances, one wonders whether the results of whatever studies are being done are not very positive, that is, they are not showing much influence of job stress on drug and alcohol abuse. If so, the tendency not to publish non-significant results might explain the scarcity of published research on drug and alcohol abuse as strains due to occupational stress. The investigation of this and other behavioral strains does seem to be a good approach to future job stress research.

TIME AND THE JOB STRESS PROCESS

Time is an important but often ignored variable in psychological measurement and method (Kelly and McGrath, 1988). Some concepts in the job stress literature have labels with a time referent, such as "chronic" stress, "episodic" stress, and "daily" hassles. The literature for the most part, however, does not explicitly recognize the importance of time in such concepts (McGrath and Beehr, 1990). In the discussion of physiological strains in this chapter, some recognition was given to the problems of time of measurement of the responses due to their half-life (e.g. in the blood stream). Some responses are more immediate than others, and some measures of the same concept need to be taken sooner than others in order for the effects of job stress to be evident. These are really measurement problems and temporal factors in measurement and research design have not been considered in the typical job stress study. I/O psychologists are often at least intuitively aware of temporal factors in psychological measures, but given these largely unrecognized problems of physiological responses, perhaps it is remarkable that they ever find any relationships with physical strains.

McGrath and Beehr (1990) argued that stress producing environmental circumstances (stress producing events and conditions), or SPECs, need to be classified in a way that could explain their relationships to temporal factors. These SPECs are the stressors in the terminology being used in this volume, that is, the work environment characteristics or stressors in the model in Figure 1.2 where this program of research on occupational stress is characterized. Figure 5.2 illustrates some of the suggestions from McGrath and Beehr regarding temporal factors in stress.

The left side of the figure indicates that there are at least two important time facets to consider regarding occupational stressors or SPECs: frequency and duration. Furthermore, they can be recurrent or not. If recurrent, they can be periodic or aperiodic, that is, they can occur at relatively predictable intervals or not. These can also be divided into high versus low rates of recurrence. Finally, some SPECs can be irreversible, while others occur and then disappear (at least until a recurrence).

In addition, the magnitude of the consequences varies from SPEC to SPEC (e.g. a machine in the workplace causing the loss of a limb versus the loss of only a hat). In the figure, temporary (or one time) versus persistent (or recurrent) consequences also has a temporal flavor. For example, the temporary loss of a loved one (e.g. a husband who is a soldier sent overseas) versus the permanent loss of a loved one (e.g. a husband who is sent overseas and killed in combat).

Frequency and duration of occurrence of SPECs	Magnitude and persistence of consequences			
	Small consequences		Large consequences	
	One time	Recurrent	One time	Recurrent
Short, one-time event				
Short recurrent event: aperiodic, low rate				
high rate				
periodic, low rate				
high rate				
Long event, known duration				
Non-reversable change (indefinite duration)				

Figure 5.2 Some temporal facets of stress-producing environmental circumstances (SPECs) (reprinted with permission from McGrath and Beehr, 1990).

These temporal factors in occupational stress are merely suggestive and probably do not complete the picture about time and stress. As indicated above, time can affect appropriate times for measurement, because different strains are likely to manifest themselves at different temporal distances from the stressor and because some strains need to be measured periodically in order to establish a reliable reading. Furthermore, different stressors have temporal features that it is unwise to ignore. While temporal factors seem important, research has not yet been conducted that could tell us much about it. A great deal of study is needed in this area. Figure 5.2 could help as a taxonomy of temporal factors to guide such research. The uncertainty theory of occupational stress (from Beehr and Bhagat, 1985a) explained in an earlier chapter also could help guide such research, as it is one of the few job stress theories to explicitly consider a temporal factor: duration of the stressor (or SPEC, in Figure 5.2).

SUMMARY

Individual strains are the outcomes that, because of their association with job stressors, define the existence of a job stress situation. The distinguishing features of strains are that they are harmful to the individual and that they are caused by workplace factors called job or occupational stressors. They come in three types: psychological, physical or physiological, and behavioral.

Job stress research in organizational psychology has focused primarily on the psychological strains, however, and it is easy to speculate why. They are the least expensive to measure and their measurement is probably the most familiar to organizational psychologists. Expense can be manifested in many ways, including amount of time needed by people in general or especially of time needed from people with expertise, type of equipment needed (as well as skilled people's time to use the equipment), and so forth. Saying that psychological strains are the least expensive means that, in practice, the types of psychological strain measures used by researchers tend to be relatively inexpensive. Instead of using questionnaires, they could, for example, have psychiatrists do a full clinical work-up of each individual in the study (at much greater expense), but they do not. It should be noted that it was not stated that psychological strains are the "easiest" to measure. This might have implied that their cheap measurement is as accurate as the more expensive measurements of physical and behavioral strains. The discussion of the measurement problems associated with physiological strains, however, indicates that there may be more problems in measuring physiological strains than meet the eye of the typical I/O psychologist. There are stable, transitory, and procedural threats to the accuracy of the measurement of physiological strains. Furthermore, regarding behavioral strains, behaviorists might say something similar about the self-reports of these.

It is interesting that there are also frequent attempts at inexpensive measurement of physical and behavioral strains, that is, questionnaires are often used to ascertain illnesses and behaviors of the people in the study. At any rate, the use of self-reports does pose potential problems for the measurement of psychological strains. Other measurement problems regarding psychological strains derive from the use of self-reports. They include the potential for contamination of strain measures with stressors, the use of the word "stress" in questionnaire items, and the use of job dissatisfaction as a strain measure. Although there is no need to abandon self-report measures, serious examination of the likely meaning of the items is imperative each time they are used.

Among physical strains, cardiovascular responses are the most frequently discussed in research, speculation, and popular press. Several other physiological responses are potential strains, but much less is known about them. Future research should investigate them the way past research seems to have settled on the cardiovascular system for stress responses. That is, research is needed on sets of responses in the alimentary system, the respiratory system, or nervous system.

Time has only occasionally been addressed explicitly in studies of occupational stress, although a few theoretical models have advocated its importance (e.g. Beehr and Newman, 1978; Beehr and Bhagat, 1985a). It has not been addressed yet in my own empirical work, which is why it does not appear in the model illustrating my own program of research (Figure 1.2). Yet temporal factors seem to be inherent in many of the discussions of measurement problems and in a few of the concepts and theories regarding stress. Future research is needed that considers these. McGrath and some of his colleagues have been noting and speculating about temporal factors in social psychological research and this work offers a taxonomy of temporal factors in the job stress process. This taxonomy, presented here as Figure 5.2, can be used to guide future research into this as yet unexplored territory.

Chapter 6

Organizational outcomes of occupational stress

The examination of job stress in organizational psychology focuses on individual outcomes. The very definition of stress or stressors used here includes the requirement that individual strains are the defining outcome. This is in contrast to many other research topics in industrial and organizational psychology, where the traditional emphasis has been on organizational outcomes. Even job satisfaction as a criterion may not be an exception to this rule, because of the long history that the field has had trying to show that satisfaction (an individual outcome) was causally linked to job performance (an organizational outcome). That is, job satisfaction was apparently not important enough by itself for many researchers to consider it the "final" outcome. Job stress, as an area of study and practice, may at times be subject to the same phenomenon, that is, theoreticians and researchers "want" to show that it is important because it can lead to organizationally valued outcomes.

Perhaps it is obvious that I/O psychology has a tendency to focus on what is good for the organization first and what is good for the individual second. In any event, the study of job stress from an organizational psychology standpoint represents the other approach, that is, focusing on the individual's outcomes first. It is still very important, however, to determine whether such stress also affects the organization's well-being. It is not enough to assume that healthy individuals add up to a healthy organization. The organization's welfare and very existence depend on things other than or in addition to the health of its individual members.

WHAT IS AN ORGANIZATIONAL OUTCOME?

Strains, or individual outcomes of job stress, are those outcomes that have a more direct impact on the individual than on the organization. Organizational outcomes of job stress, in comparison, are those outcomes that have a more direct impact on the organization than on the individual. In order to have an impact on the individual or the organization, the outcome must be something important to or valued by the individual or the organization. It would be uncharitable to assert that organizations do not care about individuals' strains – the mental and physical health of their employees. Indeed, because organizations or their representatives often do care, there is sometimes difficulty in identifying an outcome as primarily organizational or primarily individual.

The issue is, however, whether the organization or its agents care as much about the individual's health as the individual does – and whether this health is as crucial to the well-being of the organization as it is to the individual. It would be convenient if the two interests were always perfectly congruent, but organizational life is not always convenient.

As implied above, an organizational consequence of stress is an outcome that is of primary importance to the organization, that is, an outcome that has a more direct impact on the organization than on the individual employee. In I/O psychology, there are several outcomes that have traditionally been considered "criteria" for judging the success of I/O programs or systems – selection systems, for example. Success has been explicitly or implicitly defined as outcomes that are good for the organization and therefore they are obvious examples of organizational outcomes. Job performance, absenteeism, and turnover are among the most typical of these criteria. In addition, profits, sales, earnings, early retirement, ability of the organization to recruit good new employees, ability to obtain necessary raw materials or other inputs, ability to control relevant sectors of the environment, innovativeness or creativity of employees, employee strikes, amount of influence of supervisors, and grievances filed are possible organizationally valued outcomes (Beehr and Newman, 1978). Few of these have been linked to job stress in rigorous studies, although it is easy to speculate about their likely relationships with stressors. While physical stressors are often studied in relationship to performance in the engineering psychology approach to occupational stress, performance has not been studied nearly so often in relation to the social psychological stressors of interest in the organizational psychology approach to stress.

WHY WOULD JOB STRESS BE RELATED TO ORGANIZATIONAL OUTCOMES?

By definition, job stressors tend to be linked to individual strains, but it is not always clear why one would expect them to be related to organizational outcomes as well. As noted in an essay by Shore (1979), the patrons of I/O psychology over the decades have been those with the money and budgets, which means the organizations or their representatives rather than individual members of organizations. It is sobering to realize that from I/O psychology's beginnings in the early 1900s with Scott and Munsterberg until Kahn *et al.* in the 1960s the field searched for variables that improve organizational criteria without coming up with the types of job stress of concern in this book. This may be taken as a simple indicator that there is little reason to expect job stressors to be strongly and simply related to organizational consequences. After all, if they are, why did stressors not become the focus of many I/O psychology studies much earlier?

Figure 1.2, which illustrates the research program described in this book, shows organizational consequences as one set of possible results from the stress process. They do not necessarily emanate only from the organizational stressors or only from the individual strains or human consequences, but instead they can result from the process or perhaps from either stressors or strains. Role ambiguity as a stressor, for example, might be expected to lead to lower productivity in some jobs simply because the workers do not know how to direct their efforts most efficiently. Physical illness as a strain, on the other hand, might also affect the organization through lost person-hours as workers take sick leave.

How might job stressors be related to organizational outcomes? One possibility, already noted, is that individual and organizational welfares are necessarily congruent with each other. Some organizational psychology theories lead one in this direction. Theories espousing the organizational utility of treating individuals as worthwhile human beings usually argue that this treatment benefits the organization as well as the individual in the long run (e.g. Theory Y, System 4). On the other hand, when given the chance, some organizational leaders historically have opted to do quite the opposite, running sweatshops, dangerous factories, or even employing slave labor. Certainly this approach to running organizations still exists in some quarters today and would be more prominent if it were not for modern laws. Apparently, the implicit organizational theories of some leaders of organizations, presumably those people with the most first-hand experience, do not include the idea that individual and organizational interests are necessarily congruent.

Besides the theories that organizational and individual welfares are positively correlated and that they are negatively correlated, there is the obvious possibility that they can be independent. Given this situation in which there are potentially quite diverse theories about the relationships between individual and organizational welfares, it is most prudent to assume that there is no necessary relationship between all variables indicative of individual and organizational outcomes of job stress. In fact, it will be assumed here that it is necessary to investigate each individual outcome, each organizational outcome, and their relationships with particular stressors in order to determine the likely relationships between organizational stress and the congruence of individually and organizationally valued outcomes of stressors in the workplace. It seems possible for some stressors to be positively related to some organizational outcomes, negatively related to others, and not related at all to still others. As is apparent from the discussion of Beehr and Franz (1987), organizational stress is a loosely integrated research topic covering a great diversity of occupational stressors and individual strains. The main integrating theme is the interest in social psychological stressors in the workplace that lead to individual ill health. Organizational stress has many faces. Limiting it to the social (organizational) psychology stressors helps narrow the topic somewhat, but there still appear to be many variations on this general theme. There is little reason to believe that stressors discovered under such a broad definition will all be related to organizational outcomes in the same manner.

JOB STRESS AND ORGANIZATIONAL OUTCOMES

An important question in this issue is which organizational outcome one is considering. Beehr and Newman, in 1978, noted that there had been some research on the relationship between job stressors and two general types of organizationally relevant outcomes: job performance and employee withdrawal. These are probably still the two most frequently studied categories of organizational consequences of job stress.

Job performance as an organizational consequence of job stress

Research on job performance as an outcome of occupational stress is sometimes cited that has used self-reports of something resembling job performance. Examples include questionnaire measures of effort toward quality and effort toward quantity of work (Beehr et al., 1976), of job performance (Borucki, 1987), of vocational strain (Osipow and Davis, 1988), and of personal accomplishment (e.g. from the Maslach Burnout Inventory; Maslach and Jackson, 1981 used, for example, in Jackson et al., 1986). Generally, these are moderately, weakly, or not related to job stressors measured with questionnaires, with good performance negatively associated with stressors. The one exception is a self-reported measure of performance quantity, which was found to be related positively to one job stressor – role overload. In spite of problems with these types of measures, this result was interesting because it implies an almost compelling logic that people experiencing more workload tend to do more work. In general, such measures, used as measures of organizational outcomes of occupational stress, are suspect because of their measurement and the likelihood of bias in reporting one's own performance. For the most part, the potential for self-reports of performance to have some validity has not been maximized, because most of these measures were not constructed in a meticulous manner that would give more confidence in them (e.g. as outlined in Kane and Lawler, 1978). In these studies, performance was not the focus, but the early studies of this nature might have provided the best guess about the effects of the organizational psychology types of stressors on performance. Future research on job performance as an outcome of occupational stress should probably not rely on such measures of performance, however.

Perhaps the best known theory about the relationship between stress and performance is the one apparently derived from the turn-of-the-century Yerkes–Dodson law regarding drives and motivation (Young, 1936). This approach to job stress usually maintains that the level of autonomic arousal predicts task performance via an inverted, U-shaped curve and that job stressors create this arousal, as in Figure 6.1 (e.g. Ivancevich and Matteson, 1980; McGrath, 1976). There are three inverted U-shaped curves in the figure to illustrate the relativity of the concept. For task A, optimum performance is reached at lower levels of stressors than for tasks B and C. This implies that the nature of the tasks can affect the placement of the curve, even though its shape remains constant. Furthermore, it is easy to surmise that a number of factors could function to move the curve to the left or the right, including individual differences, task difficulty, task importance (which might influence the intentional effort and concentration of workers), and various context factors. As long as such factors only move the curve but leave its shape essentially unchanged, the theory seems to have credence.

As noted in an earlier chapter, much of the emphasis on performance as an outcome from stress has come from engineering psychology and the typical stressors from that approach include physical conditions (Beehr and Franz, 1987). If one considers some extreme cases of physical stressors, it seems that the theory must be correct at the stressors' scale end points, where low performance is expected. If temperature is the stressor, for example, then the person would freeze to death in extreme cold and burn to death in extreme heat. Under such situations, performance is certain to be quite low, lower than it is at some points of temperature between. Extremes of light and

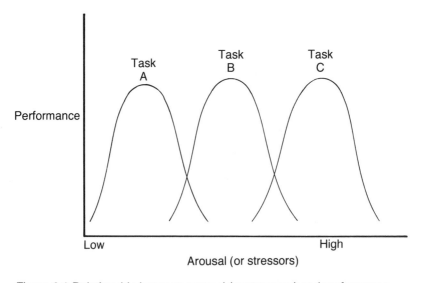

Figure 6.1 Relationship between arousal (or stressors) and performance.

maybe levels of noise that do not normally occur in the workplace might have similar results.

Of course, one would like to know whether differences in stressors that normally occur in the workplace today, not just the potential extremes, have effects that fit an inverted U. In addition, one would like to know the relevance of the theory for the types of social psychological stressors of interest in organizational psychology. Even if there is some evidence or logic to this curvilinear relationship for physical stressors, the same may not hold for social and psychological stressors. The logic used above regarding extremes of temperature relies upon fairly quick, serious physical health consequences to lead to performance changes. It is more difficult to argue that role ambiguity, at the extremes (no ambiguity and total ambiguity) would lead as quickly to death of the person. Indeed, many of the types of job stressors of interest here have been labeled "chronic" (e.g. Beehr and Franz, 1987), and there seems to be an implication that their effects take a long time to manifest themselves (more explicit in some theories than in others, e.g. Beehr and Bhagat's duration factor; 1985a). Furthermore, while one could easily argue that total ambiguity leads to large performance decrements, total clarity seems less likely to do so.

A few studies (Choo, 1986; Jamal, 1984; Anderson, 1976) have focused on the possibility that organizational psychology stressors are related to performance in a curvilinear manner. This theory is, in some ways, difficult to refute, because any finding would fit some point on the curve. That is, a study finding a positive relationship between stressors and performance could have measured stressors at the left side of the curve, those finding a negative relationship could have measured stressors at the right side of the curve, and those finding no relationship could have measured stressors at the center of the curve. A few illustrative studies, however, are instructive.

One study of 433 practicing auditors in Australia found support for the inverted-U shaped relationship between "job stress" and performance (Choo, 1986). That study used the job-related tension index of Kahn *et al.* (1964), which asks mostly about being bothered by role conflict and ambiguity as the measure of stress and used a specially constructed rating scale of job performance completed by both supervisors and the auditors themselves. The curvilinear relationship was found for both performance measures. Although the Kahn *et al.* job-related tension index is still frequently used, it should be noted that it was critiqued negatively in a previous chapter because the items tend to mix stressors and strains in each item, thereby leaving uncertainty regarding the nature of the items' meaning.

In a Canadian study (Jamal, 1984) of 440 nurses in two large hospitals, four self-reported job stressors (role ambiguity, role overload, role conflict, and resource inadequacy) were negatively correlated with supervisor ratings of three types of job "performance" (performance, motivation, and patient care). Of these twelve relationships thus obtained, two showed evidence of curvilinear relationships, those of role ambiguity with performance and role ambiguity with motivation.

In the US, Anderson (1976) reported an inverted U-shaped relationship between perceived stress of ninety-three small business owner-managers following a flood and interviewer ratings of organizational performance. Actual financial losses due to the flood, intended to be a more objective measure of the stressor, did not relate to performance, however.

Five other studies apparently did not look for a curvilinear relationship between stressors and performance and reported no or very weak (linear) relationships of stressors with job performance. Blau (1981) studied perceived P–E Fit stressors specific to urban bus drivers and performance measures coded from incidents in the organization's records. Bedeian *et al.* (1983) looked at two types of role ambiguity, two types of role conflict, and supervisors' ratings of the performance of hospital nurses. Kaufmann and Beehr (1986) investigated both perceived role stressors and P-E Fit stressors in relation to supervisors' ratings of performance among hospital nurses. Motowidlo *et al.*, (1986) examined frequency and intensity of self-reported stress at work and supervisor ratings of several performance-related aspects of nurses' behaviors in a sample of 1200 nurses in five hospitals. Spector *et al.* (1988) studied situational constraints, role ambiguity, role conflict, and role overload in relation to supervisors' ratings of university secretaries' performance. They also used (lack of) autonomy as a stressor and this was related to performance more strongly than the other stressors, but autonomy is more often considered a motivator (e.g. in work redesign theory; Hackman and Oldham, 1980) than a stressor. It is interesting that these studies did not examine their data for U-shaped relationships, considering that the idea is well known. Each study had, however, a primary focus other than the relationship between stressors and performance (e.g. focusing on social support as a moderator or focusing on multiple measurements of stressors or strains). Future researchers could benefit the field by being alert to opportunities to examine the hypothesized inverted U-shaped relationship between job stressors and performance when such data are collected. The low or non-significant linear relationships in these studies could even be understandable if the U-shaped relationship were in the data.

In data from the Beehr *et al.* study (1990; described in more detail in the chapter on social support), the results of preliminary analyses were much the same. Two hundred and twenty five registered nurses randomly selected from seven hospitals were surveyed regarding their role conflict, role ambiguity, effort-to-performance, and performance-to-outcome uncertainties (Beehr and Bhagat, 1985a), and their supervisors were asked to complete a performance rating form for them. As in most of the other studies, linear relationships between the self-reported stressors and supervisor ratings were weak or nonexistent.

Jackson and Schuler's (1985) meta-analysis summarized the few studies that had been done at the time regarding job performance and two job stressors, role conflict and role ambiguity, and reported the mean correlation between role conflict and job performance, whether objective performance, others' ratings, or self ratings. These mean correlations were all very small (all less than 0.10). For role ambiguity, the mean correlations were the same except for self-rated performance, for which the correlation was –0.24. At present, it might be safest simply to conclude that the results are at best somewhat mixed regarding the effects of occupational stress on perform-ance. In any event, perhaps there is little reason to expect all job stressors to be related to all types of job performance in the same way.

A somewhat older laboratory study of undergraduates doing anagrams (Sales, 1970) illustrates some of the complications that can occur. Both overload and underload were conceived as stressors and it does not seem logical to expect them to lead equally to performance decrements (especially within normally encountered ranges of underload and overload in the work-place). People in the overload condition received more anagrams to work on than those in the underload condition and they decoded more of them. In terms of percentage of work completed, however, overloaded people decoded about two-thirds of their anagrams, while underloaded people decoded about 90 percent of theirs. The number of errors also varied, as might also be expected. Furthermore, subjective or perceived workload was not related to any performance measure.

The relationships between job stressors and performance may depend very much on what the stressor is, what the performance measure is, and what other variables are present in the setting. Future research on the topic should probably consider all of these carefully. It would be beneficial at this point to develop theories or at least mini-theories about such relationships to guide future research. Researchers following the Person–Environment (P–E) Fit model of occupational stress have suggested this regarding the P–E Fit theory (e.g. Caplan, 1987) and it could be applied to any model of occupational stress.

Employee withdrawal as an organizational consequence of job stress

The thinking regarding the relationships of withdrawal behaviors to occu-pational stressors is quite simple and straightforward and it is very similar to the thinking about the relationship between job satisfaction and withdrawal. Basically, if the workplace is unpleasant, the employee is expected to want to get out and stay out of the workplace. Contrary to the theorizing about an inverted U-shaped relationship between job stressors and job performance, this is much simpler and resembles the usual basic expectation of a linear relationship between job stressors and individual strains. The only question is whether the withdrawal is more likely a direct result of the stressors or of the strains, as pictured in Figure 6.2.

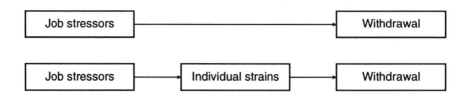

Figure 6.2 Common alternative relationships of withdrawal and occupational stress variables.

It is probably unrealistic to expect employee withdrawal to be strongly predicted from stressors or even from strains. Absenteeism and turnover, for example, have been studied in great detail for a long time and they seem to have multiple causes; job stress will only be one. Furthermore, the approach of occupational stress being a cause of withdrawal takes, at best, only half of the equation into consideration – the repulsion half.

These behaviors are potentially motivated by both attraction and repulsion. Everybody has to be somewhere, but we often think of absent or terminated people as simply gone from the focal organization without considering where they are or what they are doing. The attraction of alternative places and activities may be as much or more of a reason for absenteeism or turnover as anything that goes on the workplace. What occurs in the workplace is only the repulsion half of the equation and occupational stressors are only a part of that half. Non-stressful but still unattractive working conditions can also presumably lead to employee withdrawal.

Furthermore, attractive alternatives to attendance at work could abound for some people. Examples would include having out of town visitors, opening day at the baseball park, an attractive late night activity before the morning's work and so forth. These could easily lead to absenteeism quite apart from any stress in the workplace. Turnover, of course, could also be caused by attractive alternatives as well as or more than by stress in the workplace. Examples would include "better" jobs, but also might entail not working at all for a while in order to take advantage of an opportunity for an extended vacation, to attend school or retrain to better one's long-term employment possibilities. The nature of the job (e.g. stressors) is only one factor in determining people's withdrawal from an organization.

One would certainly expect job stress to be related to employee withdrawal, but withdrawal is not a strain or individual outcome. By definition in this book, stressors lead to individual strains, but they may or may not lead to organizational outcomes such as performance, absenteeism, and turnover. If job stress is related to the organizational withdrawal outcomes, however, there is even more reason for organizations to be concerned about it.

There are at least four types of employee withdrawal that could logically be related to occupational stress, given the simple idea that stressful occupations are painful and there will be a tendency to want to get away from them. The four types of withdrawal are lateness, absenteeism, turnover, and psychological withdrawal, and they tend to be positively and moderately related to each other (Beehr and Gupta, 1978).

Tardiness as an organizational consequence of job stress

Research on tardiness as a consequence of occupational stress has been rare. Jamal (1984) found that the self-reported job stressors, role ambiguity, role overload, role conflict, and resource inadequacy were all positively related to recorded tardiness (r's =0.35, 0.25, 0.23, and 0.34, respectively) among hospital nurses. The four stressors in that study, however, were from the Kahn *et al.* (1964) job-related tension index, which is composed of items that ask about a mixture of both stressors and psychological strain. Therefore, as noted previously in this book, it is uncertain just what these results mean. It can be argued that the rate of approaching a location in which pain is usually found would be slow. If job stress is painful and causes people to be slow getting ready for work, driving to work, and so forth, then they might be expected to be late to work more often than others who do not experience stress at work. In general, there is little research on lateness or tardiness in industrial and organizational psychology outside of the job stress field, let alone inside it.

Research on the process of lateness could investigate some interesting possibilities. For example, on the day shift, do workers who are tardy tend to set their alarms, awaken, and get up later than others, or do they simply use more time getting to work? Do they tend to live farther from the workplace than those who are not tardy? Basically, this is asking some of the same questions that we do not ask often enough about absenteeism. What are the employees doing while they are not at work?

Lateness would no doubt be a complicated variable to study, however. Indeed, there is probably a wide variation in what tardiness means from job to job and employer to employer. For example, are professors late only when they arrive for the day's first class or first meeting late, or are they late when arriving on campus later than 8.00 a.m.? Many salaried workers do not have close monitoring of their times of arrival. Many managers arrive well before the official starting time of the company. When they arrive "only" at the official starting time, are they late? Compared to expectations, maybe they are. At any rate, much lateness probably goes unrecorded, although it might be related to occupational stress and might influence organizational effectiveness.

Specifically regarding occupational stress and its potential relationship with lateness, the issue also seems likely to be complex. The simple idea that people might avoid stressful work and therefore be late can easily be questioned, because of the special differences between tardiness and other forms of withdrawal. Being late to work in many jobs might make the work more painful than being on time and the consequences are more immediate than for absenteeism. For example, if employees are late, they may receive some formal or informal punishment immediately, that is, as soon as they arrive at work. The supervisor or even co-workers might simply berate the person in some way, or the employee might be officially notified of a penalty for being tardy. Anticipating such negative and immediate effects of being late, employees might feel the work situation is even more aversive than before. Therefore, they might "decide" to be absent rather than late. Why hurry to work only to be late and get punished? Instead, it might seem better at the time to stay home and try to find a good excuse for absenteeism. Overall, little is known about the relationship between job stress and lateness and research on the topic could be interesting but complicated.

It might be possible to use self-reports to measure lateness for such research, because one study (Beehr and Gupta, 1978) has shown that self-reported lateness during the previous two weeks was related to a single-item supervisory rating of lateness over an unspecified time period (r=0.39). The use of self-reports, of course, could make it easier to study this variable, in relation to job stress or other characteristics.

Absenteeism as an organizational consequence of job stress

Not coming to work because of occupational stress seems to be one way to avoid the pain of stress. Research on absenteeism has usually found only weak relationships between absenteeism and job attitudes such as job satisfaction (or dissatisfaction). There are at least two reasons, however, to think that job stress might be related to absenteeism at least as strongly as job dissatisfaction is. First, the intensity of the negative response to job stress is, almost by definition, stronger than attitudes such as dissatisfaction. Although it is rarely diagnosed thoroughly in the job stress research, psychological strains are supposed to include clinical depression and anxiety and any number of mental health disorders. In addition, physical or physiological illnesses can be strains that are due to job stress. These sound much more aversive and debilitating than "merely" being dissatisfied with the job.

Second, companies recognize that some absenteeism is officially due to illness and it is often labeled this way in the company's official records as sick days. If job stress is a cause of these illnesses, then there should be some relationship between job stressors and absenteeism that is classified as sick days. Even this relationship will not necessarily be strong, however, because some people will try to fight through illness in order to come to work, while everyone will of course be ill sometimes (probably most of the time) when it is not due to job stress.

The specifics of measurement of absenteeism, therefore, can be important in studies seeking to understand occupational stress. Measuring absenteeism specifically due to illness could be important. It would be interesting to measure absenteeism in this way as well as in others and to see which is most strongly related to stressors on the job.

Even if one makes the decision to and is able to measure absences due to illness separately from other absences, there are other categorizations of absenteeism measures that could be taken into account. Muchinsky (1977) identified about forty measures of absenteeism that have been and could be used in psychological research. Chadwick-Jones *et al.* (1973) and Dalton and Mesch (1991) have argued for a distinction between absenteeism that is controllable and that which is not controllable by management. Further-more, it is usually argued that I/O psychologists should focus their research on absenteeism that management can do something about, because this would be most practical. It is interesting to note that absenteeism due to illness is specifically placed into the category of absence management can do nothing about and that therefore could be ignored by I/O psychologists. Here we argue that some of these illnesses are precisely the ones that should be measured because they might be stress-related.

Two of the more popular measures of absenteeism in I/O psychology are its frequency or its duration. During any given time period (e.g. a year or six months), people can be absent for a number of times or events (frequency) and also for a total length of time (duration). Two employees might both be absent for thirty-one days during the past year, but one of them was absent for thirty-one straight days, while the other was never absent two work days in a row. These would represent two extremes of absence frequency (one time for the former and thirty-one times for the latter employee), while having exactly the same duration. In cases this diverse, the meaning of and the reasons for the absences were probably quite different. If company records are used as the source of absenteeism data, the researcher is some-what at the mercy of the employer's record-keeping system, but if it is possible, the obvious solution is to record absenteeism in terms of both frequency and duration so that the relationships of each to stressors or other variables could be ascertained. In general, it seems that many psychological variables tend to be a little more closely related to frequency of absenteeism than to duration of absenteeism and perhaps this is because frequency tends to tap into another categorization of absence – avoidable absences (Dalton and Mesch, 1991). Avoidable absences are those that are similar to volun-tariness for turnover. Employees could have attended work, but they did not. It has also been argued that avoidable absences (and therefore frequency) would likely be related to variables of interest to I/O psychologists (Dalton and Mesch, 1991). This is likely to be true of job stressors also, because they are psychological in nature. Therefore, it might make sense for future research to measure both absences due to sickness and avoidable absences. If avoidable absences cannot be measured, however, frequency of absences might serve as a surrogate for them.

Besides the measurement of categories of absenteeism such as sick days versus other reasons for absence and frequency versus duration, a third measurement issue is whether to measure absenteeism by self-reports, employer records, or some other source. Whereas measurement of performance by self-reports requires great care, the measurement of absenteeism may be, within limits, somewhat easier. Self-reports of absenteeism have been found in one five-organization study to be correlated with absenteeism in the records of the organizations (Beehr and Gupta, 1978). Self-reported absenteeism for the one month prior to the self-report was correlated 0.38 with records for that month and 0.62 with recorded absenteeism during the six-month period after the self-report. The larger correlation was probably due to the improved reliability of the records measure (that is, six months probably gives a more reliable measure than one month).

When to measure absenteeism is also an issue. If it is expected to be caused by job stressors, then it should probably be measured after the measurement of the job stressors. Although this seems obvious, it is easier (and therefore often done) to collect the absenteeism measures at the same time as the measurement of the job stressors. Collecting absenteeism data at the same time usually means collecting data about absences that actually occurred *prior* to the measurement of stressors, since the data usually cover some past time period.

Gupta and Beehr (1979), following up eighteen months later on the sample used in my dissertation and described in an earlier chapter (Beehr 1976), collected new data from a subsample of employees from three of the original five organizations. Absenteeism data (frequency) were collected from the organizations' personnel records in two forms: the frequency of absenteeism in the month prior to the original interview and the frequency of absenteeism during the month subsequent to the original interview. Four self-reported stressors from the interviews (role ambiguity, role overload, underutilization of skills, and resource inadequacy) were related to the subsequent month's absenteeism measure, but not to the prior month's absence measure. Furthermore, for three of the four stressors, all but role overload, the correlation with prior absenteeism was significantly weaker than the correlation with subsequent absenteeism. Even though the correlations with subsequent absenteeism were weak (in the mid-teens), the fact that they were stronger than the correlations with prior absenteeism might be taken as some evidence for causation from stressors to absences. These results reinforce the obvious recommendation to measure the presumed consequences (e.g. absenteeism) after the presumed causes (e.g. job stressors) in longitudinal studies.

The median correlation between stressors and absenteeism in the Gupta and Beehr study was only about 0.15. Jackson and Schuler's (1985) review reported an average correlation between role ambiguity and absence as 0.09 and between role conflict and absence as –0.01. Again, we should probably not expect job stressors to be strongly related to absenteeism. A well-known model of employee attendance lists over twenty variables expected to affect absenteeism, of which role stress is only one and not a direct one (Steers and Rhodes, 1978).

As previously noted, Gupta and Beehr (1979) found that self-reported job stressors were weakly related to subsequent absenteeism obtained from company records among 651 employees in five organizations. Kaufmann and Beehr (1986) found a correlation among 102 hospital nurses of 0.24 between self-reported underutilization of skills and prior sick days obtained from records but no relationship between this absenteeism measure and a conglomerate stressor composed of workload and job future ambiguity. Spector et al. (1988), in a study of 181 university secretaries, reported a correlation of 0.17 between self-reported role ambiguity and self-reported sick days in the prior three months. The other seven self-reported stressors were not related to absenteeism. Furthermore, none of the eight job stressors assessed by supervisors of the secretaries were related to this sickness-absence measure. Jamal (1984) used four stress measures from the combined stressor–strain job-related tension index from Kahn et al. (1964) and found that they were related to subsequent (four month period) absenteeism among his 440 hospital nurses (r's =0.34, 0.27, 0.23, and 0.37). Overall, there is mixed evidence that job stressors are related to absenteeism, but the relationship may depend upon when and how the absenteeism is measured.

Turnover as an organizational consequence of job stress

As with absenteeism, the logic of an expected association between job stress and turnover is the basic withdrawal hypothesis, that is, if it is painful to be at work, then people will try to avoid the workplace. Turnover is logically a more extreme step than simply staying away from work for a day (as with some absenteeism). One approach to turnover suggests that turnover is a rational decision. That is, turnover occurs because the employee has better alternatives. This obviously applies only to voluntary turnover. While I/O psychology historically seemed to treat turnover as a negative organizational consequence, something to be reduced, it can also be positive or neutral from the organization's perspective. While there are costs of recruiting, selecting, and training associated with turnover if the organization needs to replace the person who left, in other ways turnover may not be negative. In recent years American manufacturing organizations have frequently sought to downsize, sometimes through offering retirement incentives to people (Colarelli and Beehr, 1993). In these instances, turnover might be quite welcome for the welfare of the organization. Furthermore, aside from retirement and situations in which companies are seeking to downsize, some turnover can still be good or functional for the organization (Dalton *et al.*, 1982). If the employee is a poor performer and/or costly to keep and if the labor market is overflowing with people who have relevant skills, then the organization can probably replace the poor employee with a good one and be better off rather than worse. Logically, this should depend upon the labor market in the geographic area and in the relevant skill area, the cost of the current employee (e.g. pay) versus the cost of a new employee and the cost of recruiting, selecting, and training the new employee. For present purposes, however, if the organization will either benefit or be hurt by any turnover that might be due to job stress, the turnover is an important organizational consequence. It is only when the turnover has a neutral effect that it is of no consequence to the organization.

The same question arises regarding turnover that arises regarding absenteeism. The concept of turnover comes from the organization's point of view, that is, the employee has gone away, never to return. But the employee has not disappeared from the face of the earth, only from this organization. Since everyone has to be somewhere, a logical question is, where is the former employee?

This all leads to the conclusion that, as with absenteeism, turnover can at best only be weakly related to job stress. There are lots of reasons why people quit their jobs, and they can be divided into two categories – repulsion and attraction. Employees can be attracted to better alternatives, and that is a likely set of reasons for turnover (e.g. models by Hulin *et al.*, 1985; Mobley *et al.*, 1978). They also can be "driven" out of the organization (repulsion) by something unpleasant in the organization itself. Job stress is one reason, but only one. There are so many other reasons for turnover that we should not expect job stress to be strongly related to turnover.

In spite of this, there is some evidence that job stressors are related to turnover, however. A fairly early study of 156 hospital nurses by Lyons (1971), for example, found that role ambiguity was related to employee turnover after ten months ($r=0.21$), and Gupta and Beehr's (1979) study, described earlier regarding its absenteeism results, found that underutilization of skills was related to turnover after about one and a half years ($r=0.23$). We, however, found no relationship between the study's three other stressors (role ambiguity, role overload, and resource inadequacy) and turnover. The relationships between job stressors and turnover appear to be very modest.

The study of turnover and job stress requires a somewhat longitudinal approach because one must usually wait for some time to pass before it is known who has left the organization. Rarely do people quit their jobs at the first sign of job stress. In addition, participation in a stress study by the organization's representatives is different and in some ways greater than if only a questionnaire were used, because someone in the organization must report who has terminated employment (or allow researchers to have access to records). While these constraints on research also apply to absenteeism, more turnover research has resorted to self-reports. Specifically, employees are asked, at the time of the self-report measurement of stressors, to indicate the likelihood that they will leave the organization within a future time period (often one year). These self-reports of intended turnover have been shown to be moderately correlated with actual turnover (e.g. r=0.39; Beehr and Gupta, 1978). There are some potentially meaningful differences in the specific wording of such items, because some of these indices have items asking whether people are likely to look for new jobs while others ask whether people are likely to quit their current jobs. Not enough is known about the meaningful differences between such wordings, however, to make definitive statements at present and all such indices are referred to here as turnover intentions.

Jackson and Schuler's (1985) meta-analysis concluded that the mean correlation between role ambiguity and turnover intentions was 0.18, while the relationship between role conflict and turnover intentions was 0.21. In some more recent research, the median correlation between role ambiguity (self-reported) and turnover intentions was 0.25 (i.e. Beehr and Drexler, 1986; Beehr and O'Driscoll, 1990; Jamal, 1984; Mayes and Ganster, 1988; Spector *et al.*, 1988), and the correlation between role conflict and turnover intentions was 0.27 (i.e. Beehr and Drexler, 1986; Beehr and O'Driscoll, 1990; Jamal, 1984), only a little stronger than the previous studies reviewed by Jackson and Schuler.

Other job stressors besides role conflict and role ambiguity have been investigated in relation to turnover intent. Self-reported role overload has been correlated with turnover intent in five studies (median correlation about 0.24; Beehr and Drexler, 1986; Beehr and King, 1986; Gupta and Beehr, 1979; Jamal, 1984; Spector *et al.*, 1988), constraints such as resource inadequacy in three studies (median correlation about 0.24; Gupta and Beehr, 1979; Jamal, 1984; Spector *et al.* 1988), and underutilization of skills in two studies (median correlation about 0.335; Beehr and King, 1986; Gupta and Beehr, 1979). In addition, one study reported a correlation of 0.50 between interpersonal conflict and turnover intent (Spector *et al.*, 1988). Compared to the other stressors reported here, this last one is a very strong correlation and suggests that this relatively ignored stressor merits more study.

Spector *et al.* (1988) also looked at supervisors' reports of their subordinates' (the focal people in the study) stressors and found that only two of them, constraints and interpersonal conflict, were related to turnover intentions (r's =0.19 and 0.16, respectively). These relatively weaker correlations suggest that supervisors cannot accurately rate subordinates' stressors and/or that some sort of response bias accounts for much of the relationship between job stressors and turnover intent.

The Beehr and King (1986) study was somewhat unique in that it looked at employees' intentions not just to leave the organization, but to leave their professions all together, which they labeled occupational abandonment (Beehr and King, 1986). Underutilization of skills was related to this intention in a sample of ninety-two mental health center therapists (r=0.38), but role overload was not. This type of turnover has rarely been studied (see Lane *et al.*, 1988), and could use more investigation.

Overall, the evidence is mixed regarding whether job stressors are related to turnover, but they do seem to be related to intentions to quit. The relationship with quitting is probably an indirect one in any case and so these results are not surprising.

Psychological withdrawal as an organizational consequence of job stress

In addition to lateness, absenteeism, and turnover, it can be argued that a more mild form of withdrawal from the workplace is psychological withdrawal (Beehr and Gupta, 1978). That is, although an employee is physically present at work, he or she is absent in spirit. Lack of interest in the job might tend to lead people to be absent in spirit and thought. Examples of I/O psychology variables that might overlap with the concept of psychological withdrawal would be reduced job involvement (psychological withdrawal from the job) and reduced organizational commitment (psychological withdrawal from the organization). Jackson and Schuler's meta-analysis reported the average correlation of role ambiguity with organizational commitment as –0.27 and with job involvement as –0.28, and they reported the average correlation of role conflict with these variables as –0.24 and –0.16, respectively.

These variables, especially organizational commitment, are probably closely related to turnover intentions and some measures of commitment even contain items that ask about turnover intentions. Therefore, the similar findings are expected. There are probably withdrawal behaviors that are associated with psychological withdrawal, but these have not been studied. The theme would be withdrawal from the surroundings while still being in them. For example, slowness or failure in returning phone calls to others in the organization, keeping one's office door closed and one's phone on call forward, missing or being late for staff meetings, avoiding eating lunch with others in the workplace, and so forth. These no doubt have many causes other than job stress, but they also may in part be caused by it. If so, they seem to have a withdrawal from the job or from the organization component to them. Future research is needed to illuminate this possibility.

SUMMARY

It is obvious that the study of organizational consequences of occupational stress has lagged behind the study of individual consequences in the organizational psychology approach to job stress. That is, however, as it should be, given the organizational psychology definition of work stress. Job stressors, by definition, lead to individual strains, but they do not necessarily lead to organizational outcomes. Whether and the extent to which these stressors lead to organizational outcomes is an interesting and important question, but it is not the primary expected result of the stressors.

Because of this, it is not surprising that the research indicates that job stressors are only weakly and perhaps inconsistently related to organizational outcomes. To complicate matters further, a common theoretical relationship between job stressors and one organizational outcome, the inverted, U-shaped curve between job stress and performance, is not necessarily theoretically appropriate for the other organizational outcomes. Future research could expand the current knowledge about occupational stress and organizational outcomes by including both organizational outcomes and individual outcomes in the same studies, by using theory to guide research (the inverted U-shaped curve and the concept of withdrawal may both need further theoretical refinement), and by measuring some of these consequences with non-self-report techniques. When all of this is done, however, we should still expect weaker results with these criteria than with the ones around which the definition of job stressors is built – the individual outcomes.

Part IV

Alleviating aversive effects of occupational stress

This part of the book examines the adaptive responses of Figure 1.2 from Chapter 1. Adaptive responses, or treatments for the alleviation of the harmful effects of occupational stress, abound in quantity and variety. It is not known very clearly, however, if they also abound in their quality or effectiveness. One only hopes that there is little truth in the statement that treatments are many, but cures are few. Research can provide answers to the questions about the effectiveness of occupational stress treatments, but good evaluations of these treatments have been far more rare than the treatments themselves. This is an area where research still has much that it can offer to society.

Chapter 7 overviews treatments for occupational stress and research on them. Treatments can be divided into those that focus on changing part of the individual and those that focus first on changing part of the organization in which the individual works. The individual level treatments have dominated practice in the domain and reasons for this are explored in the first chapter of this section.

Chapter 8 looks intensively at one potential type of treatment that has been a favorite in the organizational psychology approach to job stress, the use of social support. Supportive people and support groups abound and are frequently recommended for all sorts of purposes related to stress. The many studies of social support in combination with workplace stress have suggested that there may be some good effects from social support. There have been inconsistencies and even anomalies in the research, however, particularly in the research on the popular "buffering" hypothesis. Thus, it is still not clear how, when, and whether social support is usually helpful in situations related to occupational stress and several recommendations are made for illuminating its effects.

Chapter 7

Treating occupational stress

In one sense, treatment of occupational stress has far outstripped research. That is, the application of treatments and the espousal of many of these treatments go far beyond what research can claim to know about them. And of course, there are almost certainly more treatments of occupational stress than there are studies of such treatments. It is probably a fact of life that when there is a psychological problem, in organizations or elsewhere, many treatments will become available quickly. In the case of occupational stress treatments, however, rigorous evaluation research on these treatments has lagged far behind their implementation. Of course, this means that many treatments, while well-intentioned, are proceeding without the benefit of strong evidence of their effectiveness.

This chapter is concerned with a variety of potential ways of dealing with the problems arising from the core relationship of occupational stress in the figure depicting this program of research (Figure 1.2 in Chapter 1). The use of the word treatment is not intended to limit the coverage to formal, carefully planned treatments, nor is it intended to limit the coverage to professional "treaters." Instead, a broader view still seems appropriate. That is, until it can be ascertained with more certainty what treatments are the most effective, it seems prudent to be willing to consider virtually all manner of ways that people deal with occupational stress. These might be called stress treatment programs, coping techniques, adaptation, defense mechanisms, or they may have no labels at all, but it is important at this stage of learning about occupational stress to keep an open mind and to consider many possible actions and reactions to job stress for their potential beneficial effects.

Research methods that are most appropriate for examining occupational stress treatments include both experimental and quasiexperimental designs and have been described more extensively elsewhere (e.g. Beehr, 1984; Beehr and O'Hara, 1987; Beehr and McGrath, in preparation). True experiments on occupational stress treatments have been rare and quasiexperimental designs have been used primarily with treatments delivered by outsiders rather than with treatments that have been labeled coping. There is a blurring of distinction between the external treatments and coping, but coping is a term that is used more often when the individuals on their own undertake to deal with the stress.

There can be an ethics dilemma in attempting to use experiments or quasiexperiments to study the effects of stressors. The problem is the intentional exposure of people to stressors or stimuli that are expected to be harmful to them. For example, a researcher might be tempted to randomly assign people to stressful and non-stressful work situations over a period of time. As noted in the previous two chapters, however, stressors, by definition, have harmful psychological and physical effects on people. Furthermore, there might be organizational consequences as well. The manipulation of the independent variables, stressors, raises ethical questions.

A way out of the ethics dilemma can be had by focusing on manipulations aimed at improving a situation instead of manipulations aimed at creating stressors, however. Stress treatments, adaptations, or use of coping techniques all are expected to reduce stress and therefore to improve the condition of research participants rather than increase stress and worsen people's situations. In many cases, researchers could manipulate such stress treatments without great ethical risk of harming people. A study by Ganster *et al.* (1982) took this approach and it came closer to being a true experiment on occupational stress treatments than almost any other done in the field. This shows that field experiments on this topic can be done, even though they rarely are.

In studies of occupational stress and especially in studies of its treatment, it has been common to use samples of convenience. One research need that would enhance external validity in particular is the need for samples that are more representative of incumbents in jobs in general, or even just samples that are representative of the incumbents of a single job. The common reliance on volunteers in studies of occupational stress (e.g. Ganster *et al.*, 1982; Kaufmann and Beehr, 1986), on attendees at workshops or conferences (e.g. Kaufman and Beehr, 1989), or on other types of convenience samples often means that the samples have unknown properties compared with people in general. For example, the samples may be heavily loaded with people with large amounts of occupational stress, with people with small amounts (because the truly stressed people are too busy and anxious to volunteer), with people who are sensitized to and have their own definitions of stress, with people who volunteer for everything, and so forth.

COPING

Sometimes stress treatments have been classified with value-laden terms that imply one type of treatment is better than another. The terms coping and defense are examples. Coping techniques such as altering the objective environment by reducing the stressor can be inferred as superior to defense mechanisms that "only" alter perceptions. It can be argued, however, that any way of dealing with stress that has beneficial effects is useful. Having beneficial effects generally means that strain, the aversive outcome that defines the stress process, is reduced or is less severe than it would have been without the treatment. Thus, the strain outcomes that were caused by job stress are used as criteria for judging the effectiveness of the treatments. An alternative would be to use a theory or the power of expert authority to classify treatments as good, bad, or indifferent. Thus, a theory might label some treatments as coping and assert that they are effective while other treatments are labeled defense and are assumed to be ineffective. Instead, it is recommended here that the examination of stress treatments proceed without a prior conception of what good, effective, or legitimate treatments are. In this way, one might avoid bias regarding some outcomes.

A revelant issue is what ways or categories of ways there are for dealing with occupational stress. Typologies abound in the literature and although there is not complete agreement, there fortunately is some overlap among them. Two, three, and sometimes four or more category typologies are common.

One commonly used dichotomy is emotion-focused and problem-focused coping (e.g. Folkman, 1982; Folkman and Lazarus, 1980). Coping is usually a self-imposed and self-directed treatment rather than a formal treatment "program" developed and implemented by experts. Coping techniques are, however, sometimes taught in treatment programs and they are ways of dealing with occupational stress. Problem-focused coping behaviors are attempts to change the situation. The most obvious such behaviors would be attempts to alter job stressors, usually by reducing their strength. An employee might try to reduce inter-sender role conflict, for example, by getting the senders together and having them come to a common understanding about what to demand of the focal person. If role ambiguity were the stressor, then the focal people might try to get the role senders to clarify their expectations. Emotion-focused coping behavior tries to reduce the emotional strains directly without altering the stressors. Examples might be the focal people trying to convince themselves that the situation is not as bad as previously thought or in some way trying to put the situation out of their minds so it would not bother them any more.

Problem-focused and emotion-focused coping do not seem to exhaust the categories of ways for dealing with job stress, however, and it might also be possible to break them down into finer or at least different categories. While this approach labels each behavior coping, another two-category distinction of ways to deal with occupational stress includes coping as the label for one alternative and defense for the other. One of these forms, changing the objective environment, is somewhat similar to the problem-focused coping, but there is not a clear, one-to-one relationship between this dichotomy and the previous one of problem-focused versus emotion-focused coping.

This psychoanalytically based categorization has been used in job stress literature in House's (1974) model of occupational stress and Caplan's (1987) P-E Fit perspective on occupational stress. Coping behaviors are attempts to alter one's objective environment or one's objective personal characteristics, while defense represents attempts to alter one's subjective environment or subjective view of one's self. In both cases, the goal would be to make the person and the environment (either objective or subjective) match or fit each other better (this is most explicit in the P-E Fit theory). When the coping versus defense terminology is used, it is often explicit or implicit that coping is more effective than defense for relieving stress, because it gets rid of or reduces the strength of the "real" cause. Once some techniques become labeled coping and others defense, therefore, one would presumably know which would be better to use. Although it seems wise to try to alter the objective causes of occupational stress, this labeling may not be helpful if it leads people to try to use coping in all cases and never to use defense. For example, if the stressful work situation is one that the employee cannot control, defense may at times be better than nothing. To reiterate, it is probably best at this point to keep an open mind regarding the effectiveness of most techniques for dealing with occupational stress until their effectiveness has been evaluated objectively. In this chapter, the word coping will be used interchangeably with more general terms such as treatment, adaptation, strategy, and intervention. Thus, coping will not be used in a restrictive sense as some theories use it. The often pejoratively used term, defense, will not be used to label any of these treatments.

Besides these two-category typologies of ways for dealing with occupational stress, there are also some three-category classifications of treatments labeled coping. Latack (1986) named and found (via cluster analysis) some evidence for control (somewhat similar to problem-focused coping) and escape (somewhat similar to emotion-focused coping). She also had a measure of a third type of coping, which was labeled symptom management, which was the attempt to alter symptoms directly (e.g. by drinking, resting, taking medicine). Symptom management was more similar to emotion-focused coping than to problem-focused coping, but overall, this three-category distinction does not appear to fit precisely into the previously used dichotomies.

Another three-category typology came primarily from studies of women's inter-role conflicts between home and non-home roles (e.g. work roles): structural role redefinition, personal role redefinition, and reactive role behavior (Beutell and Greenhaus, 1983; Hall, 1972). Structural role redefinition seems to be similar to problem-focused coping and control, because of an emphasis on modifying the situation. Personal role redefinition might be somewhat similar to emotion-focused coping and perhaps to Latack's escape, because of its emphasis on altering the meaning of the situation. Reactive role behavior, however, seems different from the others, because it focuses on attempting to meet all of the stressful role demands, even though they may be overloading, conflicting, or ambiguous.

A review of coping research trying to make sense of such typologies, especially in relation to stress due to the combination of work and non-work situations, concluded that there were three types of coping reactions (Greenhaus and Parasuraman, 1987). These were modifying the situation (which is somewhat similar to problem-focused, to control, and to structural role redefinition, above), controlling the meaning of the situation (which is somewhat similar to emotion-focused, to escape, and to personal role re-definition, above), and managing stressful situations (which is somewhat similar to symptom management, above). Even this does not clearly cover the category of reactive role behaviors, above, however. While the literature on ways of dealing with occupational stress should not be classified as chaotic, neither is the issue of how to categorize such techniques entirely settled. Again, there is reason to keep an open mind regarding the potential effectiveness of a wide variety of treatments for occupational stress, and solid evaluative research on a variety of such techniques should be encouraged. Most of the stress treatments discussed thus far have been from the set labeled coping and these will be discussed and illustrated in more detail later in the chapter. There are still other types of occupational stress treatments, however, besides those that have commonly come to be labeled coping. One example of a broader categorization is from Newman and Beehr (1979).

A TAXONOMY OF OCCUPATIONAL STRESS TREATMENTS

Instead of a two or three-category typology of strategies for dealing with occupational stress, Newman and Beehr provided three dimensions along which such treatments can be placed: the primary target, the agent or entity who performs the adaptive response (coping tends to assume that the stressed person is the agent), and the degree to which the response is curative versus preventative (Figure 7.1). It does not appear thus far that one or a few of these types of treatments are necessarily superior, but it is interesting that some of them have been tried or at least reported much more than others.

The primary target refers to the first thing changed in the adaptation process. Typically, this would be either an aspect of the person or of the organization. Regarding the person as the primary target, a presumed causal aspect of the person could be changed, such as Type A behavior, or a presumed effect of occupational stress on the person could be the primary target, such as hypertension. In the former case, the strain could be improved because the person's own behavior (Type A) was causing the strain, while in the latter case, the strain itself was changed directly.

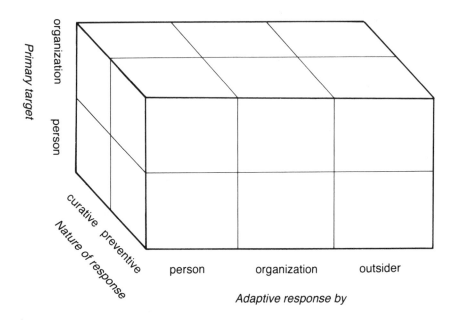

Figure 7.1 A general matrix for a review of adaptive responses to job stress (reprinted with permission from Newman and Beehr, 1979).

Regarding organizationally versus individually targeted treatments, it is argued subsequently in this chapter that more organizational targets are virtually never used in occupational stress treatment programs. It makes sense to target both the individual responses to and the organizational causes of work stress. A two-pronged attack is needed, but the organizational side is usually ignored. In order to address the organizational side, the stressors in the work environment illustrated by Figure 1.2 need to be identified so they can be addressed. If role ambiguity were the culprit, then role clarification would be a logical treatment. If interpersonal conflict were identified as a stressor, conflict resolution would make sense, and so forth.

The treatments of organizational targets are specific to the stressors, while the treatments of the individual targets are usually specific to the strains. Thus, individually targeted treatments include medication, psychotherapy, and relaxation training. Treatments employing both targets make the most sense if power is important. That is, the simultaneous attack on both cause and effect seems likely to have the strongest effect.

Regarding the agent who performs the treatment, this is usually the people themselves or the organization, but it could also be a third party outside the organization. People can take the initiative to try to help themselves, the organization can try to improve the situation of the focal person, or some outside person or agency can try to help.

Also regarding the agents of change, the person would usually have little power to change the organization in stressful situations. If they are able to clarify roles and resolve conflicts, that is likely to be one of the first things tried. If successful, the stressful situation will disappear quickly – perhaps so quickly that it will not be very stressful and is unlikely to be noticed by stress researchers and practitioners. While treatments of individual targets might be accomplished by the individual person, treatments of organizational targets seem likely to require additional agents. Examples would especially include agents from the organization itself, often in the form of various human resources specialists. In addition, special consultants can be hired by the organization to help the individual. These would include consultant-experts who might be similar to organization development specialists, but who are instead experts regarding stressful situations. Just to illustrate the range of potential outside agents, they could include outside agents with the power to force the organization to change. An easy example would be government, which could legislate against unhealthy social psychological job stressors in the way that it regulates occupational safety of the physical workplace.

The stress treatment can also be more or less preventative versus curative. The adaptive responses to occupational stress can vary according to time, among other things. For example, one can develop a treatment strategy that actually "responds" to such stress before it happens. Information "treatments" that enroll all employees, whether they are currently experiencing stress or not, for example, might be considered preventative, while treatments that wait until after stress has some harmful effects are more likely to be curative.

Regarding curative versus preventative treatments, it seems obvious at first blush that we should prevent the ill effects of job stress rather than wait until they have already begun. From a cost-effective perspective, however, some of the job stress treatments, especially the individually targeted ones, might be more efficiently used if they could be limited to those who need or will need it. That is, if there is no problem for the individual, why use costly treatments for them? Unfortunately, it is not clear how to target these people until after they show the symptoms or strains. Using the treatment at that point is then more curative than if it were used prior to the evidence of strains.

Although Figure 7.1 is drawn to suggest that there are twelve discrete categories of stress treatments, one often experiences difficulty in placing a specific treatment unambiguously into one of the categories. This is both because some activities are difficult to classify clearly as, say, preventative versus curative and because there are combinations of treatments in which more than one category is clearly in effect. At least two of the three categories, the primary target and the curative or preventative nature of the adaptive response, are probably most accurately considered to be dimensions along which treatments can vary simultaneously, as in Figure 7.2. Even the agents can be multiple, that is, more than one (person, organization, and outsider) can initiate and take responsibility for the response, but these appear to be more discrete than the other two dimensions. A given adaptive response can be located anywhere in this three-dimensional space and it would be instructive if there turned out to be relationships between such placement and general effectiveness of a treatment. Research comparing these treatment types has yet to be done, however.

THE PRIMACY OF THE PRIMARY TARGET

In 1979, Beehr and Newman organized their review around the agent of the treatment first, discussing the primary target and the nature of treatment (curative versus preventative) second. This chapter is organized primarily around the the primary target. This change of emphasis is due to some

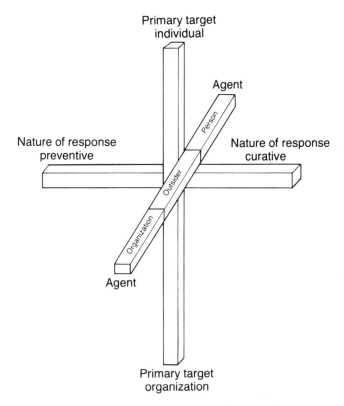

Figure 7.2 Primary target of adaptive response, nature of adaptive response and agent performing adaptive response as continuous variables.

informal observations of and conclusions about occupational stress treatments since 1979.

The primary target, that is, the immediate focus of or target of change, is either an element of the organization or of the person. On the surface, it would seem that either the organization or the individual would be a likely target of occupational stress treatments and that treating both would make the most sense and have the most potential. Instead, in practice, most of the treatments focus on changing the individual directly rather than the organization, often leaving the organization unchanged. A review by Ivancevich *et al.* (1990) found only four reports of organizationally targeted occupational stress treatment programs. The 1979 (Beehr and Newman) review even labeled some treatments as organizationally targeted that, in retrospect, it makes more sense to categorize as individually targeted. Primarily, these were in-house, organizationally sponsored wellness programs, fitness programs, and employee assistance programs. In that previous review, these had been categorized as organizationally targeted, because the first visible change when they are born is that there is a new organizational unit – therefore the primary or initial change was in the organization. This probably misses the point of the classification, however, because the main effort of these types of programs, *their* primary targets in stress-alleviating efforts, is almost always the individual. They tend to aim either at treating individuals' problems or strains after they have occurred (a curative approach) or at making the individual better able to withstand the stress of organizational life if and when it occurs (a preventative approach). Most accurately, these programs are probably, in principle, neither organizationally nor individually targeted, because they can choose any target. It is in practice that they have seemed to choose the individually targeted approaches to treatment of occupational stress.

The individually targeted approaches to treating organizational stress seem to have increased in recent years, and there is still little evidence of many organizationally targeted approaches in use today. Furthermore, many of the organizationally targeted programs found in the literature were not implemented but were simply recommended by researchers and experts in job stress at the time. This is in contrast to the individually oriented programs, many of which have been in widespread use for a long time. To have a whole, large category of potential occupational stress treatments virtually ignored in practice is interesting and this chapter emphasizes this by having the primary target as its major division.

The effectiveness of *combinations* of treatment strategies, including combinations of personal *and* organizational strategies, needs to be evaluated. Even more to the point, organizational strategies need to be attempted more in order to evaluate them either alone or in combination with personal strategies. Possible reasons why this is not happening are offered later in the chapter.

THE INDIVIDUAL AS THE PRIMARY TARGET

From the foregoing, it is obvious that individually targeted treatments have been by far the most popular approach to occupational stress management. These are treatments whose immediate effect is to change some aspect of the personal facet or the human consequences facet in the Beehr–Newman (1978) model in an earlier chapter.

If aimed at an element of the personal facet, an individually targeted treatment would be attempting to change a fairly stable characteristic of the person that is thought either to be causal in the stress process or that interacts with job stressors to cause strains. An example would be programs attempting to change people from being Type A to being the presumably less coronary-prone Type B. This approach to reducing the risk of coronary heart disease has been strongly recommended in many camps since at least 1974, when the best selling book, *Type A Behavior and Your Heart* (Friedman and Rosenman, 1974) was published. Type A behavior is thought to be a cause of coronary heart disease (in the book, it is claimed to be the primary cause), and therefore reducing it should logically lead to less risk of this potential job stress-related disease.

If a stress treatment is aimed at an element of the human consequences facet, it is focused on relieving or preventing a strain directly. An example would be muscle relaxation training, in which muscle relaxation is thought to be accompanied by reductions in physical strains, for example catecholamine secretion, and maybe mental strains such as depression (e.g. Ganster *et al.*, 1982).

The difference between individually targeted stress treatments aimed at the personal facet and the human consequences facet is important. In the first place, one is aimed at the cause or a partial cause of the problem and the other is aimed at the outcomes or effects of the problem. Treating the outcomes, if successful, should have immediate effects, but changing the cause (the elements of the personal facet) should have longer lasting effects. As long as the cause remains, then an effects-oriented treatment such as relaxation training will need to be implemented permanently. On the other hand, if the relatively stable personal characteristics of the personal facet are changed, such as changing from a Type A person to a Type B person, this presumably results in a new stable disposition of the person and the treatment is completed once and for all.

Of course, it is never quite that simple. It is an especially difficult process to change what is considered a relatively stable trait of the person. Changing such traits may require long-term psychotherapy with only modest expectations for success. By definition, a stable characteristic is long-lasting and difficult to change.

Examples of evaluations of individually targeted treatments

The left column of Table 7.1 indicates potential ways of dealing with occupational stress that could be labeled individually targeted. Most have not been evaluated rigorously as remedies for job stress.

Many laboratory experiments have been conducted on some types of individual treatments that are amenable to laboratory work, with varying degrees of success. Common examples include biofeedback, relaxation, and meditation training (Beehr *et al.* in preparation). Here, we are interested in studies that purport to show the effectiveness of these techniques for dealing with occupational stress, however, and most of the laboratory experiments do not clearly do that. There is actually some reason to question the relevance of almost all of the studies of the individually targeted treatments as occupational stress treatments, but this issue will receive more attention later in the chapter.

Efforts to introduce physical relaxation have been popular as individually

Table 7.1 Individually and organizationally targeted treatments of occupational stress

Individual targets	Organizational targets
Meditation	Mastery of environment (including stressors)
Manage desires, ambitions, drives	Leaving stressful situation permanently
Increase self-understanding	Human relations training
Organization provide health services	Planning, organizing day's activities
Vicarious stress reduction (e.g. audience activities)	Find more suitable job
Relaxation techniques	Redesign jobs
Acceptance of less than perfection	Alter organizational structure
Tension release (laughing, crying, attacking)	Change evaluation, reward system
Seeking medical, psychological, other professional help	Change work schedules
Attempts to alter behavior or personality	Clarify roles
Use of biofeedback techniques	Refine selection and placement procedures
Think of work as less important	Clarify career paths and promotion criteria
Getting sufficient rest	Improve organization's communication
Quitting drug intake	
Physical activity	
Diet	
Increased religious activity	

targeted treatments of occupational stress. The main idea is that bodily tension is a factor in strain, and therefore if one can resist or combat this factor by making the body relax, then the strains will be lessened in some way. There are several popular forms of delivering this relaxation training. It can be done by verbal instruction (sometimes on tape), with the aid of biofeedback equipment, or as meditation, often with a somewhat mystical quality using a mantra or chant.

Jones *et al.* (1988) reported two studies that gave videotaped instructions to hospitals' employees and found that two measures of performance (medication errors and malpractice frequency) were reduced. The videotapes, however, contained many things in addition to relaxation instructions (general stress information, nutrition information, exercise information, and information about health habits), and there were severe control problems in the studies. Furthermore, the outcomes were job performance measures rather than individual strains, which are usually expected to be the primary outcome of relaxation. Unfortunately for present purposes, it is quite difficult to know what to conclude from this study regarding the effectiveness of relaxation on strains.

A second study combined progressive relaxation, in which volunteers from a hospital equipment facility were taught to relax parts of their bodies separately and together in order to get to a very deep state of relaxation, with focused meditation (Bruning and Frew, 1987). Eight- to ten-hour training sessions during one week led, several weeks later, to lower pulse rates and systolic blood pressure compared to a control group that was given general information about stress (which might also help to test for a placebo effect). Diastolic blood pressure and galvanic skin response were not affected.

A third study of muscle relaxation was another field experiment in which muscle relaxation was introduced to employees of a public agency (Ganster *et al.*, 1982). At the end of the study, epinephrine and one psychological strain (probably depression) were reduced and these results tended not to fade much after the passage of four months. These results did not, however, replicate with the waiting-list control group in a subsequent quasi-experiment. There were no effects on norepinephrine, irritation, anxiety, or somatic complaints. The muscle relaxation treatment was combined with cognitive reappraisal, in eight two-hour sessions over an eight-week period, and therefore the effects cannot be said to be attributable solely to relaxation.

Murphy and his colleagues have reported three studies using both relaxation and biofeedback treatments and control groups. Using a randomly assigned, waiting-list control group with thirty-eight highway maintenance workers, there were generally no effects on a variety of psychological and physiological strains overall, but there was a suggestion of some effects on specific days (Murphy, 1984). In that study, the treatment was provided in six one-hour daily sessions. In another report of forty-five volunteer highway maintenance workers with a randomly assigned waiting-listed control group and a non-random control group, treatments were provided again during six days, and muscle relaxation had reduced the absenteeism rate during a one-year post-treatment period, but there was no apparent effect on job performance, accidents, or injuries as measured from personnel records (Murphy and Sorenson, 1988). Furthermore, the effects on absenteeism were not maintained six months later. Finally, twenty-eight nurses were assigned (random assignment was not specified in the article) to biofeedback, progressive relaxation training, or a self-relaxation (placebo or non-specific effects) control group (Murphy, 1983). No treatment was very superior to the others and there were no apparent strong, overall effects on a variety of psychological strains, self-reported behavioral strains, and self-reported performance in the short-term or three months later.

A few things are noteworthy in these three studies. First, the groups tended to be very small, making it necessary to have big effects in order to obtain statistically significant results. Second, many of the potential outcomes of the studies were things other than individual strains. This is good in the sense that the variety might allow the discovery of wide-ranging effects of biofeedback, relaxation, and meditation programs. One should be cautious in interpreting the relative lack of significance, however, because some of the outcomes are not necessarily expected to be affected by treatments of job stress; by the definitions used here, only strains are clearly expected to be affected by a successful treatment. Overall, however, the weak results of these studies do not lend much confidence to the use of these forms of treatment for job stress.

The studies taken as a whole (not just the last three) do not suggest strong advocacy of these types of treatments (relaxation training, biofeedback training, and meditation) for dealing with occupational stress. In general, the effects were small or non-existent. It must be again noted, however, that many of the studies suffered from a variety of problems, including small numbers of people, probably rather weak interventions (over short periods of time, for example), lack of controls of various sorts, and the reliance on non-strain measures for dependent variables.

There have also been evaluations of a few other types of individually targeted job stress treatments. These were, however, often combined with the other treatments, listed above. In another study by Jones *et al.* (1988), the videotapes constituting the intervention included general stress information, nutritional information, and information on exercise and health habits as well as relaxation. In yet another study, the same tapes were employed plus a slide-tape presentation explaining the relationship between stress and stress-related malpractice. It is very difficult, therefore, to say what the active ingredient(s) of the treatments might have been. The Bruning and Frew (1987) study included separate management skills training and aerobic exercise groups, both randomly assigned. As with the relaxation and meditation group, these also had effects on systolic blood pressure and pulse rate. The management skills training was based in part on Meichenbaum's (1975) cognitive behavior modification strategy, as was part of the treatment in the Ganster *et al.* (1982) study. In Ganster *et al.*, however, the treatment was combined in the same treatment group with relaxation, and therefore separate evaluations of the treatments were not possible.

Coping as an individually targeted treatment

A special example of an individually targeted job stress treatment is coping. Coping as an occupational stress treatment was briefly addressed earlier in this chapter. Coping is often a term used for treatment of job stress when the individual is the agent of the treatment and is not instructed by an outsider in the treatment's use. There are exceptions in the use of the term coping, but most uses in the research literature will fit with this description. There have been some recently reported studies of coping with occupational stress, and these usually include the individual as the target of the treatment – but not always. An individual experiencing a stressful situation at work can attempt to cope with it by changing the stressors. In fact, this is the frequently advocated problem-focused approach to coping. While changing the organization's stressful situation may sound like an organizational strategy, this approach to coping still puts all the onus and responsibility on the individual person. They must change the organization or job in order to cope effectively. The immediate target is individual; they must change their own behavior first, even though the new behavior is aimed at alleviating the stressors.

Unfortunately, studies of coping with occupational stress have rarely gone beyond creating or confirming categorizations or typologies of coping styles. Therefore, it is even more difficult to say how effective various occupational stress coping techniques are than it is regarding some of the other individual treatments discussed above. Studies of coping do not usually manipulate coping. Instead, the designs are usually non-experimental and therefore evidence regarding causality is weak or non-existent.

Recent studies have factor or cluster analyzed lists of potential coping items, formed coping indices based on these results, and correlated these indices with other variables (usually potential outcomes of coping). Kuhlmann (1990) found that one of his four coping indices, unstable submission, was positively related to self-reported work-related stress, somatic complaints, exhaustion, and time span for recreation among ninety-nine male public transport employees in Germany. His other coping indices, positive self-instruction, suppression, and active prevention, were not related to these outcomes, however. Latack's (1986) study of 109 managers and professionals found that control was negatively correlated with some strains, while symptom management and escape were positively related to them. Dewe and Guest (1990) found that there was little relation between coping indices and strains among 223 administrators and supervisors, but that control was correlated negatively with some and escape was correlated positively with some strains. Beutell and Greenhaus (1983), in a study of 115 married women with children, found that reactive role behavior was negatively correlated with a one-item measure of perceived success in dealing with occupational stress.

Some of these studies have taken the typology of Hall (1972) as a starting point and have focused on females in potential situations of work–home conflict. This accounts for the female samples and the labels for the coping factors. Furthermore, they have, in a sense, found what they were searching for. That is, certain types of coping were expected, based especially on Hall, and they were found. While it is not necessarily so, there is a tendency for one to get what one looks for in factor-analytic studies of coping, however. There is probably room for studies that are not necessarily based on preconceived types of coping. If one does not use a preconceived categorization of coping types, a logical strategy would be to elicit the types of coping from the subjects themselves. This could be done with open-ended interviews, after which coding of the responses would determine the final categories into which the responses are grouped. These data could then be used to address substantive questions regarding the coping types. A related approach would begin by conducting preliminary, open-ended interviews with a small sample of people who are similar to those the researcher wishes to study. In this case, the interviews can subsequently be used as input into the development of questionnaire items for the main study of coping.

One such study was unique in that it looked for coping styles among a group of both police (596 married officers in two east coast metropolitan police forces) and their spouses (n=441; fewer than the officers due to non-responses and some officers who did not want their spouses contacted) as they each dealt separately with their own stressors (Beehr et al., 1989). The coping items were derived from a combination of sources, including previous literature on coping and occupational stress and preliminary interviews with police officers. By avoiding the limiting of questions to a set of a priori categories, we were entertaining the possibility of some activities that are not always considered to be coping in other research. The questionnaire that was developed for the primary study therefore included some item content and phraseology that was rare among occupational stress coping studies, notably items regarding the use of religious activities, some semi-macho reactions, and drinking as forms of coping.

Since coping is supposed to be a response to stressors, and according to some theories a response to appraised occupational stressors, the respondents were presented with a potentially stressful situation in a written vignette and asked how they would respond in that situation. A randomly selected half of the officers responded to each of the following vignettes:

When you come home irritable and emotionally drained from what is your worst shift your family confronts you with overwhelming family demands. For example, your children want you to help them. Your spouse/mate is not available or is being very demanding. No one seems to be sensitive or to care about what you have been through.

A supervisor finds fault with your on-duty behavior. You explain that your actions were reasonable and proper under the circumstances. You feel that you are being treated unfairly, probably because of departmental politics or who you are.

All of the spouses responded to the following vignette:

Your spouse comes home irritable and emotionally drained from what is his/her worst shift, your day has also been difficult and you have things that demand his/her immediate attention. Your spouse does not want to be bothered and is not sensitive to your needs.

One reason that it seemed important to ask about potential coping activities undertaken in the context of stressful situations was that there would be at least some face validity to the idea that these behaviors really were linked to stressful events. This is an idea to which we shall return shortly. The officers' vignettes were purposely varied to include both a work–home role conflict stressor episode and a work-only stressor episode. For the spouses, a work-only episode did not make sense, because many of them were not employed. There was little obvious difference in responses of the officers to the two vignettes, and those data were therefore analyzed together (Beehr *et al.*, 1989).

As a first step, the nature of the stressors was investigated via factor analyses (principal components with oblique rotations), as in the other studies described above. Two differences, though, were that a fairly wide range of activities were considered as potential coping responses to stressors and that factors were derived from both employees (police) and their spouses. The results of the factor analyses are in Tables 7.2 and 7.3. It was desirable to find similar factors so that subsequent parallel analyses could be performed on the two types of respondents (police and spouses). The spouses' factor analysis seemed cleaner and more interpretable, and it is presented first (Table 7.2), while the factor analysis of the officers' responses to the coping questions is presented second and the order of the columns of factors in the table are rearranged for easier comparisons with the first table (Table 7.3).

In each case, six factors resulted using the criterion of eigenvalues greater than one, and five of the six were somewhat similar. In order to have identical coping indices in each sample, five coping indices were formed as determined by the combination of the factor loadings and rational judgment. Two items that did not load on the same factor in both samples were eliminated and rational judgments were used to determine the more appropriate index for two other items. The resulting indices were labeled problem-focused, avoidance, rugged individualism, religion, and self-blame.

Table 7.2 Factor analysis of spouses' coping activities (reprinted with permission from Beehr *et al.*, 1989)

Item	FACTORS					
	I Problem focused	*II* Avoidance	*III* Rugged individualism	*IV* Turn to religion	*V* Self-blame	*VI* (Unnamed)
Try to figure out what needs to change and do it	0.75	−0.05	0.08	−0.07	−0.05	−0.03
Try to work it out with the other people involved	0.70	−0.16	0.06	−0.02	−0.23	−0.10
Make a plan of action and follow it	0.70	0.02	0.01	−0.15	0.22	0.10
Avoid getting upset by not thinking about it	−0.07	0.69	−0.06	−0.02	0.01	−0.01
Try to act as if nothing is bothering you	−0.17	0.67	−0.05	−0.09	−0.15	0.02
Look for the silver lining, so to speak; try to look on the bright side of things	0.30	0.60	0.05	−0.18	−0.08	−0.17
Do something that takes your mind off the situation	0.11	0.54	0.04	−0.02	−0.03	0.10
Make it known how you expect to be treated	0.09	−0.14	0.82	−0.02	−0.09	−0.11
Make sure no one pushes you around	−0.08	0.08	0.82	0.06	0.06	−0.03
Do what you have to do for yourself	−0.02	0.21	0.45	0.04	0.26	0.12
Rely on your faith in God to see you through	0.02	0.16	0.03	−0.89	0.06	−0.07
Think what God would want you to do in this situation	0.05	0.06	0.00	−0.90	−0.05	0.05
Pray or meditate	0.05	−0.04	−0.03	−0.89	−0.06	0.09
Try to please everyone	−0.01	0.29	0.18	0.03	−0.66	−0.18
Hope that if you wait long enough, things will turn out OK	−0.21	0.35	0.01	−0.04	−0.51	0.09
Blame yourself	0.11	−0.04	−0.16	−0.06	−0.74	0.12
Stay away from everyone; you would want to be alone	−0.09	−0.11	0.04	−0.01	−0.25	0.65
Drink	0.02	0.10	−0.03	−0.03	0.19	0.73
Put the situation in perspective so things won't look so bad	0.61	0.34	−0.02	−0.13	0.18	−0.08
Talk to someone about how you are feeling	0.23	−0.17	0.42	−0.11	−0.08	0.06
Laugh it off or joke about it	0.29	0.30	0.03	0.23	−0.17	0.23
Yell and scream at the family or spouse	−0.39	−0.27	0.34	−0.04	0.23	0.24
Eigenvalue	3.87	2.35	2.09	1.83	1.27	1.02
Cumulative percent variance	17.6	28.3	37.8	46.1	51.8	56.5

Table 7.3 Factor analysis of police coping activities (reproduced with permission from Beehr *et al.*, 1989)

Item	FACTORS					
	VI Problem focused	I Avoidance	IV Rugged individualism	II Turn to religion	V Self-blame	III (Unnamed)
Try to figure out what needs to change and do it	−0.47	0.24	0.14	−0.08	0.29	−0.27
Try to work it out with the other people involved	−0.54	0.05	−0.01	−0.01	0.13	−0.05
Make a plan of action and follow it	−0.19	0.30	0.27	−0.04	0.07	−0.32
Avoid getting upset by not thinking about it	0.14	0.52	−0.12	−0.03	0.00	−0.01
Try to act as if nothing is bothering you	0.20	0.40	0.07	0.00	0.03	0.25
Look for the silver lining, so to speak; try to look on the bright side of things	−0.30	0.55	−0.07	−0.12	−0.03	0.17
Do something that takes your mind off the situation	−0.07	0.48	0.09	0.00	−0.02	0.01
Make it known how you expect to be treated	−0.25	−0.08	0.51	−0.14	−0.22	−0.07
Make sure no one pushes you around	0.01	0.11	0.65	−0.05	−0.26	−0.06
Do what you have to do for yourself	−0.23	0.01	0.37	−0.02	−0.14	0.09
Rely on your faith in God to see you through	0.03	0.05	0.00	−0.91	−0.04	0.06
Think what God would want you to do in this situation	0.08	0.02	−0.01	−0.88	0.05	0.02
Pray or meditate	−0.01	−0.08	0.02	−0.79	0.05	−0.01
Try to please everyone	−0.09	−0.01	−0.06	−0.01	0.33	0.45
Hope that if you wait long enough, things will turn out OK	0.10	0.03	0.07	−0.01	0.03	0.59
Blame yourself	−0.02	0.01	−0.08	−0.04	0.37	0.01
Stay away from everyone; you would want to be alone	0.35	−0.07	0.46	−0.01	0.21	0.06
Drink (and party with other officers)	0.02	−0.03	0.28	0.17	0.04	0.10
Put the situation in perspective so things won't look so bad	−0.32	0.49	0.02	−0.03	0.04	−0.02
Talk to someone about how you are feeling	−0.53	−0.05	0.07	−0.10	−0.20	0.07
Laugh it off or joke about it	−0.11	0.23	0.06	0.04	−0.09	0.47
Yell and scream at the family or spouse	0.11	−0.25	0.26	−0.04	0.19	0.25
Eigenvalue	VI 1.07	I 3.78	IV 1.99	II 2.16	V 1.21	III 2.13
Cumulative percent variance	56.1	17.2	45.7	27.0	51.2	36.7

The label for the first index, problem-focused, was chosen because the items were judged to be very similar in content to problem-focused coping from other literature. Of the other four indices, avoidance was judged to be the most obviously emotion-focused, but the other three were probably also emotion-focused coping indices. The items about turning to religion des- cribed behaviors that might be expected to have a calming effect. Rugged individualism could deal with emotions such as pride or anger, and self- blame might deal with emotions such as guilt and shame (Beehr *et al.*, 1989).

These five coping indices were not strongly related to each other (the range of their correlations was –0.15 to 0.28, with a median of 0.125 for police; –0.05 to 0.33, with a median of 0.115 for spouses), indicating that they might be used relatively independently of each other. The problem-focused and self-blame activities had the largest number of significant correlations with the strains, with the signs of the correlations being consistent with the interpretation that the problem-focused activities are somewhat successful (that is, they might reduce strains) and that self-blame is somewhat un- successful and maybe harmful (that is, it might increase strains). To the extent that rugged individualism has an influence, it may be a deleterious one in the police sample, because it had weak but positive relationships with strains. As in other coping studies, the strengths of these relationships were relatively weak. The largest multiple r for the five coping indices predicting a strain among police was 0.38, predicting somatic complaints. Among spouses, fewer strains were measured in the study (somatic complaints for spouses were not measured), and the largest multiple r was 0.27 for experi- enced stress (Beehr *et al.*, 1989).

This study seems to indicate that some typical coping activities can be fairly specific to groups of people or occupations. The specific resulting indices were not restricted solely to those advocated by the general literature on coping, although they can be compared with those (e.g. problem-focused and emotion-focused). Overall, this study suggests that "generic" typologies of coping methods, such as problem and emotion-focused, might be operationalized in more than one specific way. Furthermore, a relatively unresolved issue concerns whether the specific operationalizations of these generic types of coping tend to vary by occupation or by organization. For example, the rugged individualism of the Beehr *et al.* (1989) might be unique to the police occupation because of their occupational and organizational cultures.

Extensions of employee alcoholism treatment programs

Besides treatment techniques that go under the rubric of coping, another set of potential treatments for occupational stress are derived from employee alcoholism treatment programs. Employee alcohol problem treatment pro- grams have been around for quite a while and there is increasing suggestion that such programs, or programs modeled after them, could be useful in treating occupational stress problems. The Employee Assistance Program (EAP) movement might be able to move in this direction. Treating work-related stress at the worksite has intuitive appeal and in many ways this idea seems promising. There are also some potential drawbacks, however.

There are probably many quite different variations in the nature of EAPs, making it difficult to refer to the exact nature of *the* EAP. Employee counseling is a part of all EAPs (Winkelpleck, 1984). For this reason, they have the potential to implement the individual approach to occupational stress treatments and this seems to be the usual approach used when they treat job stress.

One potential problem is that, considering that the traditional area of expertise of most such programs is alcoholism, it does not necessarily follow that they would naturally lend themselves to use for occupational stress. It is easy to see, in reviewing of occupational stress research, that there is no great amount of evidence that alcohol abuse is caused by occupational stress. While occasional statements can be found in the popular press and elsewhere that alcoholism and alcohol abuse may be a result of occupational stress, rigorous research has not shown this to be the case very clearly at all. Therefore, in spite of impressions one might gain from the popular press, the EAP's historically strongest area of expertise is not clearly related to occupational stress.

A second potential problem with EAPs or employee alcohol problem programs moving toward treating occupational stress is simply that it is not entirely clear that they have been successful in treating the problem of their primary focus (employee alcoholism and alcohol abuse). Weiss's (1987) review provided some provocative conclusions about corporate alcoholism programs. He presents evidence that the typical figures on employee alcoholism are probably not as high as the 5–10 percent usually cited by government and private agencies working in the alcohol abuse areas. Furthermore, Weiss argues that there is actually little evidence that alcoholic employees are especially poor performers on the job. Therefore, in addition to the problem (in the context of this chapter) that alcohol abuse may not be caused by job stress, the problem being treated by such programs (whether caused by occupational stress or not) may not be as serious as is being claimed. Finally, given the rigor and results of the research on the topic, it is not clear that many of the employee alcohol treatment programs are especially effective at reducing alcohol abuse.

While these conclusions about corporate alcoholism programs do not necessarily mean that the extension of this general format and approach to occupational stress treatment programs will fail, neither do they engender enthusiasm. At any rate, such approaches to occupational stress, given the EAP's traditional emphasis on counseling techniques, are likely to be individually targeted.

Why consider individually targeted treatments to be treatments of occupational stress at all?

A careful review of the individually targeted treatments for occupational stress provokes a curious question, stated in the subheading above. There is at least one common weakness of most of the reported studies of the individually targeted approaches to occupational stress. Simply put, it is not clear that many of them have anything whatsoever to do with occupational stress. The individually targeted psychological approaches are usually forms of employee counseling. Many of the individual approaches could very well be medical and/or counseling programs that happen to be available primarily to employees of a specific organization. These programs do *not* generally fit very clearly under the rubric of occupational stress, considering the definition(s) of occupational stress discussed in Chapter 1. Just because an individual is employed and ill does not mean that employment caused the illness, and just because a medical or psychological treatment is offered to people in a work setting does not mean that the work setting caused the problem. Most treatments in the literature make no effort to determine whether any occupational stressors are involved and yet they label the stress treatments "occupational." Many of these treatments have been used for a long time. It seems that when job stress became a popular concept, however, the treatment continued as before but with a new name: stress treatments.

As defined there, occupational stress is a situation in which elements of the work (occupation, job, organization) known as stressors cause strain or ill health (broadly defined) for the job incumbents. In the recent examples of evaluations of individually targeted treatments (see this heading, above), virtually none of the examples clearly assessed any stressors. Murphy's 1984 study had survey measures of "work environment job stress," but these appear to be questions asking about individual outcomes rather than job stressors. The studies by Jones *et al.* (1988) may have assessed stressors in their measures of "organizational stress," but it was not entirely clear what those were. There was no hint of a diagnosis of job stressors in the other studies. Failure to examine stressors in studies of individually targeted job stress treatments is the norm rather than the exception. It seems to be assumed that if one does a treatment of certain illness-related variables (psychological or physical) for employees in the workplace, then the treatment is an occupational stress treatment. When the treatment occurs elsewhere, it is simply medicine or counseling.

It is a fallacy, however, to assume that the place of treatment is the key to whether or not a treatment is an occupational stress treatment. This is not to say that such treatments cannot be useful. It is simply the case that there is no reason to think of them as occupational stress treatments. If one took a different approach to defining occupational stress, one in which, for instance, the secretion of catecholamines into the blood stream is defined as stress, then treatments aimed at lowering these levels could be labeled stress treatments by definition. Of course, even then one does not usually know that these secretions were caused by a factor in the workplace; therefore one does not know whether occupational stress or some other type of stress is being treated. This is not the usual definition of occupational stress in the organizational sciences, however, nor the one used in this book.

What would an individually targeted approach to treating occupational stress look like, then? To answer this question, first, some assessment of the work environment stressors would have to be at least attempted. Even perceptual, self-report measures would be better than nothing at all. Second, in conjunction with this, some attempt would have to be made to obtain reasonable evidence that the work enviromental factors thought of as stressors may be having an influence on the individual strains. At a minimum, these stressor measures should be found related to the strains.

Logically, a successful individually targeted treatment should affect the things it targets and these have in practice usually been the person's strains (although it could be other facets of the individual). If an organizational stress assessment found, for example, that some expected stressor such as role overload was positively correlated with a potential strain such as hypertension, then an individually targeted treatment might be implemented (such as biofeedback, meditation, relaxation, or medication). If successful, one would expect such treatments to affect the blood pressure levels. Furthermore, there is little reason based on the choice of treatment to expect the role overload to be reduced. If it were reduced, one would have to wonder why and do further research. These effects could be assessed with the types of experimental and quasi-experimental designs used in some of the studies discussed above. The evidence that role overload is causing hypertension would not be very strong, because that part of the study would be non-experimental. Nevertheless, this would make it more clear than is usual in such studies that the treatment was a work stress treatment rather than simply medicine or counseling being offered to people who happen to work for pay.

While most of the studies of individually oriented occupational stress treatments are not clearly treatments of occupational stress, a somewhat larger percentage of studies of coping have more overt relevance to it. At a minimum, some (but not all) of the coping studies asked people to report how they act when they experience things at work that one might expect to be stressful. The Beehr *et al.* (1989) study presented police and their spouses with vignettes describing what might be stressful situations and asked them to report how they behave under such conditions. The Latack (1986) study asked people how they behave when confronted with specific stressors such as role conflict, role ambiguity, and role overload.

As with any research area in the social and behavioral sciences, it is wise from time to time to step back and look at the overall picture to get some perspective. When this is done with many of the purported occupational stress treatments and studies, the question arises, "Where is the occupational stress?" It is easy to get involved in certain important details such as measurement of variables, design of experiments, and so forth, and to forget the overall topic. In many studies there seem to be no obvious work-related stressors. This does not mean that the treatment could not be useful or that the study has no meaning, but its use for or meaning for occupational stress is cloudy.

THE ORGANIZATION AS THE PRIMARY TARGET

Contrasted with the typical individually targeted treatment, organizationally targeted treatments almost necessarily diagnose the job or organizational stressors. Based on this diagnosis, specific stressors are likely to be chosen for change. Occupational stress interventions in which some element of the organization (usually a job, workplace, or occupation stressor) is the primary target are very rarely seen in the literature. A 1987 (Ivancevich and Matteson) review of stress treatments as reported in behavioral medicine, health psychology, applied organizational behavior, stress, management, and organizational development, observed that very few studies of these have ever been reported.

Murphy and Hurrell (1987) outlined a program in which one element was the creation of a stress reduction committee in the workplace whose function it was to make recommendations regarding stress problems. Presumably, this could include programs to reduce stressors as well as strains. It commissioned a job stress survey by the study's authors and the report from that survey recommended some organizationally targeted treatments, including improving task orientation, improving clarity of expectations, and increasing employee autonomy and supervisor support. Outcomes of or even actions taken based on these recommendations were not reported, however.

Jackson (1983, 1984), in a frequently cited study of an organizationally targeted treatment with the potential for dealing with occupational stress, took advantage of a naturally occurring event in which the outpatient facility of a university hospital began holding twice per month staff meetings. She obtained cooperation from the organization in setting up a Solomon four-group design, including a four month follow-up. This treatment, while not undertaken for the purpose of controlling occupational stress, can be conceived as a step toward participative management, which could alleviate some stressors such as role ambiguity. Both role conflict and role ambiguity appeared to be reduced by this intervention, which is very encouraging for the future of organizationally targeted interventions. As part of the study, a path analytic model was also developed and tested, but the data were not totally supportive of it. Unfortunately, some problems prevented adequately testing the validity of a revised model (Jackson, 1984).

Bruning and Frew's (1987) previously mentioned management skills training had at least some implications for organizational treatments. They tried to get people to change their own work environments by exploring their own work and personal values and goals. Although it was called management skills training, which may sound like an organizational intervention, it was implemented by having the people who might be experiencing stress change their own behaviors. Thus, again, the individual was the primary target rather than the organizational environment.

Obviously, it is very rare for organizations to implement these types of stress-treatment interventions. At this point, it can be said that these types of recommendations have been around long enough to be implemented. As far back as 1955, Neel noted that the industrial programs aimed at worker maladjustment had primarily emphasized individually targeted treatments in which the individual is treated so that they will be able to adjust to conflicts and tensions (job stressors) in the workplace. Twenty four years later, Newman and Beehr (1979) made similar observations. Today, we can make them again.

Potential philosophies behind the frequent choice of the individual instead of the organization as a primary target

Why have organizationally targeted treatments for occupational stress not been developed and implemented more widely? The idea of organizationally targeted treatments of occupational stress are obvious in the very definition of job stress, definitions in which the two equally important facets are job stressors and individual strains. Furthermore, the idea of such treatments has been around a long time, at least since Neel's 1955 article, and it has been prominently repeated in the modern job stress research literature. Treatments in which elements of both the individual and the organization are targeted have been recommended many times over the years (e.g. Ganster et al., 1982; Murphy, 1987; Neel, 1955; Newman and Beehr, 1979), but they are apparently not taken seriously by those who actually do the implementation. It is time to examine potential reasons for this. In doing so, ways to change this situation may become more apparent.

Of course, one can only speculate why this situation in job stress treatments has developed, but there are at least a few possibilities. First, there have been, for centuries, entire professions focusing on treatments of individual illnesses, whether these are considered the results of job stress or not. There are some things that have always been done by the medical profession to treat illness. If the illnesses are due to job stress, they can be treated in the same ways as if they have any other causes. Other professionals treating individual maladies of various sorts include clinical psychologists, social workers, and counselors. They can do for those suffering from occupational stress just what they have been doing for those suffering from physical and mental problems due to any other cause. These are all individually oriented treatments and they have a long history of ready availability.

A second possible reason for focusing on individually targeted stress treatments while ignoring organizationally targeted treatments is the difficulty in changing organizations. Actually, it may in some instances be just about as difficult to get individuals to change some of their behaviors or their strain symptoms, but it does seem to be easier to get them to try and/or to get someone to pay for these individually targeted treatments. There are usually are no insurance companies ready to cover the cost of an organizational treatment; thus the so-called third-party payments might be directing the types of treatments of job stress that are dominant. Those with authority in organizations need to be willing both to allow or encourage change in the organization and to absorb any costs that may be incurred in the change effort. It is even possible that a part of the resistance to changing the organization hinges on those with authority being quite happy with the organization (or their parts of it) just as it is. They may even feel that they have had a hand in creating some parts of the organization and have some psychological investment in its current state. If they did not create the current situations, at least they probably feel that they have been successful in the organization as it now exists – so why change it?

A third possibility for the paucity of organizationally targeted stress treatments may be somewhat covert but inherent in the process of targeting the organization for treatment. If an organizational stressor is targeted for change, it could be seen as an implicit or even explicit admission of guilt on the part of the organization that it is responsible for causing the employees' ill health. Focusing on changing the individual carries with it no such inherent implication of guilt. If anything, there is a logic built into the individual treatments for assuming that the individual, not the organization, is at fault. After all, it is apparently the individual who needs to be changed. Those managers with enough authority to implement organizationally targeted treatments may tend to have the organization's welfare at heart more than any individuals' and they might even fear that the organization accepting the blame in such a manner could leave it more susceptible to successful lawsuits or workers' compensation claims related to organizational stress. In what appears to be an increasingly litigious society, this is not far-fetched.

As noted by Ivancevich and Matteson (1987), the overemphasis on the individually targeted treatments has probably retarded potential research and applications of organizationally targeted stress treatments. This is obviously one of the biggest needs for job stress research currently.

METHODOLOGICAL ISSUES IN RESEARCH ON JOB STRESS TREATMENTS

Unlike the study of what causes occupational stress, the study of treatments designed to reduce or eliminate stress lends itself readily to experimental and quasi-experimental designs. This is because the treatment is an intervention that can be the manipulation of an independent variable in an experiment. Furthermore, it is a manipulation that is expected to be helpful to people. When one studies occupational stressors, it is more difficult to manipulate the stressor, in part for ethical reasons. In that case, the researcher would be purposely exposing people to a situation thought to be harmful to them. The research methods available for studying stress treatments, therefore, are those of the true experiment and the quasi-experiment (e.g. Cook and Campbell, 1979; Cook et al., 1990), and their relevance to this research topic has been discussed by Beehr and O'Hara (1987). There are some other research issues that have not often been discussed in relation to research on occupational stress treatments, however.

One such issue regards the quality of past research in relation to the findings of such research. Murphy (1987) has noted that there is a negative relationship between the rigor of past research on occupational stress and the reported success of the treatments being evaluated. One hopes Murphy has not stumbled onto a general principle regarding organizational psychology interventions, but this is reminiscent of the conclusion by Terpstra (1981) that the reported success of organizational development interventions varies negatively with the rigor of the evaluation study. Murphy's conclusions regarding treatments of the occupational stress were derived from reviewing treatments that were virtually all individually targeted. Studies using the non-rigorous pre-experimental designs, in Cook and Campbell's (1979) terminology, have very consistently found that nearly any type of individually targeted treatment was successful, while true experiments were getting more ambiguous results.

This is very discouraging for the implementation of stress management programs, because it means that one is not very sure that they are working. Because of the way that many of the studies were done, these results could be due to non-specific or placebo type effects. Future research should especially employ additional control groups that control for these types of effects. The disturbing relationship observed between methodological rigor and successful results, if the observation is correct, reinforces very strongly the need for using solid research methods in future studies in this area.

A second issue that has rarely been discussed in relation to treatments for job stress is borrowed from the personnel psychology area – utility analysis (e.g. Cascio, 1991). Methodological issues abound in using utility analysis to evaluate treatments of job stress. Methods for estimating costs of the human consequences of job stress to the organization are rough. Although it is easy to find published estimates of the cost of poor employee health to the organization, these estimates are partly based on assumptions and estimates of unknown accuracy. In addition, we are interested here only in the costs of poor health that is caused by occupational stress and this makes it much more difficult to develop an accurate estimate. Research methods that allow even a crude estimate of this would have to at least find the strength of association of employee health problems with stressors (and this ignores the basic premise that correlation does not prove causation). Furthermore, the same requirements would hold for examining any potential organizational outcomes of job stress. In fact the process of costing the individual outcomes of stress to the organization is the transformation of the individual outcomes to organizational outcomes. If, for example, employees' anxiety due to job stress does not affect their job performance, absenteeism, use of the company-paid health insurance, and so forth, there is no cost to the organization. As discussed in the previous chapter, if turnover is caused by job stress, that can be a negative, positive, or neutral outcome to the organization. It is not easy to turn these outcomes into dollar figures that are relevant to the organization.

Cascio (1991) has noted problems with estimating costs and benefits of employee assistance programs and wellness programs. These programs treat and try to prevent illnesses, focusing only on the individual targets and causes. It gets even more complicated if we try to do this for job stress specifically. Although it has not been seriously attempted yet, a successful program might be very beneficial and so it is a topic ripe for future research.

As noted in an earlier chapter, estimates are frequently offered of the costs of occupational stress to the nation. At times, such estimates are no doubt offered regarding the costs to a given organization also. As further noted previously, there are certainly problems with trying to make such estimates. It is a further leap of inference (and faith) to offer estimates of the cost effectiveness of treatments aimed at alleviating occupational stress and yet, in the workplace, this is what must be done, at least implicitly, in order to make decisions about implementing such treatments.

It is very important to know how successful occupational stress treatments can be and research design is important in addressing this issue. Beyond that, however, even if the treatments are successful, decisions about implementation of such treatments depend in part on what the benefits are and who benefits from them, and what the costs are and who pays for them. Even if the company pays for them directly, it is fair to ask what the alternative uses of that money would have been. For example, is occupational stress treatment seen as a way of improving business functioning, or is it seen as an employee fringe benefit (as are other health-related benefits)? If it is seen in the former manner, then the employer would usually be willing to foot the bill. If it is seen as the latter, however, it may end up being "taken out" of the total compensation package that employees would receive. The question of utility to these two parties is important for the likelihood of the programs being implemented and it is an area in need of research.

Traditionally, utility analyses assess the costs and/or benefits of various organizational programs to the organization in dollar terms and Bobko (1987) has suggested ways for using these techniques to assess the cost effectiveness of occupational stress management programs. The basic idea, of course, is that measurable outcomes of a program need to be assessed and translated into dollar value. If this value is positive, then it would be compared with the costs of the program to the organization in order to arrive at an estimate of the worth of a program.

This type of analysis, while not totally precise, can help to estimate the value of a program to the organization and therefore can help in making decisions about the program's implementation. Partly because of the difficulty of getting accurate estimates, it is customary to make somewhat conservative estimates. In this way, the program's advocates would be less likely to be in a position of overselling something whose results would not live up to expectations. Utility analysis of occupational stress management programs is another area in need of research.

CONCLUSIONS AND FUTURE DIRECTIONS

A beginning has been made to correct the deficiency in the quantity of research on occupational stress treatments but there are major deficiencies in the amount of research in certain areas. The research that has been done has usually taken an approach that makes it unclear what the treatment has to do with occupational stress. Basically, the studies look at illnesses or symptoms among people who are employed and these are treated, often in the workplace. This appears to be the practice of medicine or clinical/counseling psychology in the workplace generally rather than occupational stress treatment specifically. While treating illnesses at work or anywhere else seems to be a useful and laudable function, these studies usually tell us little that is very directly concerned with occupational stress or how to treat it.

There is no question, however, that this has come to be accepted as the primary way to implement and study occupational stress treatments. It is time to take a step back and look at the bigger picture, time to remember why we are looking at these things at all. If the reason is that we are interested in learning about and treating occupational stress, then some other courses of action need to be pursued in future research. Some evidence about occupational stressor variables needs to be incorporated into the research. Because of this almost totally dominant paradigm in the existing research, it is still true that there has been a paucity of research on occupational stress treatments, over a decade after this problem was noted by Newman and Beehr (1979) and almost three decades after it was noted by Neel (1955).

It is best at this point to keep an open mind about potentially useful treatments and to evaluate them rigorously before accepting or rejecting them. As Murphy (1987) noted, there is some suggestion in the literature that even the dominant, accepted approaches to dealing with occupational stress have not fared all that well when evaluated rigorously. The need for continued efforts at rigorous evaluation is great.

Typologies of occupational stress treatments can help direct future research, once one begins to plug existing research into the categories of a typology. Using individually targeted versus organizationally targeted treatments, for example, it becomes immediately apparent that research on occupational stress treatments for which the primary target is the organization is almost non-existent. This type of research is currently one of the biggest needs in the field. Perhaps the biggest part of this problem is that such treatments simply are not undertaken. That is, it is difficult to study and evaluate something that does not exist.

It is hard to say for certain why organizationally targeted treatments of occupational stress are not undertaken more often, but there are several possibilities, including the fact that there are ready-made professions capable of administering the individually targeted programs, the difficulty in changing organizations or even getting them to try to change, and the implicit blame placed on the organization when organizationally targeted treatments are introduced. In order to get some such treatments seriously considered, these problems might have to be overcome.

Chapter 8

Social support as a form of treatment

The previous chapter discussed types of treatments of or adaptations to (Beehr and Newman's term; 1978) occupational stress. That discussion was broadly focused, covering very disparate ways of dealing with the problem, including what is usually labeled coping as well as adaptive efforts that are more usually called treatments. This chapter focuses on one very specific adaptation, coping technique, treatment, or situation that seems especially dear to the organizational psychology approach to occupational stress: the effectiveness of social support in ameliorating the potentially harmful effects of work stressors. In terms of the model in Figure 1.2 that outlines this job stress research program, social support is an adaptive response.

The importance of other people in one's work life is an essential assumption in most organizational and social psychology theories, and this is true in the case of the organizational psychology approach to occupational stress. The theory used most often to explain and study job stress, especially in the early research, is from social psychology and sociology – role theory. There is a natural tendency for researchers steeped in the organizational psychology approach to job stress to believe in the importance of other people in occupational stress episodes and situations.

This might account for the quick, widespread acceptance of the buffering hypothesis in regard to social support and work-related stress. This hypothesis, which basically proposes a specific type of interaction between job stressors and social support predicting individual strains, will be discussed shortly, but it was for some years the dominant theme of the social support–work stress literature even though its existence has never been strongly supported by research.

Using this as a historical perspective, organizational psychology adherents should perhaps be wary of overly quick acceptance of other findings regarding social support and job stress. In many areas of psychology other than industrial and organizational psychology, research and enthusiasm about social support as an all-purpose treatment and research variable peaked during the late 1970s, with its original promise as an all-purpose cure-all unfulfilled (Vaux, 1988). Although it continued to get some attention in conjunction with workplace stress, it is finally becoming clear that straight-forward, simple conclusions about its effects in this research domain are also rare. With this as a caveat, several observations about the work stress–social support research literature are offered in this chapter, and some theory and recommendations for future research are discussed.

Social support has long been a topic of study and theory in organizational psychology, even before occupational stress became a topic of frequent study in this field. Versions of social support went disguised under names such as supervisor support, leader consideration, and group cohesiveness, to name but a few. Rather than job stress, however, the focus of earlier research on these types of support was usually either job performance, job satisfaction, or both. One reason why it is easy to conclude that this earlier literature was studying social support, sometimes under different labels, is that when social support began to be studied in relation to stress, it was defined and operationalized in a very wide variety of ways (Beehr, 1985b). These ways easily encompassed supervisor support, supervisor consideration, group cohesiveness, and other such traditional organizational psychology variables.

WHAT IS SOCIAL SUPPORT?

Definitions of social support have been inconsistent, diverse, vague, and even contradictory (Beehr, 1985b; House, 1981). As Vaux (1988) noted, "people assist each other in an astonishing variety of ways" (p. 17), and most of these have been labeled social support at one time or another. The most intuitive meaning of social support is probably what is called *emotional* support in the literature, that is, the provision of sympathy, evidence of liking, caring, and listening. This is far from the only type of support that people can offer to each other in the context of occupational stress, however, and other types in the literature have labels such as tangible support, instrumental support, appraisal support, and informational support. Furthermore, this is only a short version of the list (for further discussion, see Beehr, 1985b; Cohen and Wills, 1985; House, 1981; Vaux, 1988). The mere existence of other people in institutional or structural relationships (e.g. spouses) has sometimes been used as evidence of the existence of social support. Given the looseness of definitions in the literature, it is perhaps as difficult to say what social support is not as to say what it is. Social support would usually not be present, however, if nobody has any spatial or structural relationship with the stressed person or if the relationship is hostile. Other than that, some sort of social support could probably be said to exist in almost any situation, according to some published definition or other.

Social support is truly a metaconstruct, as noted by Vaux (1988), composed of many theoretical subconstructs. This may be the problem with the conflicting results over the years of research on it. Within the domain of *occupational* stress specifically, there may not yet be enough research on specific aspects of social support to summarize how the different sub-constructs affect the stress process, but that will eventually be needed. Considering the inclusiveness of previous social support definitions and operationalizations, it has become necessary to categorize social support into types. It has become difficult to address a topic so diverse; therefore it must be recognized that researchers theorists, and practitioners alike are probably talking about several different things.

Types of social support

A couple of categorizations of social support are commonly used in the literature and yet they are quite different from each other.

Structural and functional social support

Cohen and Wills (1985) divided social support into two categories, structural and functional. Their review was of general life stressors, however, rather than being focused on work-related stressors. Structural social support referred to the existence of a social network within which the person was imbedded, for example the existence of connections of the person with neighbors, relatives, and community organizations. In this regard, most employees have some structural social support. That is, they are usually part of an organized set of people who have relationships with each other. The number or frequency of contacts with such people is often the indicator of structural social support used in the structural social support research orientation.

Functional support, on the other hand, refers to definitions and measures of social support requiring an indication that the socially supportive person or people serve a function for the focal person. Examples of such functions include the provision of esteem, information, or companionship, or of being instrumental for the accomplishment of the focal person's tasks (Cohen and Wills, 1985). Virtually all known studies of social support in relation to work-related stress have used functional measures of social support. Both emotional and tangible support, discussed next, are forms of functional support.

Emotional and tangible social support

Within the occupationally oriented stress literature especially, the two functions most often studied may be labeled emotional and tangible (or sometimes, instrumental) social support (e.g. Caplan *et al.*, 1975). Of the two, emotional support is the one that most people think of when the term social support is mentioned. Many early thoughts about the subject were that emotional support would be the one that would help alleviate the effects of occupational stress better, but this has not really been borne out by research. Alleviating stressful effects usually means that the strains are reduced more, either through a buffering effect or a main effect on the strains. One reason for this may be that some of the questionnaire measures of social support that are frequently used in the job stress literature (i.e. those from Caplan *et al.*, 1975) do not empirically distinguish very well between the types of support if the source of support is controlled. That is, when questions ask about different types of social support such as emotional and tangible emanating from one potential source of support, such as a supervisor, these types are usually strongly correlated. There are several studies in which this was found (e.g. Caplan *et al.*, 1975; Kaufmann and Beehr, 1986, 1989; Mattimore, 1990), and it has become common to combine these types of support, thus keeping the sources of social support separate but not the types of support in occupational stress studies (e.g. Dunseath and Beehr, 1991; Ganster *et al.*, 1986).

These measures of emotional and tangible support that correlate so highly tend to be what Cohen and Wills (1985) labeled "global" measures, that is, each question in the index asks about emotional or tangible social support in a fairly non-specific way. The items do not ask, for example, about specific actions that supportive people have undertaken. Examples of emotional and tangible support items, respectively, from Caplan *et al.* (1975) are "How *easy is it to talk with* each of the following people," and "How much does each of these people go out of their way to do things to *make your work life easier* for you?" The "people" listed would then be specified as the supervisor, the co-workers, or people outside the workplace (spouse, family, and friends). These are very generally worded items and do not explain very precisely what actions the supportive people take. Thus, they can be labeled global emotional support and global tangible support (Cohen and Wills, 1985).

An obvious direction for future questionnaire studies of job stress and social support is to identify more specific forms of support. One recent study that measured family emotional and instrumental support much less globally, however, still reported a strong correlation between the two ($r=0.62$; Mattimore, 1990). This occurred even though the indices consisted of many items (45) that were somewhat more specific than those in the indices more often used in job stress research.

One approach to developing questionnaire measures of social support starts with the observation that people are not simply present when supporting others; they are surely doing something. The question is what are they doing, or more precisely, which things are they doing that are helpful? This could be done by asking about more specific actions of the supportive others, actions that could help to define emotional and tangible support more precisely, for example. One could even videotape many staged episodes of potential social support and have subjects rate them for social support on the existing, global, items. Then it might be learned what people are responding to and what the operational definitions of social support in past studies mean to respondents.

Contents of communications

One such specific type of action that could be interpreted as social support is talking to or otherwise communicating with the focal person. More specific still would be the contents of these talks or communications between the stressed person and the supportive person (suggested by Beehr as early as 1976).

Two studies examined this type of activity as social support and it looks promising for future research. In Beehr *et al.*'s (1990) study of role conflict among 225 registered nurses in seven hospitals, we focused on supervisor support. A part of these data that were relevant to uncertainty was presented in Beehr *et al.* (1986) and was discussed in a previous chapter. Regarding social support, we wrote twelve items that were expected to measure the frequency with which nurses talked to their supervisors (usually head nurses) about (1) the positive things that happened at work, (2) the negative things that happened at work, or (3) non-work issues and events. A factor analysis resulted in three very clean factors of four items each, mirroring the three intended indices, and the alpha reliabilities were acceptable (0.92 for non-job-related communications, 0.75 for negative communications, and 0.80 for positive communications). Thus, it appeared possible to measure these three types of contents of communications with supervisors relatively separately. The intercorrelations of the communications social support indices subsequently formed were moderately high, however, with a median correlation of 0.55 ($p<0.01$).

We also used a derivative of a functional supervisor support measure from Caplan *et al.* (1975), a combination of emotional and tangible support, and found that it correlated with all three contents of communications, 0.40 ($p<0.01$) with non-job-related communications, 0.18 ($p<0.01$) with negative job-related communications, and 0.44 ($p<0.01$) with positive job-related communications. This suggests that the typical functional support measure might be tapping the types of communications that people undertake with the supportive person, at least in part. Apparently, it is seen as supportive on these traditional, global measures when the others are willing to talk to the stressed person about non-work things or about the positive things in the workplace, but it is only mildly supportive to talk about the negative things about work. It is interesting, however, that the negative contents of communications were not related to the functional support measure negatively. Perhaps it is even better to talk about the bad things at work than about nothing at all when stress strikes. This needs further research attention.

Fenlason (1989) and Fenlason and Beehr (reanalysis of the same data; in press) used these items to measure contents of communications of a random sample (n=173) of secretaries in a midwest state division of the Professional Secretaries Association International. Instead of addressing contents of communications with and social support from only supervisors, three of the secretaries' potential sources of social support – supervisors, co-workers, and people outside the workplace – were studied. Since the items from Beehr *et al.* (1990) had been written specifically for nurses, we made minor wording modifications in the items to make them relevant to secretaries. With the exception of the last item, they can now be used for any job. Anyone wishing to use the scale can rewrite the last item either to make it refer to the specific job or people in the sample or to be non-job-specific (e.g. "We talk about the rewarding things about this job"). The items, which are now more generally useful, are in appendix F. In order to use them with jobs other than secretaries, the final item should be adapted either to name the specific job or simply to say "about working in this job." In our secretaries' study, the reliabilities were better than in the previous study of nurses (0.93 for non-job-related communications, 0.89 for negative communications, and 0.87 for positive communications).

Three factor analyses of the contents of communications items were computed, one for each source (supervisor, co-worker, and extraorganizational). Results of all three showed strong correspondence with the three concepts. It therefore seems possible to write items about contents of communications that will hang together in intended ways. Furthermore, it was encouraging that the median intercorrelations among the three indices were much lower than in the Beehr *et al.* study (0.26 for communications with supervisors, 0.39 for communications with co-workers, and 0.27 for communications with extraorganizational sources), suggesting that it may be possible to measure these contents of communications somewhat independently after all.

Fenlason and Beehr also used Caplan *et al.*'s (1975) indices of global and tangible social support from the same three sources, and found that the contents of communications indices correlated with these more traditional social support indices in logical ways (Table 8.1). The correlations within the boxes should be stronger than the other correlations in the same columns and rows, because these compare the different types of social support measures (contents of communications and the more global functional measures of Caplan *et al.*). This is nearly always the case in the data in Table 8.1.

Some of the most striking results in this table are the correlations between negative communications and the traditional support indices. Within all three boxes, they are the lowest correlations (median r=0.175). This confirms the Beehr *et al.* (1990) finding and strongly suggests that talking with stressed people about the bad, unpleasant, or negative things in the workplace will not be perceived as supportive in the way that social support has usually been measured in workplace research. This does not necessarily mean,

Table 8.1 Correlations of contents of communications with indices of emotional and tangible support (reprinted with permission from Fenlason, 1989)

Contents of communication	Supervisor support		Co-worker support		Family & friends support	
	Emotional	Tangible	Emotional	Tangible	Emotional	Tangible
With supervisor						
Positive	0.55**	0.52**	0.23**	0.31**	0.29**	0.29**
Negative	0.20**	0.15*	0.05	0.11	0.18**	0.11
Non-job	0.55**	0.45**	0.21**	0.23**	0.26**	0.29**
With co-workers						
Positive	0.28**	0.26**	0.48**	0.45**	0.33**	0.30**
Negative	−0.09	−0.13	0.33**	0.14*	0.14*	0.04
Non-job	0.23**	0.17*	0.53**	0.31**	0.26**	0.13
With others						
Positive	0.34**	0.33	0.25**	0.27**	0.33**	0.39**
Negative	−0.05	−0.12	0.18**	0.10	0.21**	0.14*
Non-job	0.15*	0.18*	0.32**	0.35**	0.55**	0.39**

* $p < 0.05$
** $p < 0.01$
Ns range from 160–171

however, that work stress–social support researchers should not study communications with negative affect. Considering the rather contradictory and confusing results with the traditional indices of social support, the use of new and different measures could even lead to some clarification of the situation.

Along these lines, in a study of college students, it was found that students who confided in each other when they experienced stressors tended to become more depressed rather than less depressed (Cutrona, 1986). Exactly what "confiding" consisted of is unknown, but it seemed likely in the context of the study to mean talking about problems or negative things. By contrast, the provision of positive feedback in those situations tended to be followed by students becoming less depressed.

Again focusing on the three boxes in Table 8.1, it appears that there is a tendency for emotional support to be more strongly related to the contents of communications than tangible support is, because the differences between eight of the nine pairs of correlations are in this direction. The magnitude of the differences is not great, however. This is something that needs further research also. That is, to what extent are these contents of communications primarily seen as emotional?

Overall, it seems possible to study types of communications with potentially supportive people and this might help eventually to clarify the types of activities that comprise social support for stressed employees. Furthermore, this list is not exhaustive. That is, these are certainly not the only types of communications that people engage in. Cutrona (1986), for example, has begun to study "helping behaviors" among college students, including listening to confidences, offering advice, expressing points of view, expressing concern, and giving positive feedback. Future research on occupational stress and social support could expand the domain of contents of communications. There are probably many ways to categorize communications messages between people at work, and the best way to do this to help understand social support and occupational stress may not have been discovered yet.

Not only are there probably other contents of communications besides the ones covered in these studies, but there are other dimensions of communications that could be studied. First, the simple frequency of communications could be very important. There may be some optimum range of frequency of communication with a stressed worker that has the most favorable effect. Second, the emotional intensity of the communications might be important. When the contents are positive or negative, this implies that there is some affect attached to them. There is likely to be a range of intensity of expressed affect accompanying the communication episodes, and this intensity might be related to the helpfulness of the social support. Third, some of the sources of potentially supportive communication may also be sources of some of the stressors. If, for example, the supervisor is the person most responsible for overloading, conflicting, or ambiguous demands, does communicating with that person in one of these three ways (positive, negative, or non-job) have an especially strong impact on the strain experienced? And if so, is the effect positive or negative? Research on contents of communications in relation to occupational stress has barely begun, but the possibilities seem great.

The idea for examining the role of contents of communications as operationalizations of types of social support was suggested by Beehr in 1976, but it was not tried until much later (i.e. Beehr *et al.*, 1990; Fenlason and Beehr, in press). There are still other potential specific operationalizations of social support that have either not been studied or have not been studied in conjunction with occupational stress. Some of these have been named here; all of them need study. They may eventually lead job stress researchers out of the social support wilderness.

All of this again brings to the fore the issue of the definition of social support. Clearly accepted conceptual and operational definitions are usually considered essential for research and yet they could limit the scope of research in an area such as this. Rather than attempting a single clear definition, research on social support might be better off at this point accepting the current situation and simply continuing to investigate social interactions in all their complex forms to see how important they are in the process of occupational stress.

Frequency and nature of interactions

Another relatively new approach to defining social support in the workplace concerns the nature and frequency of interactions with potentially supportive others. Henderson and Argyle (1985) asked employees to select a peer at work in each of four categories: friends they know through work and whom they also see outside of work, people they get along with well socially at work, but whom they do not consider to be friends elsewhere, people they get along with well only as a co-worker on work tasks but would not spend much time with otherwise, and people with whom they do not get along. This typology seems to be a categorization of both where one interacts with others (at work and/or elsewhere) and the perceived degree of intimacy of the relationship. It was associated with twelve activities, such as helping each other at work, discussing one's personal life, and having coffee, drinks, or meals together. These activities and the typology itself may help to define social support in more specific ways compared with how it has been defined in many past job stress studies. If one wants to know what social support is and the extent to which different types of social support affect the job stress process, this study is suggestive of possible alternative measures of social support for future research.

Such research could proceed, for example, by expanding the list of activities, having experts rate the activities and/or typologies on several theoretically relevant dimensions (e.g. the likely degree of intimacy and instrumentality), and having the respondents provide frequency estimates for the activities. Introducing such measures into research on job stress and social support might help to illuminate what types of support have what effects as well as what social support is exactly. This is a promising avenue for future research.

EFFECTS OF SOCIAL SUPPORT IN RELATION TO OCCUPATIONAL STRESS

There are three general types of effects that have been proposed for social support in conjunction with occupational stress (Beehr, 1985b; Beehr and McGrath, in press). The first is a main effect of social support on stressors. That is, social support might reduce the harmful effects of job stressors by reducing the strength of the stressors themselves. The second is a main effect of social support on strains. Social support, in this view, would directly reduce the strength of the aversive effects of stressors on the person. The third contention is that there is some type of interaction effect. The most commonly proposed interaction effect in the job stress literature is the interaction between job stressors and social support to affect the level of strains.

Main effects of social support on job stressors

Of the three types of effects that social support might have, its effects on job stressors have been explicitly studied the least. Most of the occupational stress studies, as noted in a previous chapter, have used non-experimental field methods, and some of them report correlations among most or all of the variables in the study. Therefore, some information is often present regarding the possibility that social support could have an effect on the stressors. Among eight studies that did report these correlations, about thirty-eight of sixty correlations between job stressors and social supports were significant ($p<0.05$), but the median correlation (that is, the median of the eight median correlations from each study) was only -0.22 (Beehr, 1976; Beehr and Drexler, 1986; Beehr et al., 1990; Etzion, 1984; Ganster et al., 1986; La Rocco and Jones, 1978; Marcelissen et al., 1988; Seers et al., 1983; some of these correlations could only be estimated due to the nature of their reporting in the studies).

In another recent study of 181 employees of a small midwestern city, Caplan et al.'s (1975) three sources of social support (i.e. supervisor, co-worker, and extraorganizational) and six job stressors (role conflict, role ambiguity, quantity of workload, work variability, underutilization of skills, and responsibility for others) were measured (Dunseath and Beehr, 1991). Mail-back questionnaires were used in this study, which largely replicated Ganster et al. (1986), the median correlation between the social supports and stressors being -0.125.

From these results, it appears that if there is a main effect of social support on job stressors, it is not a strong one, and it is not a general one. It is not general, because the wide variety of social support types and sources does not seem to have a strong effect on a wide variety of job stressors. It is possible that some specific supports have effects on some specific stressors, but the studies reviewed did not use enough of the same stressor and support variables to begin to make such an inference. We are at the point in research development in which such inferences must be made based on logic and then used as hypotheses to be tested.

One such hypothesis is that instrumental or tangible supports might affect the stressors more than emotional supports (Beehr, 1985b). Tangible supports are, by definition, often aimed at materially helping with problems experienced in the situation. One of the major situational problems during occupational stress episodes is the stressor itself. It would be tangible social support, for example, to help the stressed people get the job's tasks done at a time during which they are overloaded. This would materially relieve the overload (the stressor).

A second hypothesis is that support offered from the source of the stressor might be more helpful than support offered from other sources. If the co-workers are the sources of stressors, for example, and they offer social support, this might be especially appreciated and tension-relieving to the focal employee.

A third hypothesis about the potential for specificity of social support's effects on job stressors is that the social support from the supervisor might be more effective in reducing stressors than social support from other sources would be. This is based on the more general hypothesis that support offered by more powerful people is more important than support offered by less powerful people when one experiences stressors in the workplace. The supervisor is the source of support with the most formal power among the sources usually studied in workplace stress research. Extending beyond prior research, however, one might hypothesize that support from people in the organizational hierarchy above the supervisor would be even more effective at reducing stressors. All of this needs more research before any tentative conclusions can be offered, however.

Main effects of social support on individual strains

Some of the earliest thinking and observations about general stress (not job stress, necessarily) and social support concerned the potential effects of social support on individuals' strains. Social support was often offered by researchers, sometimes as a post-hoc explanation, for the relatively good health (i.e. lack of strains) of people who were married, had friends or co-workers, and so forth in various stress studies (House, 1981). If it has this effect, it may be through a kind of calming effect that it has on the mind and body. Perhaps some types of social support lessen nervous system arousal and/or glandular secretions in the body, and this would directly lead to fewer stress-related health symptoms.

In the occupational stress research domain, both House (1981) and Beehr (1985b) concluded that many studies of social support have reported positive main effects of social support on individual strains, but this has been most consistent with psychological strains. In a set of ten published studies reporting correlations between various types and sources of social supports and strains, about thirty-five of fifty-three correlations between social support and types of psychological outcomes were significant (Beehr, 1976; Beehr and Drexler, 1986; Beehr et al., 1990; Chisholm et al., 1986; Etzion, 1984; Ganster et al., 1986; La Rocco and Jones, 1978; Kaufmann and Beehr, 1989; Marcelissen et al., 1988; Seers et al., 1983). In the recent study by Dunseath and Beehr (1991) utilizing three social supports (emotional and instrumental combined for supervisor, co-workers, and others) and three possible psychological outcomes (life dissatisfaction, job dissatisfaction, and depression), seven of nine correlations were significant.

Eight of the ten (Beehr, 1976; Beehr and Drexler, 1986; Beehr et al., 1990; Chisholm et al., 1986; Ganster et al., 1986; La Rocco and Jones, 1978; Kaufmann and Beehr, 1989; Seers et al., 1983) studies included various types of satisfaction measures as psychological outcomes. Satisfaction had a median correlation of about +0.15 with the various types of social support.

In the recent study by Dunseath and Beehr (1991), the median correlation between the three social supports (emotional and instrumental combined for supervisor, co-workers, and others) and two types of satisfaction (life dissatisfaction and job dissatisfaction) was +0.29. In some of these studies, there were negative as well as positive correlations, which might underscore the wide variety of operational definitions of social support.

The Beehr and Drexler (1986) study was one that used only satisfaction or its facets as criterion variables. In that study, 2,046 employees (only a 49 percent response rate, however) at all levels of a statewide banking system in a western state returned mail-back questionnaires. With that size sample, it was believed that there would certainly be enough statistical power to discover the elusive moderating effects, if they did exist. As noted in Chapter 6, however, dissatisfaction is not, by itself, an indicator of the presence of job stress. Therefore, other individual outcomes, those that can more clearly be labeled strains, need to be associated with social support in order to claim that social support might have an effect in the stress process.

A variety of psychological strains has also been studied in relation to social support. Psychological strains include measures of things such as depression, self-esteem, anxiety, and burnout. Eight of the ten studies cited above (Beehr, 1976; Beehr et al., 1990; Chisholm et al., 1986; Etzion, 1984; Ganster et al., 1986; La Rocco and Jones, 1978; Kaufmann and Beehr, 1989; Marcelissen et al., 1988) had such measures, and their median correlation with the social support measures in those studies was −0.18. People reporting more social support tended to report less severe or less frequent psychological strain. In addition, Dunseath and Beehr (1991) found a median correlation of −0.26 between their three social support measures and one psychological strain, depression. The low magnitude of these correlations is surprising. Previous reviews have often concluded that there is a relationship here, and given the criticism that negative affectivity alone might account for a substantial correlation among such self-reported measures (e.g. Brief et al., 1988), there is surprisingly little association between social support and strains in this set of studies.

Fewer published studies on occupational stress have examined the relationship of occupational stress and physical strains. Four of the job stress studies reviewed above included some measure(s) of physical strains. The measures varied from self-reports of illness or somatic complaints to measures of physiological effects, but they are summarized together here because there are so few of them. Of the five physical strain measures in these studies, the median correlation was about −0.145. Only one study measured physiological outcomes in ways other than self-reports, and it tended to find very weak relationships between blood pressure and cholesterol level and social support (Marcelissen et al., 1988). Dunseath and Beehr (1991) found a median correlation of −0.07 (ns) between the three social support measures and self-reported somatic complaints.

Overall, the potential for direct effects of social support on individual strains seems likely but weak. It also seems more likely to be found when using self-report measures of both social support and strains. There is, however, enough variety in the correlations to suggest that further research is warranted. Such research should probably examine a variety of more specifically measured social supports than has been the norm in the past. Future research could, for example, proceed along the routes suggested above regarding contents of communications and/or frequency and nature of interactions as specific types of social support.

Interactive effects of social support

By far the most interesting hypothesis about social support and occupational stress is that social support interacts with occupational stressors to affect individual strains. This is the buffering hypothesis that Ganster *et al.*, (1986) called the dominant hypothesis regarding social support and occupational stress.

The buffering hypothesis

The buffering hypothesis has been described and tested in a few different ways when considering both the job stress and life stress literatures, but one definition has dominated in the job stress literature. Figure 8.1 shows the typical buffering effect that would be expected in occupational stress research. The fact that the low social support line is above the high social support line indicates the main or direct effect of social support on strains that was discussed above. The key for the buffering hypothesis, however, is the difference in slopes between the high and low social support groups. Buffering is usually defined in the occupational stress literature as the finding of a more positive relationship between stressors and strains at higher levels of social support than at lower levels of social support (Beehr, 1985b; House, 1981). Somehow, the causal link between job stressors and individual strains is broken, or at least lessened, by having supportive others. The low social support line in the figure represents the situation for most people experiencing occupational stress, but the high social support line shows no relationship or at least a less strong relationship. The presence of social support is said to buffer or protect the person from the experience of strains in the presence of what would otherwise be stressful job situations.

Cohen and Wills (1985) reviewed the literature on social support and life stress, but in a subsection of that article, they concluded that the *occupational* stress literature provided "considerable support for the buffering model" (p. 347), even though they reviewed only three studies (House and Wells, 1978; La Rocco *et al.*, 1980; La Rocco and Jones, 1978), of which two supported the buffering hypothesis. In the same year, Beehr (1985b)

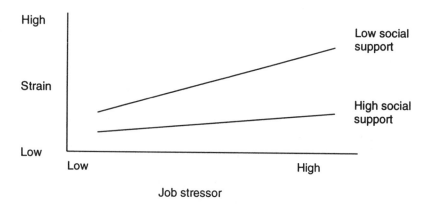

Figure 8.1 Social support's expected buffering effect in occupational stress.

reviewed seven occupational stress studies (Beehr, 1976; Blau, 1981; House and Wells, 1978; La Rocco *et al.*, 1980; House's 1981 graphing of Cobb and Kasl's 1977 data; and two studies that were unpublished at that time but subsequently published as Kaufman and Beehr, 1986, 1989), two of which were in common with Cohen and Wills, and concluded that the evidence regarding the buffering hypothesis is mixed.

One of the reasons for Beehr's (1985b) less positive view about the existence of a buffering effect in the occupational stress research literature was that he uncovered a number of results that have been labeled "reverse," or sometimes "opposite," buffering as well as the expected buffering effect and no interaction effect. That is, higher levels of social support sometimes make the relationship between job stressors and individual strains more positive instead of less positive. Two examples of reverse buffering are illustrated in Figure 8.2. The top example in the figure is drawn to show an expected main effect for social support in addition to the (reverse) buffering effect. In this case, even though the stressor is more strongly related to the strain under conditions of high social support, the individual is still better off by having less strain with higher levels of social support under any existing level of the job stressor. This situation was found by Kaufmann and Beehr (1989).

The implication of the bottom example in the figure is that people under high stressor conditions are actually worse off (more strain) with higher social support than they would be if they received less social support from their surroundings. When an interaction is present, the issue of whether receiving more or less social support would be better for the focal person depends on the point at which the lines cross. If they do not cross within the range of social support that is actually available or possible, then the person will always be better off with a little more social support. The main issue regarding reverse buffering, however, is the unexpected finding of the differences in slopes of the lines in Figure 8.2 relative to each other. For years researchers had expected that the people receiving more social support would have weaker or less positive relationships between job stressors and individual strains.

Six recently published studies, most of which were not reviewed by either Cohen and Wills (1985) or Beehr (1985b), found about twenty-six significant interaction effects between social supports and stressors among the 153 tests (Beehr *et al.*, 1990; Etzion, 1984; Ganster *et al.*, 1986; Kaufmann and Beehr, 1986; Kaufmann and Beehr, 1989; Seers *et al.*, 1983). Of these twenty-six, sixteen of the interactions were examples of reverse buffering, while only ten were examples of the expected buffering effects. The primary purpose of the two studies by Kaufmann and Beehr (1986, 1989) was the examination of buffering or interaction effects. In the 1986 study, 102 (over 99 percent) of the nurses (all female) participating in a workshop at a midwestern medical

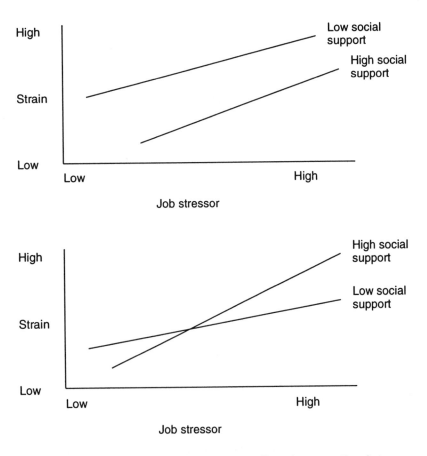

Figure 8.2 Social support's reverse buffering effects in occupational stress.

center in a small city completed a questionnaire and took each other's blood pressure and pulse readings (discussed in an earlier chapter regarding individual outcomes). In addition, absenteeism frequency specifically due to sickness and performance ratings were obtained from the personnel records, although the analyses with these were considered exploratory, because they are organizational outcomes rather than actual strains. As discussed in previous chapters, organizational outcomes are not necessarily a part of the effects of job stress.

Two stressors were measured, underutilization of skills and a combination of P–E Fit on workload and job future ambiguity (Kaufmann and Beehr, 1986). Caplan *et al.*'s (1975) six social support measures were used (three sources times two types of support). In addition, an instrumental support measure was developed that had no referent to a particular source such as supervisors or co-workers. Overall, using moderated regressions, there were seven (of a possible fourteen) significant interactions between a stressor and a social support measure predicting strains. There were also two significant interactions (out of fourteen) for absenteeism due to sickness, but none for performance. The most interesting thing about these interactions is that they were all in the opposite direction from the predictions. That is, they all represented reverse buffering effects in which the slope of the stressor–strain relationship was steeper at higher levels of support than at lower levels of support. The study therefore could certainly not be said to support the traditional concept of buffering.

In the second study we did (Kaufmann and Beehr, 1989), 121 (89 percent response rate) police officers from various agencies in a midwestern state participating in a workshop sponsored by the state police administration completed questionnaires. The workshop covered many psychologically oriented aspects of police work (e.g. selection, training, performance appraisal, as well as occupational stress), and the data were collected before the stress part of the workshop in order to minimize sensitizing the participants to the subject and potentially altering their responses inadvertently. The same questionnaire measures were used that had been used in the earlier study of nurses (Kaufmann and Beehr, 1986), but no physiological or personnel records data were collected. Based on factor analyses, the stressor measures were combined into one overall stressor and the strain measures were combined into one overall psychological strain measure. Of the seven possible interaction effects from moderated regression analysis, only one was significant, that between the instrumental support measure and the stressor. As in the previous study (Kaufmann and Beehr, 1986), this was also a reverse buffering effect.

Additionally, in Dunseath and Beehr's (1991) recent study, only two of thirty-two interactions were significant, albeit both in the expected buffering direction. Overall, these studies do not support the hypothesis that social support acts to buffer the effects of job stressors on individual strains.

These figures are not actually unequivocal accounts that are comparable across studies, because difficult judgments had to be made about which of the variables really fit the definitions of stressors, social supports, and strains in each article, and because the types of statistical analyses reported differed among the studies. Nevertheless, there are enough results here to give confidence in the conclusion that social support is not a strong, comprehensive treatment that will reduce the aversive strength of the effect of job stressors on individual strains – that is, the buffering effect of social support is not a common finding in job stress research.

In addition, one study not included in these six, because a mere counting of its results would be misleading, could be judged to be non-supportive of any interaction effect. This was a study by Beehr and Drexler (1986) in which facets of satisfaction were the primary criterion or strain variables. They found twenty-five of forty-eight significant interactions, but the median percent variance accounted for was less than one-half of 1 percent. The statistical significance was primarily due to the sample size, which was about 2,000. This study is probably most accurately said to support the conclusion that there is no real interaction effect between social support and occupational stress predicting job satisfaction. This reinforces the conclusion, above, that the typical buffering model used to explain social support and occupational stress is probably not widely found in the workplace.

If social support has any effect in the job stress process other than its main effect it certainly is not a clear, universal, and simple effect. Theoretical work needs to be done to guide future research that will have a chance to discover the more complex interactions that might exist (Beehr and McGrath, in press). One possibility is that three-way interactions exist, that is, that there are some people or situations for which buffering (or reverse buffering) occurs reliably. Two studies searched for three-way interactions, using sex, education, and blue-white collar as third predictive variables, but they found no good evidence for such higher order interactions (Dunseath and Beehr, 1991; Ganster et al., 1986). Therefore, if there are subsets of people or situations for which the buffering (or reverse buffering) effect is reliable, they have not yet been discovered.

Another possible reason for the inconsistent results, however, concerns the measurement of social support. The measurement of this complex variable is in need of refinement. There is no clear current agreement regarding how to measure it and the reason may be that the variable is not even close to being a single variable. Its operationalization needs to be examined more closely in future research. Instead of global measures of social support, measures that are quite specific need to be developed and their effects compared in future studies. This will result in multiple measures of social support that are diverse operationally and conceptually.

A model of occupational stress and social support

A model based on the uncertainty approach to occupational stress outlined in earlier chapters has been offered by Beehr (1985b). It will be recalled that the uncertainty theory of occupational stress proposes that a common denominator in many experiences of the work-related social psychological stress is uncertainty regarding expectancies – in combination with the importance of relevant outcomes and the duration of the uncertainties (Beehr and Bhagat, 1985a). Specifically, the types of uncertainty thought to be common to many job stress situations are uncertainty of the likelihood (expectancy) that one's efforts will lead to job performance and the likelihood that one's performance will subsequently lead to valued outcomes.

Figure 8.3 illustrates the proposed relationship between social support and this model of job stress. It addresses two types of social support that have been studied most often in occupational stress research, instrumental (or tangible) and emotional, and it allows for all of the types of effects of social support on the stress process that are discussed here: direct effects on job stressors, direct effects on individuals' strains, and buffering effects on the relationship between job stressors and strains. It does this within Beehr and Bhagat's (1985a) uncertainty framework for occupational stress. The arrows in the model show the theoretically causal direction of relationships between variables, and the signs on the arrows (plus or minus) indicate the positive or negative direction for these causal relationships.

Instrumental support is proposed to have a main (direct) effect on the job stressors (arrow A), while emotional support is expected to have a direct effect on the employee's strains (arrow B). As noted earlier, measures of these two types of support are typically correlated with each other in non-experimental field studies. Because of this, it is unlikely that one would find instrumental support *only* related to job stressors and emotional support *only* related to the strains, but it would be expected from the model that instrumental support will have a stronger effect on job stressors than emotional support and that emotional support will have a stronger effect on strains than instrumental support.

A further reason why instrumental support should be related to strains is that it is related to them indirectly through its effects on the intervening variables of uncertainty and importance. This muddies the waters a bit regarding how strongly it should be related to strains, but a hypothesis that makes sense from the model is that instrumental social support should be more strongly related to job stressors than it is to strains. Furthermore, it is likely that certain sources of instrumental support would have a greater effect on the occupational stressors than other sources. Specifically, instrumental support from people who have the power to affect stressors is more likely to have this effect than instrumental support from people who do not really have such power. The most important source of instrumental support

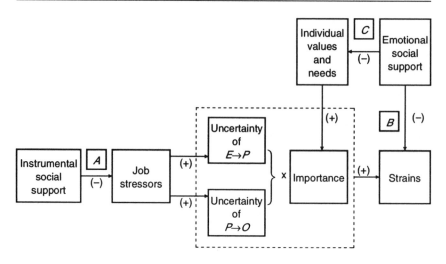

A   Main effect of instrumental social support on job stressors.

B   Main effect of emotional social support on strains.

C   Buffering effect of emotional social support on the relationship between job stressors and strains.

(+) or (−)
indicates the direction of the effect, i.e. increasing (+) or decreasing (−) the strength of the variable.

Figure 8.3 Effects of instrumental and emotional social support in the context of job stress (reprinted with permission from Beehr, 1985).

will vary according to what the stressor is, but on the average, one might expect that the supervisor's instrumental support would be the more important. This is because on the average, the supervisor is formally more powerful in the work situation than the other sources typically studied (co-workers, and family and friends). The model seems rich with the potential for such main effect hypotheses.

Emotional support, on the other hand, is proposed to have a main effect on strains. It seems intuitively obvious that providing comfort and sympathy to people could put them at ease figuratively and literally, and this could be an operational definition of emotional social support. As noted earlier in this chapter, there does seem to be a main effect of social support on emotional or psychological strains, and this model proposes that the emotional type of support does this quite directly.

Using the Beehr (1985b) model, the buffering effect is expected to occur

mainly through the effects of emotional support on importance in the Beehr
and Bhagat (1985b) model. This is proposed to happen through the effects
of emotional social support on individuals' values and needs (arrow C). The
assumption is that the importance employees place on the outcomes in a
given situation is in part a function of their needs and values. The social
information processing approach to organizational behavior (e.g. Salancik
and Pfeffer, 1978) holds that employees' needs are influenced by the information they receive from other people. Since the definition of social support
in past research has been so varied, it is easy to conclude that it could take
the form of providing information about what needs are appropriate in the
situation.

If social support can reduce the strength of the importance the person
places on the outcomes in the situation, then the link from job stressor to
individual strains will be weakened. This could happen, for example, by the
emotional support taking the form of convincing people that they need not
be so upset because the potential outcomes (e.g. lost opportunity for promotion or missed financial bonus due to a missed deadline for product
delivery) in the stressful situation are not all that important anyhow.
Basically, when the social support has this effect, then the buffering effect
might occur. This possible linkage has not yet been studied and is therefore
a topic for future research on job stress and social support.

This reasoning also suggests that if social support could make the situation, or especially the outcomes, seem *more* important, then reverse buffering
could occur. This is because the importance, which is a multiplicative factor
in part of the model, would increase the strength of that part of the model.
But why would social support do that? Again, information that is transmitted
during social support episodes is a possible key. If it leads to the employee
placing even more importance on the situation's outcomes, then the link
between job stressors and individual strains will be stronger than if no social
support had been offered.

One obvious problem with testing this model (besides its complexity and
the problem of developing measures of uncertainty noted in a previous
chapter) is the previously noted difficulty of measuring the instrumental and
emotional social supports independently. The typically strong empirical
relationship between the two types of support makes it difficult to come up
with very different results for them. The only subsequent direct test of parts
of this model to date has been a study by Fenlason and Beehr (in press).
They used the commonly employed global emotional and instrumental
social support measures of Caplan *et al.* (1975) and found that the
differences between eight of the twelve pairs of correlations were in the
expected direction, but only two of the eight were significantly different.
More specifically, each of three sources of emotional support (supervisors,
co-workers, and extraorganizational sources) was correlated both with (two)
job stressors and a psychological strain, and each of the three sources of

instrumental support was also correlated both with (two) job stressors and a psychological strain. Of the six correlations between *emotional* support and job stressors, five were weaker (less negative) than the correlation between the corresponding emotional support and psychological strain, but only one difference was significant. Only three of the six pairs of correlations were in the predicted direction for the *instrumental* support indices, however, one of which was significant. This part of the model is probably worth further research, but the first attempt by Fenlason and Beehr met with only modest success. The development of more accurate measurement of the types of social support could be an important breakthrough.

Contents of communications and reverse buffering

It was proposed (above) that contents of communications might be the key to explaining reverse buffering, and Beehr (1976) suggested that reverse buffering could be due to communication that makes the situation seem to be even worse than had previously been imagined. Beehr *et al.* (1990) followed this suggestion with their three types of communication from potentially supportive supervisors: negative work-related, positive work-related, and non-work-related communication. Based on the above discussion, one might expect the negative communication to lead to reverse buffering, but it did not. All interactions found were of the normal buffering variety, and non-work-related communications had more buffering effects than the other two forms of communication combined.

Fenlason and Beehr (in press), in a parallel study, found only normal buffering effects for two of twelve tests of emotional and instrumental social supports' interactive relationships with role stressors predicting psychological strains. The other ten interactions were not significant. Concerning the contents of communications indices of social support in that study, of eighteen moderator tests in that study, three were significant and one more was very close ($p=0.054$). Of these, there were three buffering effects and one reverse buffering effect. Two of the four concerned negative contents of communication, and the reverse buffering instance was one of these. Again, it is easy to conclude that there is more we do not know about the buffering effect than we do know.

The results continue to be confusing but suggestive that social support can be a volatile variable in the occupational stress process. In addition to the overall inconsistency of the results concerning buffering, it is difficult to discern a clear pattern regarding when buffering occurs, when it does not, and when reverse buffering occurs. The refinement of social support measures may help with future understanding in this area, and what people talk about (i.e. contents of their communications) might be important.

Social support as a dependent variable

One reason for the confusing results regarding the interactive or buffering effects of social support could be that the direction of causality has been confused or misinterpreted in these non-experimental studies. Because they are non-experimental, the ability to infer the direction of causality is always weak and highly dependent on logic, reason, and theory rather than supported by the research design.

Looking at the research methods and reading the empirical literature on social support and job stress, one could come away with the impression that social support is administered by others at their discretion or is simply present in the environment to a certain degree all of the time. That is, much of the literature seems to treat social support almost as a stable condition of the situation. The placement of the social support chapter in one book implies this sort of thinking quite directly (Gore, 1987). It is placed in a section labeled "Individual differences," a label that implies a certain stability. In fact, however, most people would probably agree that social support is not stable for many people. It varies over time as well as from person to person. It is as logical to ask what causes social support as it is to ask what social support causes. Future research needs to be directed toward this question.

One might ask, for example, why some people experiencing job stress get social support and others do not. First, focal people in job stress research are not just reactive recipients of whatever social support happens to be lying around near their working area. They are, or can be, proactive in seeking social support. Second, the potentially supportive people in the studies also have some discretion regarding their own behavior. They may or may not be willing and able to provide it.

If people seek out social support when they experience stressful working conditions, this may be a form of coping for them. One study hypothesized and found that people experiencing any of three stressors at work (role ambiguity, role overload, or underutilization of skills) tended to be especially dissatisfied with their co-workers compared to dissatisfaction with most other facets of their work situation (Beehr, 1981). A second study (Gupta and Beehr, 1979) reported that people experiencing such stressors tended to withdraw from the workplace in the form of absenteeism and turnover. Such withdrawal would of course make it less likely that the stressed people would receive support from their workplace colleagues. Furthermore, even when the stressed person is at work, they might withdraw from others because of being dissatisfied with them (as indicated above). A clear research question is whether people experiencing job stress tend to seek social support as a means for coping with stress, or whether they are more likely to withdraw from potentially supportive others.

At the simplest level, there are two types of evidence that can be easily obtained from existing research about this coping hypothesis. People can either seek and therefore presumably obtain social support when they experience stressors, or they can seek it when they experience strain – or they can do both. Therefore, previous studies providing correlations of social support with stressors and strains would have a bearing on this hypothesis. These results have already been reviewed in this chapter under the opposite assumption, that social support was having a causal effect on job stressors and individual strains, and this opposite assumption shows the ambiguity of interpreting data from non-experimental field studies. As noted earlier, these relationships tend to be low, with correlations in the teens or twenties. The correlations between social support and individual strains tended to be negative, and those between social support and job stressors tended to be negative. This is consistent with the theory of social support as a causal variable and is not consistent with the concept of social support as a dependent variable. Specifically, if people reacted to stressors and strains by seeking social support, one would expect the correlations of social support with both stressors and strains to be positive. Therefore, on the surface of the evidence, it appears that the data favor the theory that social support is a causal variable rather than a dependent variable in job stress situations.

Along these lines, in a study of life stressors, Lin *et al.*, (1979) have suggested that people seek social support as a coping mechanism under stressful conditions. In the workplace, Seers *et al.* (1983) studied 104 government employees and found instances of reverse buffering. Instead of interpreting these results as reverse buffering, however, they suggested Lin *et al.*'s coping hypothesis as an explanation, and plotted the interaction with social support on the horizontal axis and the "strain" (job satisfaction, which, it has been argued in this book, is not a very good indicator of strains) on the vertical axis. For people with high scores on the stressor (role conflict), there was a positive relationship between social support and job satisfaction, while for people with low stressors there was virtually no relationship between social support and job satisfaction. Thus, people experiencing stressors might be benefiting from social support, while social support was having no effect on those without stressors.

Novel and creative explanations of unexpected social support interactions such as this are needed. This particular one, coping, may be valuable. It no doubt needs more development, however, given that even in the Seers *et al.* (1983) study the zero order correlation between the stressor and social support was negative. This runs counter to the suggestion that high levels of stressors prompted people to seek social support.

Marcelissen *et al.* (1988) did a rare longitudinal study of social support and occupational stress in order to look for stronger evidence of causation. Their study sheds some important light on the potential for social support as a dependent variable, but it does not necessarily support the coping hypothesis about social support. In a study of 2,034 employees of twenty-one Dutch companies, this analysis indicated that social support was not necessarily a very strong cause of anything in the job stress process, but there was some evidence that social support from co-workers might be *caused by* the focal person's strains. As would be expected from the zero order correlations from the literature summarized in this chapter, the relationship was negative. Instead of the usual interpretation of social support causing reduced strains, however, it was more likely that increased strains were causing less social support! This is an intriguing possibility and deserves further theoretical and empirical investigation.

One explanation is simply that people exhibiting strains are no fun to be around. At an extreme, their suffering behavior might drive people away, thereby reducing any chances they might have had to obtain social support. Whereas it was suggested earlier in this discussion that people who are experiencing occupational stress might withdraw from others, this hypothesis is more along the lines that other people withdraw from them. While people might try to cope with their stressors by seeking social support, many will not be successful. This thinking indicates that providing social support can be a burden which is aversive to some potentially supportive people.

A simple hypothesis about human interaction is that people are more likely to interact with others when it is pleasurable to do so and will be less likley to interact with others when it is painful to do so. It is an easy inference to assume that it is not a pleasure to interact with many people experiencing stress and that it might even be quite unpleasant. Unfortunately, this puts more burden on the stressed employee not to be too difficult to interact with. Otherwise they will not be very successful in obtaining social support. This simple idea might explain some of the confusing research findings about occupational stress and social support.

Future job stress research using social support as a dependent variable will be necessary to help resolve this issue. As noted earlier, there has been a tendency for researchers to treat the existing social support as a given, at least implicitly. Instead, people experiencing job stress can seek it out and can even drive it away. Stressed people are proactive creators of their own environment and not simply passive reactors to it. Similarly, others in the focal person's environment are proactive and have some influence over the extent to which they will provide social support. As researchers continue to refine and redefine social support and its measurement, they also need to consider the different types of social support as a dependent variables. It is as important to know what causes it as to know what it causes.

SUMMARY

Social support can be seen as an adaptation or treatment of occupational stress. Popular thinking frequently recommends it and comments on the need for support groups and support systems. With organizational psychology's close ties to social psychology, a variable like social support is especially attractive as an explanation for many things, including the effects of occupational stress. It is possible that researchers have at times, because of this, been too quick to make some conclusions about its effectiveness, and the early acceptance of the buffering hypothesis might be an illustration of this.

One of the most obvious problems with the social support literature is that social support has not been operationally defined in a clear, limited, consistent way. At times it is difficult to know what would *not* be considered socially supportive behavior, because of the inclusiveness of the literature. At this point, maybe it is better in the future not to try to limit it (and it would probably not be possible to get agreement on such a limitation), but instead to make sure any *one* operationalization of it is clear and limited. In that way one will eventually be able to make comparisons about relatively known versions of social support.

Future research might focus, therefore, on developing less global measures and instead come up with a variety of specific alternatives regarding what social support might be or the forms it could take. House noted in 1981 that understanding what leads to perceptions of social support was a neglected issue. It still is. If it could be determined, for example, that social support in the form of certain activities was more beneficial than social support in the form of other activities, this would be very useful information for further research, theory development, and applications. One such set of activities is communication with the focal person, and a beginning has been made in understanding what potentially supportive types of communications could occur in the workplace and what their effects might be on the occupational stress process.

Because of the diverse and confusing results, especially regarding the buffering hypothesis, this is a good time for theory development and the use of existing theory to guide research. One such theory is the uncertainty theory of occupational stress (Beehr and Bhagat, 1985a). A beginning has barely been made in using it as a guide for social support research (Fenlason and Beehr, 1994).

It is concluded from past research on occupational stress and social support, which requires summarizing over a very wide variety of social support, job stressor, and individual strain variables, that there is a very weak or non-existent negative relationship between social support and job stressors, a weak or moderate negative relationship between social support and individual strains, and total confusion regarding interactions between social support and job stressors in predicting individual strains.

The popular buffering hypothesis has certainly not been supported overall in this literature. Most studies do not find interactions, and roughly half of the interactions discovered turn out to be in the direction opposite from that predicted by the buffering hypothesis. Future research on such interactions might be aided by a carefully reasoned specification of the types of stressors, strains, and social support activities that are expected to result in various kinds of interactions.

Considering this somewhat confusing state of affairs, one important avenue for future research is to use social support as a dependent variable in job stress research and also in research on other organizational psychology topics. The discovery of interpersonal activities and influences that are seen as supportive or that behave in understandable ways in conjunction with job stress variables would help to advance understanding and guide still other future research. Social support is likely to remain a promising and interesting research topic.

Kessler *et al.*, (1985), reviewing research primarily on main effects of social support on pathology, echo many of these recommendations for future research. Some of the observations in this chapter are not entirely limited, therefore, to the work domain. One issue that Kessler *et al.* noted, but that did not arise in the context of *work* stress, concerns the potential consequences of the administration of social support to the provider of the support. Kessler *et al.* suggested that the long-term provision of social support might be emotionally draining on the provider. Examples were primarily ones that might not occur immediately in the domain of work stress as approached by industrial and organizational psychologists (e.g. provision of social support by family members to those with long-term, serious illnesses). Nevertheless, some of the same issues could arise in the context of work-related stress if the strains were severe and long in duration.

Part V

Conclusion

It has become very clear in the chapters of this volume dealing with the various facets of the job stress process that we know some things about job stress, but there is much yet to be learned. This section summarizes some of the major conclusions from the previous chapters and indicates what needs to be done next. Furthermore, some guidelines regarding how to undertake the next research steps in this domain are outlined.

Chapter 9

Conclusion

It would be useful in future investigations to examine the effects of . . .
(Bhagat *et al.*, 1985: 212)

Future studies could incorporate these hypothesized explanatory
variables . . .
(Kaufmann and Beehr, 1986: 524)

An important area for future research . . .
(Russel *et al.*, 1987: 273)

This finding, if substantiated in future research . . .
(Tetrick and La Rocco, 1987: 541)

. . . researchers investigating job stress should . . .
(Sutton and Rafaeli, 1987: 270)

. . . future research should look directly at . . .
(Seltzer and Numerof, 1988: 444)

More work is needed . . .
(Steffy and Jones, 1988: 695)

In the future, studies should collect information on these important factors
. . .
(Martocchio and O'Leary, 1989: 499)

As has been noted in most recent occupational stress studies, including those
quoted above, more research is needed. Sometimes it seems that the more
we learn about occupational stress, the less we know. It at least can appear
that way, because we often learn that there are still other things that we do
not know or that something we "knew" is not always true after all. Future
research needs to be guided by past research results and also by theory in
order to lead to better understanding and eventual control of occupational
stress.

After an initial surge of research on occupational stress in organizational
psychology in the 1960s and 1970s, much of the field settled into a kind of

doldrums, with little innovation occurring. This was noted by Jackson *et al.* (1986: 637) in a statement about burnout research:

> Alternatively, a pessimist might predict that burnout researchers will travel the familiar and well-worn paths blazed by their forefathers in stress research, the result being that twenty years from now we will have more data but not much more knowledge.

While the situation is probably not so bleak as this pessimistic alternative suggests, the field of industrial and organizational psychology has never quite embraced the topic of occupational stress wholeheartedly. When I submitted my first job stress study to a major I/O psychology journal in the mid-1970s, one reviewer commented that the field did not need this new topic. He or she may have feared that it would be old, well-worn stuff dressed up with new words. As argued in this book, when job stress studies rely heavily on job satisfaction as a primary outcome of the stressors, this fear is well founded. To put it as a question, why call it job stress instead of placing it in its rightful place in the well-established base of knowledge about job satisfaction? Therefore, job stress researchers need to be studying and measuring something other than, and something more serious than, simple affective reactions to the job (i.e. job satisfaction).

Alternatively, the reviewer of my manuscript may have been thinking that the topic belonged in the bailiwick of another field, such as health or mental health. Indeed, one prominent I/O psychologist several years ago told me that the topic of job stress "smacks of clinical psychology," which was why I/O psychologists would never take to it strongly. In 1978, Beehr and Newman recommended that I/O psychologists had something to contribute to the knowledge about occupational stress by, for example, simply examining more traditional I/O psychology research areas in which they were interested and determining their possible relationships with employee strains. At that time, the field had almost been ignoring the type of occupational stress that is the subject of this book. A dozen years later, Ilgen (1990) noted that the health of the workforce is an issue that I/O psychology had largely ignored. "An almost identical concern – that job stress and employee health had been relatively neglected by industrial/organizational researchers – had been expressed 12 years before by Beehr and Newman (1978)" (Keita and Jones, 1990: 1137). The situation really is not as bad as it was, however. Several articles on occupational stress per year now appear in I/O types of journals and there are at least some I/O psychologists who are interested enough in the topic to study it.

Part of the problem could be that the knowledge already gained is not widely known. This at least appears to be the case in the area of practice and in the popular press. Among people who do not actively engage in occupational stress research, there is another problem, one that is probably related to the fact that occupational stress is a popular topic as well as a technical one. One hears about it in the mass media and hears co-workers and people on the street talk about it – sources that do not always have technically correct information. To paraphrase a statement often attributed to Will Rogers, it's not so much what we don't know about job stress that bothers me – it's what we know that just ain't so.

Examples of what we know that just ain't so abound. As I was writing this paragraph, I received a call from a psychological practitioner who was referred to me for my presumed expertise on occupational stress treatments. She wanted to know which treatments were the most effective for alleviating the effects of executive stress, because she was proposing such a program to a company for which she was consulting. As noted in an earlier chapter, one of the things we know that apparently ain't so is that executive positions have more stress than most other types of jobs. A second thing we know but don't is that it is clear what treatments, if any, work best for alleviating job stress. It might be recalled from a previous chapter that Murphy (1987) has noted the negative relationship between the rigor of evaluation studies of stress treatments and their reported success. I recommended that whatever she did, she should be sure to evaluate its effectiveness and I gave her references to read. In spite of such warnings that I gave, the consultant will presumably do something to try to help the company, and in order to obtain the contract and to be as effective as possible, she will probably emit confidence to the executives that the treatments are well proven – possibly spreading some misconceptions even further.

This book has described a program of research illustrated in Figure 1.2 in the first chapter. My colleagues and I think we have learned a great deal about stressors in the social psychological environment at work, the resulting human consequences or strains, moderators of the stressor–strain relationships, organizational consequences of stress and adaptive responses to it. We also realize that there is much more left to be discovered, as indicated by the quotes from others at the beginning of this chapter.

It is just as important to discover what we know that is not so as it is to discover new things about job stress regarding which we now have no firm opinions. Occupational stress myths (things we know that just ain't so) have been discussed throughout the chapters in this book and they include the idea that stress is consistently related to performance in predictable ways, that good and bad events can be equally stressful, that all jobs are stressful, and even that different experts are talking about the same thing when they use the word stress.

RECOMMENDED DIRECTIONS FOR FUTURE RESEARCH

Each chapter of this book has within it several suggestions for future research. Instead of repeating these dozens of recommendations, however, a few main themes are discussed here.

Let's organize

A clear organization of all research on occupational stress, past and future, would aid in understanding, comparing, and directing research. Future research on occupational stress would be more beneficial to the extent to which it is placed explicitly into the context of other research, and two good ways of doing this are to make sure the research either is theory-based or clearly fits into a taxonomic framework.

The use of new theories or topic areas

Role theory led researchers in one direction for quite a while after the pioneering work of Kahn *et al.* (1964) introduced us to role conflict and role ambiguity as job stressors. The direction provided by this theory seems to have hit a limit, however, in terms of its usefulness in explaining the process of occupational stress. Additional theories need to be used. Insights from these theories might add to our knowledge by providing additional information about other stressors or by providing information that can be integrated with role theory to develop a new theory – a synthesis of two others. One theory offered in earlier chapters is the uncertainty theory of occupational stress (Beehr and Bhagat, 1985a). The idea that many organizational psychology types of job stressors emit a common response among people, namely uncertainty about the effort-to-performance and the performance-to-outcome expectancies in their work, brings along with it many testable hypotheses; few studies have yet tested even parts of the theory, however, and its testing is therefore very open for future research.

Uncertainty theory suggests how strains occur and suggests potential moderator effects of duration and importance on the relationships between uncertainty and strains. Furthermore, the book in which the uncertainty theory is presented contains chapters written by active I/O psychology researchers on other I/O topics, and they suggest ways in which these other topics could be related to job stress through the mechanism of uncertainty. Such speculation can be a fruitful source of research ideas for anyone interested in the topic.

Social psychology has often been a source of theory for organizational psychology and it might serve that function again in the case of occupational stress. Role theory came to I/O psychology from that discipline and the uncertainty theory of job stress could be said to come from social psychology also, because it is a take-off on expectancy theory of motivation – a theory with a long history in social psychology. McGrath (1976), who wrote the first edition I/O handbook chapter on occupational stress, is a social psychologist and his approach can also be seen as a social psychology approach. There is nothing wrong with adopting or adapting theories from other areas if they can fit and illuminate our own interest areas; witness the rampant use of systems theory in organizational theory. Systems theory originated in the physical sciences. Social psychology is a discipline that might help future job stress research if its theories provide new ideas (Love and Beehr, 1981).

Some social psychological theories that could potentially be used in this way, in addition to role theory and expectancy theory, have been noted before: reference-group theory, cognitive dissonance theory, and interaction theory (Love and Beehr, 1981; Mettlin and Woelfel, 1974). Reference-group theory, for example, could be used to propose that people whose major reference groups are outside the organization and outside of work in general would be less susceptible to the aversive effects of occupational stress because of their lesser dependence on organizational members for important norms and standards for their own behavior. Studies comparing the fit of one job stress theory with another to empirical data have rarely been attempted. Other current topics in social psychology that are not necessarily theories include the interest areas of mood, of self (e.g. self-enhancement, self-awareness, self-appraisal, self-monitoring), and of social cognition.

Negative affectivity (NA), discussed in relation to occupational stress in a previous chapter, is related to mood. Early attempts to use NA to understand occupational stress research have already been reported (e.g. Brief *et al.*, 1988), although the focus has been on the extent to which NA is a nuisance variable that artificially inflates obtained relationships between self-reported measures of stress variables such as stressors and strains.

Schwarz (1990) notes that mood research often suggests that people in poor moods judge situations and people more accurately than those in good moods do (performance appraisals, for example; Sinclair, 1988). It makes sense that people experiencing occupational stress could simultaneously experience negative moods. If they do, then this might even suggest that their perceptions of the stressors are more accurate than the perceptions of people who are not experiencing job stress. Accuracy of self-reported measures of stressors, therefore, might vary along with the strength of the stressor itself, because stressor strength varies with the strength of strains such as depression – and perhaps also with the strength of negative *moods*.

One way out of the self-report dilemma and the factors introducing error into the reports of some variables is to make the variables more objectively observable even though they are self-reported. On the stressor side, for example, the examination of shiftwork or non-standard schedules was noted in an earlier chapter as a stressor in need of more study by organizational psychologists. Even though people might be asked to report about their shifts themselves, it seems likely that they usually can observe and will report fairly accurately the shift on which they work. Shiftwork, which has been studied as a stressor somewhat already (e.g. Zedeck *et al.*, 1983), might be a very opportune stressor for future research for two reasons: we have not studied it enough yet, and it can probably be measured easily and with little error with self-reports.

The second example of a social psychological topic that might be useful in future research examining occupational stress is the self. In self-evaluation or self-appraisal studies, for example, many people are assumed to seek information that will allow them to appraise themselves (e.g. their skills or performance). This tendency might vary with environmental situations such as high uncertainty. Strube has proposed a model suggesting that self-appraisal and Type A behavior are related to each other (e.g. Strube *et al.*, 1987). The basic premise of interest here is that Type As are more disposed to desire and seek information that can be used for self-appraisals than Type Bs are. One of the elements in the model, "uncertainty about an important ability," is likely to be related to the effort-to-performance uncertainty in the uncertainty theory of occupational stress (Beehr and Bhagat, 1985a). Uncertainty about one's own ability on job-related tasks makes it difficult to predict whether one's task-related efforts will be successful, that is, whether they will result in performance. This is the essence of the E-P uncertainty in that theory of occupational stress. Furthermore, Strube *et al.* (1987) propose that Type As are bothered by and react more strongly to uncertainty than Type Bs do. This model, in combination with uncertainty theory of job stress, can be used to tie Type A behavior directly to job stress and to develop testable hypotheses regarding processes through which job stress effects occur.

The third example of a broad topic area from social psychology mentioned above is social cognition. Beehr and Bhagat (1985a) contended that their uncertainty theory was a cognitive theory of job stress in the sense that it focused on certainty of perceptions. One use of cognitive information processing theory that is known to many I/O psychologists is Salancik and Pfeffer's (1978) argument that many of the perceptions people have about work situations are socially influenced. That is, information about the work environment is gathered from others as well as by observing the job environment directly for oneself. This has implications for self-report measures of any aspect of the job, including measures of job stressors. Further showing the importance of social information, in the job stress process in the social support literature, it has been suggested that various forms of information are passed from the supportive people to the stressed person. These are even proposed as the very essence of social support (e.g. Cobb, 1976). In Chapter 8, it was noted that Beehr *et al.* (1990) and Fenlason and Beehr (in press) reported studies suggesting that the content of what people talk about during episodes of social support is influential in affecting strains. Social information processing approaches might help direct future research in this area.

Mood, self-appraisal, and social cognition theories all appear to have links to occupational stress and further examination of them is likely to lead to new innovative research in the area. These three, however, are only a few examples from the world of social psychology and there are no doubt many other areas of research in social psychology and even in other disciplines that can be used to understand job stress in new ways. There are frequent

calls for more interdisciplinary research on job stress and the usual implication is that this means more widely varying disciplines such as medicine,
physiology, and so forth. In addition to such interdisciplinary research, we
must not forget that areas of expertise that are closer to I/O psychology can
also be useful (e.g. other areas of psychology).

The creation and use of taxonomies

Besides new unifying theories or approaches, a second way to get the prior
research organized and to direct and make sense of future research is to rely
on taxonomies. Taxonomies, in this context meaning ways of classifying
elements of the job stress process, have been mentioned and/or recommended in several previous chapters. The Beehr and Newman (1978) model,
illustrated in Chapter 1 is largely a taxonomy in which the various elements
or variables that had been studied in relation to job stress were placed. The
elements were then placed into the model, which summarized the relationships that most researchers presumed existed between the elements.

The Beehr–Newman taxonomic model is general enough to encompass
the variables from virtually all of the research done on job stress before and
since it was presented. In organizing the research at that time, it provided
one useful tool for understanding what the various researchers were saying.
Research on the topic is now at a more advanced stage, however, and
taxonomies at different levels might be more useful. That is, today's useful
taxonomies might be those that are more limited to specific parts of the job
stress process rather than an attempt at a global, all-encompassing taxonomy
of job stress.

Examples of more limited areas in which taxonomies can help to indicate
gaps in research were suggested in previous chapters. One regards categorizing stressors. Based on discussion earlier in the book, stressors could be
categorized as acute versus chronic and as perceived versus objective.
Furthermore, these two dimensions, if crossed, illustrate the areas in which
the most research has been done and the least (Figure 9.1).

As illustrated in the figure, past approaches to the study of job stress from
the organizational psychology point of view have hit this matrix like a
shotgun blast, but the center of the pellet holes is not the center of the target.
If past organizational psychology research were plotted this way, one would
no doubt conclude that we have generally hit chronic, perceived stressors
more heavily than any of the other types of stressors in our research. Since
the other types of stressors have not yet been studied very much, there is
obviously even more to be learned about them than there is about the one
"overstudied" area.

Besides the chronic or acute time limit of the stressor and the nature of the
measurement, there is a third dimension of occupational stress that has been
discussed less frequently in organizational psychology: the evaluation of the

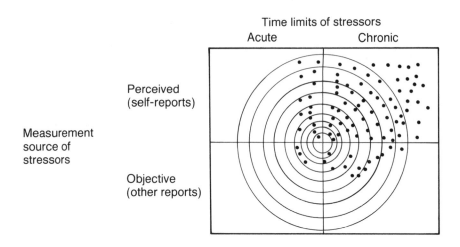

Figure 9.1 The shotgun pattern of occupational stress research.

stressor as good or bad (e.g. Beehr and Franz, 1987; Beehr and Schuler, 1982; Schuler, 1980). People evaluate some, if not all of the environmental events and states in their work lives as relatively favorable or unfavorable. Promotions, for example, might usually be evaluated as good events, while being transferred to a new geographical location against one's wishes would probably be evaluated as bad. Some stress theories, especially those from social psychology, argue that any change in life can be stressful. While the life stress research has sometimes addressed this issue (e.g. Sarason *et al.*, 1978), the job stress literature usually has not. A taxonomy can be developed from these three dimensions of job stressors, as in Table 9.1. Chronic, subjectively measured, bad (negatively evaluated) stressors have been the theme of most job stress research until now and we do not know as much about the other types. Do the various forms of job stressors as categorized in the table result in similar employee reactions, or are there reactions that are specific to the type of stressor? The answer to this unknown presently.

Even more specific taxonomic development was suggested in Chapter 3 within two single chronic stressors, role ambiguity and role conflict. These two job stressors have been studied more often than any others in organizational psychology. They have too often been studied together, accompanied by identical hypotheses about their relationships with third variables. This is probably a mistake, however, and it is time to stop treating them alike. Furthermore, it is probably time to stop treating each of them as a unitary construct. When they were introduced to I/O psychology as stressors, role conflict was divided into several types (Kahn *et al.*, 1964). Except for one

Table 9.1 A taxonomy of stressors

Time limits	Nature of measurement	Evaluation of stressor
	Objective	Good
		Bad
Acute	Subjective	Good
		Bad
	Objective	Good
		Bad
Chronic		
	Subjective	Good
		Bad

very specific type, inter-role conflict among women, subsequent research has generally treated role conflict as a single undifferentiated variable. Future research is needed that will determine the potentially different effects of different types of role conflict – including what causes the different types, where or among whom they occur most frequently, and what their relative effects are.

Role ambiguity, by contrast, has not historically been differentiated into subtypes, theoretically or operationally. A taxonomy of the subtypes of role ambiguity was proposed in Chapter 3, based on the source of the ambiguous role messages: impersonal sources, organizational members as sources, and non-organizational members as sources. Furthermore, subtypes of two of these three were proposed. No research has been done on the potential differential nature of these types of role ambiguity and so there is much to be learned. Furthermore, other taxonomies of role ambiguity have not been proposed but might prove as insightful and useful.

Besides taxonomies categorizing stressors, it can be concluded from Chapter 8 that new taxonomies of social support would help to direct future research on occupational stress. It was suggested that social support research in the occupational stress domain should get away from the sole reliance on global measures (Cohen and Wills's term; 1985) of social support to identify more specific forms. More specificity, especially in terms of behavioral descriptions, might lead social support research out of its current state of confusion.

Questionnaire items from Fenlason (1989) were presented in Chapter 8 that were derived in conjunction with Beehr *et al.* (1990), and these focused on the content of what people talk about during potentially supportive episodes at work. These consisted of talking about the bad things about work, about the good things about work, and about non-work things. The typical categories of social support in work stress research concern two dimensions: the source of support (what person or people) and the nature of support (emotional versus instrumental or tangible). The measures of social support that have been used in previous job stress research have often been purported to be separate measures of these, although empirically they often do not separate well. Even though these distinctions are often followed in developing measures, the resulting indices are usually global in the sense that they require the respondents to make summary judgments about unspecified actions that represent emotional and instrumental support to them.

Social support has been defined so loosely in the literature that a wide variety of specific activities could be instances of social support. Taking the two basic forms of emotional and instrumental support, Table 9.2 offers examples of categories of behaviors that could be experienced as these types of support. Regarding emotional support, a supportive person could at a minimum take the time to listen to the stressed person. The common notion of a listening ear being soothing and calming suggests this would be emotionally supportive. This is familiar to many I/O psychologists from research topics other than job stress and therefore should not be all that foreign to researchers. Measures of leader behaviors, for example, often include items that ask about supervisors being willing to listen to the subordinate's problems.

Table 9.2 Taxonomy of specific forms of social support for stressed people

Structural forms of support	*Functional forms of support*	
	Emotional	*Instrumental*
Mere presence	Listening	Helping work
		Doing work for person
	Talking	Joining person to
Frequency of presence	Saying person is good	work together
	Saying person is right	Getting resources for
Duration of presence	Urging person to act	person
	Saying it is unfair	
	Saying it is not so bad	Helping escape
	Saying future will be better	Helping find new job
	Talking about non-job topics	Helping to be absent
	Touching	Informing
		How to work

People other than supervisors, of course, can also do this and it is likely to be an example of an emotionally supportive behavior.

In addition to listening to the stressed person, which might seem somewhat of a passive behavior, the supportive person can take a more active role by talking or touching the stressed person. If one talks to the stressed person, the contents of such communications may be important. It is possible, however, that talking could be supportive even though topics of conversation do not matter much. The phrase "being there" for someone has become common in our vocabulary; it could literally mean simply being there, saying anything (or nothing). This recalls the old "mere presence" idea from social facilitation theories of the past (Ferris *et al.*, 1978).

While mere presence might not be the best explanation for social facilitation phenomena, it could by itself be part of the social support. Aside from mere presence of potentially supportive others, frequency of contacts and duration of such contacts might be variables that are important elements of social support. Mere presence, frequency, and duration could all be studied for their supportive influence on stressed people. In addition, of course, the contents of the communications between stressed and supportive people need study. Listening is one form of communication and touching can include forms of non-verbal communication, but the major form of communication suggested in Table 9.2 as a form of emotional support is talking. The table lists some examples of things that can be said to a stressed person.

Some elements of the contents of conversations with stressed people have been addressed in Chapter 8, especially in reviewing the empirical studies by Beehr *et al.* (1990) and Fenlason (1989). Those communication contents were talking about good things about work, talking about bad things about work, and talking about non-work things. As can be seen from the examples in Table 9.2, however, there is more to such communications than these three categories.

The table also suggests that there are more specific forms of instrumental social support than have been measured in most past studies. Three categories are suggested in the table: helping to get the work done under stressful circumstances; helping to escape the stressful work situation; and providing information that might help the stressed person do the work or deal with the stressor. Again, the specific items in the table listed under these categories are only examples. Many other specific types of instrumental supportive behaviors are also possible and all of them are in need of research. These types of support have been largely unexplored in relation to occupational stress.

Taxonomic work can sometimes benefit research areas that seem to have hit dead ends, because it can indicate areas that still need work and areas that had not even been considered for research previously. Topic areas in need of research were noted throughout this book and further suggested research directions are apparent in this section.

Remembering the proactive person

In addition to organizing through taxonomic development for future research attacking job stress problems, one simple observation could encompass
many of the suggestions. This is the observation that people are proactive as
well as reactive. That is, they not only are done unto, but they also do things
themselves. Although it might not seem necessary to point this out in most
contexts, one could look through the occupational stress research literature
and conclude that people doing work are basically recipients of various
treatments. That is, they are experiencers who react to situations rather than
choosing, creating, or altering them. This includes job stressors and also
treatments such as social support. An exception might be the literature on
coping, which tends to assume that many people can alter their own situations.

The recognition of the proactive nature of people includes the observation that they have goals. It has been suggested that job stress research
should move its emphasis from roles to goals, that is, from its origin in role
theory to a more proactive view of humanity in which people are assumed
to have goals of their own (Beehr, 1987). If people are goal-oriented in their
lives in general and in work in particular, then job stress might be conceived
as situations that hinder progress toward important goals. The uncertainty
theory of job stress (Beehr and Bhagat, 1985a), discussed in a previous
chapter, takes this approach. Expectancy theory of motivation was used to
develop that job stress theory and expectancy theory is basically a proactive
theory of human behavior.

The well-known Person–Environment Fit theory of job stress (e.g. Caplan,
1987) also can be seen, in part, as taking the proactive person into account.
Part of the theory concerns the fit between the person's needs and the
organization's resources. The person's needs include conscious preferences
that appear to be similar to goals and therefore part of the P–E Fit theory of
occupational stress can accommodate the view of an employee as a proactive person.

Besides the uncertainty theory and the P–E Fit theory of job stress, there
may be other ways of incorporating the notion of proactive people into stress
research. There are certainly a great many psychological models, theories,
and research topics regarding human behavior that assume proactive people.
Industrial and organizational psychologists do not have far to search in order
to locate these. A prominent example is goal-setting theory, which proposes
that one of the best ways to explain people's job performance is to determine
their conscious goals (e.g. Locke, 1978; Locke *et al.*, 1981). The focus of or
criterion for goal-setting theory has usually been job performance and the
theory therefore has nothing to do with job stress as defined here – that is,
there are usually no strains involved as criteria in the goal-setting theory and
research. Some major principles derived from goal-setting research are that
people perform better when they have high goals than when they have low

goals, and that they perform better when their goals are specific than when they are more general. Furthermore, it is suggested that people perform better or at least are more likely to meet their goals when they accept the goals than when they do not, and perhaps that people are more likely to work hard toward goals that are set participatively than goals that are assigned – although research does not always support this (Locke *et al.*, 1981).

The proactive person assumption that people work toward goals could be used in occupational stress research and theory development by incorporating some of the goal-setting theory variables: goal difficulty, goal specificity, goal acceptance, and participation in goal-setting. Difficulty in reaching or failure to reach one's goals is likely to be frustrating and therefore is intuitively stressful. Some uncertainty in the uncertainty theory of job stress can be interpreted this way. Goal difficulty and goal specificity could logically be linked to the likelihood of goal attainment and therefore to the frustration potential of goals. Goal acceptance (which might be related to importance in uncertainty theory) could moderate the potential effects of the other goal variables on employee strains. In addition, participation in goal-setting seems to resemble autonomy in some key ways (e.g. degree of control over the work environment), which has often been proposed as a moderator of the stressor–strain relationship (e.g. Beehr, 1976). Therefore, goal-setting activities and variables could be active in the job stress process, but research investigating its relationship to stress is currently lacking.

Another potential job stress research approach based on proactive assumptions about people begins by assuming that people can create their own stressors. The theme here is not that people react differently to the same environmental stressors, nor is it only that people might differentially select themselves into stressful jobs. Instead some people are actually able to redesign their own jobs to an extent that they can introduce more stressors into them than would otherwise be there. People with a tendency toward hard work, for example, might overload themselves rather than the workplace forcing the excess work on them. Perhaps Type A people might do this more than others, for example. There are probably still other individual differences among people explaining who would create their own job stressors. People who tend not to get along well with others might create their own interpersonal conflict, which a previous chapter noted is a recently studied job stressor. The recognition that people are proactive suggests that the focal person as the source of their own job stressors needs to be studied in future research.

The potential research avenues opened by an explicit focus on the proactive nature of people are no doubt numerous, but another one that was mentioned previously in Chapter 8 is related to social support–occupational stress theory and research. Since the focal people are proactive, they are likely to be influential in obtaining social support. That is, some people seek it more than others, or the same person might seek social support more in some stressful situations than in others. It is frequently recommended by practitioners and in the popular press that social support networks should be joined, created, and maintained for use in situations that would be judged stressful. This is a potential way of helping oneself to cope with the stress. If people can actually do this, that is, if they can actually join, create, and maintain social support networks, that is another way of saying people are or can be proactive in obtaining social support. This support-seeking activity of proactive people could use more research. As indicated in Chapter 8 also, although not in these terms, support *givers* are also proactive. That is, they can choose to give or not to give social support, they can choose to give more of it or less of it, they can choose to give it to some people and not others, and they can choose to give it more in one form or another. *Giving* social support to stressed people in the workplace is the other side of the coin of social support and we have only limited understanding of it presently.

The process facet: filling in the blank

The process facet in the Beehr–Newman (1978) job stress model depicted in a previous chapter was not very thoroughly researched when it was first described and that remains true today. While most of the other facets in the model can be described theoretically and verified to some extent empirically, the process facet is still relatively blank by comparison. It seems most likely to consist of both psychological and physiological processes, but evidence regarding the nature of these processes in relation to the kinds of occupational stressors studied by organizational psychologists is scant.

Regarding the psychological processes, it seems likely that perceptual processes and decision making or response selection processes occur when people encounter such stressors. Since most organizational psychology studies have measured job stressors perceptually (i.e. via self-reports), they have essentially measured parts of the process facet. The problem is that these studies have generally not, in addition, measured job stressors more objectively. Therefore, there is usually no link shown between the objective job stressors in the environmental facet and the perceptions in the process facet. While the perceptions of the environment have often been measured in past research, the processes of decision making or response selection have not been. Research on the psychological processes needs to address what leads to the perceptions of a stressful environment, the nature of information used, and how this information is used to make decisions under stress.

Regarding the physiological processes, some fields interested in occupational stress have measured physiological responses that might be considered part of the process facet. As noted in Chapter 5, researchers in some fields have measured catecholamines (epinephrine and norepinephrine) in the blood or urine as measures of stress. By themselves, catecholamines would seem to be neither harmful nor healthful and therefore would not need to be considered strains (parts of the human consequences facet). They could be the intermediate process link between stressors and strains, but researchers studying stressors from the organizational psychology point of view have rarely obtained such measures.

Catecholamine levels are only one possible physiological process involved in occupational stress situations and episodes. It was noted in a previous chapter that Selye (1956; 1975) proposed that there were common, physiological first mediators in response to various stressors, although he never was able to identify them. If such responses could be identified, they also would be physiological elements of the process facet. Research still needs to be done on the intermediate physiological processes related to the types of organizational stressors of interest in this volume.

It's about time

Not enough research about time has been done in conjunction with occupational stress. There have been some attempts to integrate temporal factors into job stress models and theories, but there has been little or no explicit attempt to test these parts of the models in the empirical research.

Time has been proposed as having some influence on the job stress process (e.g Beehr and Newman, 1978; Beehr and Bhagat, 1985a; McGrath and Beehr, 1990), although the model was not very explicit regarding exactly what this effect is. Beehr and Newman recommended two things. First, in order to provide better evidence about causality in non-experimental field studies, longitudinal research designs were recommended in which stress-type measures would be repeated over some time period. Thus, the addition of time as an element in empirical studies was recommended. This is a common recommendation found in research discussions even today, but it still is rarely done.

A second way in which time needs to be employed in job stress research was made explicit by McGrath and Beehr (1990). Specifically, there is a temporal sequence from stressor to strain to coping that is inherent in most approaches to job stress. There is necessarily some delay or latency period between each of these causal job stress elements and the thing that causes them.

McGrath and Beehr label the stressors as SPECs (stress producing environmental circumstances or stress producing events and conditions). Every SPEC does not necessarily result in every strain immediately. Instead there is a delay. Furthermore, there is no reason to imagine that the latency period is equal for all possible pairs of SPECs and strains. Our research, however, rarely if ever allows for this. Most of the job stress research in organizational psychology uses non-experimental designs and most of it is cross-sectional rather than longitudinal. Many inferences from the data of these cross-sectional studies, because they collect all data at one point in time, assume equal latency periods across pairs of SPECs (stressors) and strains. For example, any implicit or explicit inference from the results of such studies that one stressor (say, role ambiguity) is more strongly related to one strain (say, anxiety) than to another (say, hypertension) is based on the assumption that both strains occur in response to role ambiguity with equal speed. There is little theoretical or empirical evidence to think that this is true, however.

Similar arguments can be made about the temporal link between any pairs of specific strains and coping activities (labeled adaptive responses in Figure 1.2). Some strains probably lead fairly quickly to the use of some coping activities or treatments, while others might be deemed more tolerable and take much longer for the focal person to enact efforts to treat the problem. Making comparisons and testing hypotheses about people's likely coping responses to job stress is fraught with potential problems due to the probable variable latency effects of the different coping responses.

Obviously, the latencies described here are currently unknown and therefore, the appropriate time period between measurements in non-experimental field studies is also unknown. One logical solution, however, consists of longitudinal designs measuring each element of the job stress process at several points in time. Furthermore, any results suggesting different latency periods for different pairs of job stress variables should be replicated by more studies.

> Given that most stress research has disregarded temporal factors, it is a wonder that researchers find any consistent relations between putative stressors and stress related outcomes, and not surprising that observed relations between stressors and stress related outcomes (both statistically viewed) are usually small.
>
> (McGrath and Beehr, 1990: 103)

This suggests the need for a great deal of future research. Further discussion of research problems related to time and its methodological implications is available from Kelly and McGrath (1988).

One final way in which time is important in occupational stress conceptualizations and research concerns the types of stressors referred to as acute and chronic. These labels refer to the length of the time period during which the stressor occurs. In job stress research, most studies have assumed and apparently measured chronic stressors (Beehr and Franz, 1987). Self-reported role ambiguity and role conflict items, for example, ask about the extent to which or the frequency with which some types of conflicting or ambiguous events or states occur. Although the items don't directly say that these have been occurring for a long period of time, this does seem to be a clear implication. The items seem to imply that these are the states of affairs generally on the job and respondents can easily infer that the items mean states that have been present continuously.

Acute stressors, on the other hand, are more likely to consist of events rather than states and the events themselves are time-limited in some way. One example would be that the tax deadline for tax accountants is a specific day and this appears to be stressful for them (as well as for the tax payer, of course; Friedman *et al.*, 1958). Another example that has been studied as a stressor is graduate nurses' first experience with providing comprehensive patient care (e.g. Eden, 1982). Obviously, something can happen for the first time only once and so this is an example of a one-shot, time-limited event. Not many of these shorter time, potentially stressful events have been studied as job stressors to date, but they seem likely to occur more frequently in the workplace than the amount of research on them would imply. The life stress research has been filled with such stressors and yet the job stress literature has almost ignored them.

It should be noted that some theories of job stress would not cover these short-term stressors very well without revision. The uncertainty theory (Beehr and Bhagat, 1985a), for example, proposes duration of stressor as a variable that would be positively related to occupational stress. It is not clear how the theory would account for short-term stressors that might have strong effects on strains and yet be of very short duration themselves.

Thus, time is probably an important variable in occupational stress processes, even though it rarely has been taken into account in empirical research. It can be important for at least three reasons: because longitudinal studies could be useful in getting better information about the likely causality in non-experimental field research, because there are likely to be currently unknown but widely differing latencies involved in cause–effect relationships, and because there may be both time-limited (acute) and stable (chronic) stressors.

"If you can measure it, that ain't it" (Kaplan, 1964: 206)

Kaplan's observation applies to few research areas any better than it does to occupational stress. Whole sets of measurement problems permeate this research topic. Furthermore, it seems that we are only gradually becoming aware of many of them.

Potential problems with self-report measures

One measurement issue that job stress research has in common with many other research areas in organizational psychology concerns the potential measurement problems with perceptual or self-report measures. One question is concerned with whether these measures, when they are intended as measures of the person's environment, are very accurate representations of that environment. This can be a philosophical issue, in part, because it is arguable whether anyone ever knows the environment objectively. If everybody but one person sees things the same way, that does not necessarily mean that person is wrong. This abstract issue about accuracy, however, is not the only important issue regarding perceptual measures and occupational stress research.

Any perceptual biases or even random measurement errors would not increase Type I errors of inference very much if they were not correlated with measures of other variables. In occupational stress research, however, both theoretical causes (e.g. job stressors) and their theoretical outcomes (e.g. individual strains) are often measured perceptually. As noted in a previous chapter, when one then seeks to determine whether these stressors and strains are related to each other, spuriously strong relationships due to correlated measurement error might result. Most organizational psychology researchers probably believe that this is a problem, but there is disagreement regarding the size of the problem. That is, there is disagreement about the degree to which such relationships are inflated in organizational psychology research in general (e.g. Spector, 1987b; Williams *et al.*, 1989), and this applies also to job stress research in particular. It could certainly bear further study.

As noted previously, a recent development in this issue is that one possible reason for the correlated method bias is negative affectivity, a stable individual difference or trait that would lead people to perceive everything more or less negatively (e.g. Brief *et al.*, 1988). While the potential problems with the research supporting this view were noted in an earlier chapter, the concept is not to be dismissed lightly and requires more research.

The most obvious and frequently recommended solution to the potential problems of perceptual measures is to make sure studies measure at least some of their important variables with non-self-report techniques. This use of multiple sources of data is likely to eliminate many of the concerns noted here.

One such other source of data requires obtaining physiological measures. If these are related with perceptual measures, correlated measurement bias is not likely to be as viable an alternative explanation for relationships discovered among variables. Unfortunately, there are many potential problems with physiological measures as well and many of these probably are not as readily recognized by the typical I/O psychologist (Fried *et al.*, 1984). In order to make modest improvements in job stress research using physiological measures, more careful, more timely, and more relevant measurement might be necessary. Some simple techniques could help improve upon past research, however, such as statistically controlling potential covariates of some of the physiological measures (even simple ones such as age and sex).

Aside from the potential measurement problems with physiological responses to job stress, research also needs to consider whether all of the relevant physical responses have been studied yet. There had been a pre-ponderance of emphasis in stress research on cardiovascular responses. Although these are important, the entire spectrum of physical strain respon-ses may not have been fleshed out yet. More research on other physical outcomes may be as important as additional information on the same outcome.

Also related to the potential response bias problems of self-report meas-ures, behavioral measures could be used more than they have been in past occupational stress research. Research could, for example, use behavioral measures of stressors (e.g. behaviors of others in the workplace that make it stressful), of strains (e.g. withdrawal from the organization, doctor visits, and changes in the way the focal person reacts to other people in the workplace), and of social support (e.g. what people talk about and how frequently they interact during potentially supportive episodes). As noted in previous chap-ters, some of this has been done in past research, but not nearly enough. There is a need for some creative research developing new behavioral measures of old stress constructs in order to assess and reduce the potential problems of self-report measures.

Measurement of job- and occupation-specific stressors

Aside from self-report measures, there are some potential problems with the widespread adherence to the use of generic measures of stressors. That is, we have generally tried to develop and use the same measures of stressors in all situations – role ambiguity and role conflict, for example. If one studies a given occupation or job intensively, differences between it and other jobs often become apparent, but no such differences usually seem to strongly affect our choice of stressor measures. Closer observation of specific jobs or occupations might lead to the study of stressors that we have not considered before because they are not common to all jobs. While there is merit to finding common stressors, much might also be missed by not attempting to discover stressors that are more specific to certain focal jobs or occupations.

What is "stress" anyway?

A final measurement issue noted in a previous chapter concerns the word "stress" and its meaning. Theorists and researchers in job stress have not used or defined the word consistently, which can lead to some confusion. To make the confusion worse, some recent job stress research is beginning to use the word "stress" or its cognates in self-report questionnaire items. It is crucial to determine what this word means in such questionnaires. It may be better simply not to use the word and avoid the ambiguity, but another approach to the problem is for future research to study the issue directly. This has been done recently (Jex *et al.*, 1992), but more such research could yield important information for interpreting past studies that have used such self-report items. While I/O psychologists act as if they think that they know what "satisfaction" means to people, they probably have not yet reached this stage of confidence with the word stress. It is time to obtain some more data on the issue.

THE CHALLENGE AHEAD

Occupational stress research has been a strong growth industry for the last fifteen years or so and it does not look as if the growth will slow down now. Research in growth areas sometimes seems to continue as if it has a life of its own and it is almost mandatory that research reports end in a call for more research. The key, however, as in most industrial/organizational psychology topics, is to have future research that is directed in effective ways. That is, research is needed that is not redundant with areas in which a great volume of studies have already been conducted. We need research answering questions that still remain after past efforts have cleared up some other issues and we need research explaining why some previous research results are contradictory. These types of studies would bring new and useful knowledge about the fascinating topic known as job stress.

There has been so much research now that it is time to step back and take a second look at what we, as job stress researchers, are doing. In order to make sense of the volumes of past research, it would be useful to organize it. Several of the chapters in this book offered ways of organizing at least parts of this research topic and this chapter urged other people interested in the topic to help future researchers and research consumers by organizing the past in at least two ways. First, theories can be borrowed or developed in order to make sense of the past research and this will also then help to indicate future research directions. When research has tested some parts of a theory and not others, obvious gaps appear that could be incorporated in future research on job stress. A second way to get organized for productive and informative future research is to develop taxonomies of job stress variables and processes. That will help to indicate how consistent results from past research studies have been with each other and it is another way of highlighting both inconsistencies that can be resolved by future research and gaps in current knowledge.

Job stress topics ripe for more research were noted throughout the previous chapters. Aside from organizing past research to direct future studies, four other themes appear to need rigorous examination. These are a focus on remembering that people are proactive, figuring out what the process facet of job stress is all about, the explicit incorporation of time as a research factor, and a variety of measurement issues and themes.

Inspection of most occupational stress research taking the organizational psychology approach reveals methods that seem to assume that people are simply passive recipients of life. That is, we seek to see how many or how serious were the job stressors that people were exposed to and what was done to these people. While we know that people can also control some of their own destinies and that they make choices determining what they are exposed to, this knowledge has not crept into job stress research very often – with the frequent exception of stress-coping research. Research designs and measurements that allow for people selecting and/or creating their own degree of stress would be useful now.

The contents of the process facet of the Beehr–Newman (1978) model of job stress was relatively unknown when the model was developed, and this is still true today. Of all the things that we call stress, even limited to the organizational psychology approach, what processes do they have in common? We have tended to take a black-box approach in which we are searching for environmental stressors entering the black box (the person) and for ill health and welfare exiting from the box. What happens between is a mystery. Research discovering any common psychological, behavioral, or physical (physiological or neurological) intervening processes common to all job stress situations would be groundbreaking. As noted in a previous chapter, we are currently stronger on theories than on sound research results identifying such processes.

The element of time is another factor needing more attention in job stress research. While it is common to call for more longitudinal research on occupational stress in order to justify stronger inference about causality, this is not the only important use of time that is in need of attention. There is likely to be latency between many of the causes and effects involved in occupational stress and such latencies are likely to vary among the many different pairs of causes and effects. Such cause and effect pairs would include stressors–strains, stressors–coping activities, and strains–coping activities, for example. These varying latencies or time periods can lead to quite inaccurate conclusions about the relative strength of potentially causal relationships among different pairs of variables (McGrath and Beehr, 1990). This is a research problem whose solution will require innovation and creativity – and almost certainly longitudinal research designs.

Finally, it was noted in previous chapters that a large set of research issues revolve around measurement. Measurement problems in organizational psychology job stress research seem truly to know no bounds. They include measurement of all types of stressors, of strains (including physiological measures), and of adaption or coping attempts. As noted previously, one particularly interesting but totally ignored issue is what the word stress itself means to the public. While we researchers can carefully define it in our studies so that we can communicate with each other, researchers often do not define it consistently with each other. Now that some occupational stress researchers are beginning to use the word in self-report measures, we must also wonder what the respondents think it means. The confusion about such a basic question seems remarkable, but this relatively new turn of the research now demands that we determine what respondents mean by it. It is ironic that researchers do not agree on its definition and yet we expect the general public to know what it is. This problem probably arises from the study of a topic and the use of a word that is so intuitively interesting and popular among the general populace. The study of popular topics apparently brings with it special problems.

Overall, occupational stress is a fascinating and important topic and the need for research that is meaningful and informative has not dissipated over the relatively short time of its life in organizational psychology. Its future should be as exciting as its past.

Appendices

APPENDIX A

The ten best effort-to-performance (E→P) uncertainty items (alpha=0.82). (Beehr, T. A. (1987). "The themes of social psychological stress in work organizations: from roles to goals." In A. W. Riley and S. J. Zaccaro (eds), *Occupational Stress and Organizational Effectiveness*. New York: Praeger Press, 71–102. Reprinted with permission.)

Items in order from best to tenth best

The amount of work I get done depends on how hard I work.

If I did not try as hard as I do, my job performance would suffer.

My job performance would not improve even if I worked more hours.

My job performance would not change regardless of how hard I work.

I could do better work if I worked more hours at my job.

The quality of my work is related to how hard I try.

If I were not corrected for my mistakes, my job performance would suffer.

People where I work could do better work if they tried.

I know what I am supposed to try to do at work.

If I loafed at work, my work would suffer.

Response categories:

(Ninth Item) Strongly disagree, disagree, slightly disagree, neither agree nor disagree, slightly agree, agree, strongly agree;

(Other items) Very unsure, unsure, a little unsure, neither sure nor unsure, a little sure, sure, very sure.

Questionnaire directions for "sureness" scale:

For the following questions please give two answers. First, circle T or F to indicate whether you think the statement is true or false. Then circle a number from 1 to 7 indicating how sure you were in answering true or false.

Example: I will graduate in four years. T F 1 2 3 4 5 6 7

Scoring: UC scoring involves only the number circled and not T or F.

APPENDIX B

The ten best performance-to-outcome (P→O) uncertainty items (alpha=0.84). (Beehr, T. A. (1987). "The themes of social psychological stress in work organizations: from roles to goals." In A. W. Riley and S. J. Zaccaro (eds), *Occupational Stress and Organizational Effectiveness*. New York: Praeger Press, 71–102. Reprinted with permission.)

Items in order from best to tenth best

People where I work would get more rewards if they performed their work better.

My co-workers will think highly of me if I do my job especially well.

Doing a good job will get me a promotion.

I will receive recognition when I perform well in my job.

If I did better work my pay would increase.

People where I work would lose out if they did poor work.

My job performance will result in a particular reward.

Pay increases have nothing to do with the quality of my work.

Doing a good job will get better pay for me.

The harder I work the more accomplishment I feel.

Response categories:

Very unsure, unsure, a little unsure, neither sure nor unsure, a little sure, sure, very sure.

Questionnaire directions for "sureness" scale:

For the following questions, please give two answers. First, circle T or F to indicate whether you think the statement is true or false. Then circle a number from 1 to 7 indicating how sure you were in answering true or false.

Example: I will graduate in four years. T F 1 2 3 4 5 6 7

Scoring: UC scoring involves only the number circled and not T or F.

APPENDIX C

Role ambiguity (Beehr, 1976).

I can predict what others will expect from me tomorrow.

I am clear what others expect of me on my job.

On my job, whatever situation arises, there are procedures for handling it.

I get enough facts and information to work my best.

(Response alternatives: very true, somewhat true, a little true, not at all true)

APPENDIX D

Work-family inter-role conflict items for role-based conflict (Beehr *et al.*, 1993).

My work and family lives seem to get in the way of each other.

Some members of my family want me to do things that might not be good work practices.

Sometimes at work I act just like I do with my family.

What I should do on my job and what my family wants of me are two different things.

My family expects me to do things at work that conflict with my own judgment.

The following two items were designated High Family Expectations.

My family has high expectations for me when I am doing my work.

My family is especially concerned that I do a good job at work.

(Response alternatives: strongly agree, agree, slightly agree, neither agree nor disagree, slightly disagree, disagree, strongly disagree)

APPENDIX E

Occupational abandonment or occupational turnover items (Beehr and King, 1986).

I am thinking about leaving mental health work altogether.

I do not want to remain in the mental health field.

If I had it to do all over again, I would not become a mental health professional.

I wish I had chosen another line of work.

(Response alternatives: strongly agree, agree, neither agree nor disagree, disagree, strongly disagree)

APPENDIX F

Contents of communication indices from Fenlason and Beehr (1994) for supervisor, co-worker, and extraorganizational social support.

People talk about a variety of subjects on and off the job. The following sets of questions ask you to rate *how often* you talk about these subjects with different people.

Please circle the number that best represents *how often* you talk about these subjects with *your boss or supervisor.*

Please circle the number that best describes *how often* you talk about particular subjects with *your co-workers.*

Now please circle the number that best represents *how often* you talk about these subjects with *your friends and family.*

We discuss things that are happening in our personal lives.

We talk about off-the-job interests we have in common.

We share personal information about our backgrounds and families.

We talk about off-the-job social events.

We talk about how we dislike some parts of our work.

We talk about the bad things about our work.

We talk about the problems in working with bosses.

We talk about how this organization is a lousy place to work.

We talk about the good things about our work.

We share interesting ideas about performing our jobs.

We talk about how this organization is a good place to work.

We talk about the rewarding things about being a secretary.

(Response alternatives: very often, fairly often, sometimes, occasionally, rarely)

References

Abdel-Halim, A. (1978). "Employee affective responses to organizational stress: moderating effects of job enrichment characteristics." *Personnel Psychology, 31,* 561–79.

Adelmann, P. K. (1987). "Occupational complexity, control, and personal income: their relation to psychological well-being in men and women." *Journal of Applied Psychology, 72,* 529–37.

Anderson, C. R. (1976). "Coping behaviors as intervening mechanisms in the inverted-U stress-performance relationship." *Journal of Applied Psychology, 61,* 30–4.

Argote, L. (1982). "Input uncertainty and organizational coordination in hospital emergency units". *Administrative Science Quarterly, 27,* 420–34.

Balick, L. R. and Herd, J. A. (1987). "Assessment of physiological indices related to cardiovascular disease as influnced by job stress." In J. M. Ivancevich and D. C. Ganster (eds), *Job Stress: From Theory to Suggestion.* New York: Haworth Press, 103–16.

Barling, J., Bluen, S. D. and Fain, R. (1987). "Psychological functioning following an acute disaster." *Journal of Applied Psychology, 72,* 683–90.

Baruch, G. K., Biener, L. and Barnett, R. C. (1987). "Women and gender in research on work and family stress." *American Psychologist, 42,* 130–6.

Bedeian, A. G., Mossholder, K. W. and Armenakis, A. A. (1983). "Role perception-outcome relationships: moderating effects of situational variables." *Human Relations, 36,* 167–84.

Beehr, T. A. (1976). "Perceived situational moderators of the relationship between subjective role ambiguity and role strain." *Journal of Applied Psychology, 61,* 35–40.

—— (1981a). "The Beehr–Newman model of occupational stress: applications to criminal justice research." Paper presented at the First National Conference on Burnout, Philadelphia.

—— (1981b). "Work-role stress and attitudes toward co-workers." *Group and Organization Studies, 6,* 201–10.

—— (1984). "Stress coping research: methodological issues." In A. S. Sethi and R. S. Schuler (eds), *Handbook of Organizational Stress Coping Strategies.* Cambridge, MA: Ballinger.

—— (1985a). "Organizational stress and employee effectiveness: a job characteristics approach." In T. A. Beehr and R. S. Bhagat (eds), *Human Stress and Cognition in Organizations: An Integrated Perspective.* New York: Wiley, 57–81.

—— (1985b). "The role of social support in coping with organizational stress." In T. A. Beehr and R. S. Bhagat (eds), *Human Stress and Cognition in Organizations.* New York: Wiley, 375–98.

—— (1986). "The process of retirement: a review and recommendations for future investigation." *Personnel Psychology, 39,* 31–55.

—— (1987). "The themes of social-psychological stress in work organizations: from roles to goals." In A. W. Riley and S. J. Zacarro (eds), *Occupational Stress and Organizational Effectiveness.* New York: Praeger Press, 71–102.

Beehr, T. A. and Bhagat, R. S. (1985a). *Human Stress and Cognition in Organizations.* New York: Wiley.

—— (1985b). "Introduction to human stress and cognition in organizations." In T. A. Beehr and R. S. Bhagat (eds), *Human Stress and Cognition in Organizations.* New York: Wiley, 3–19.

Beehr, T. A. and Drexler, J. A. Jr. (1986). "Social support, autonomy, and hierarchical level as moderators of the role characteristics-outcome relationship." *Journal of Occupational Behavior, 7,* 207–14.

Beehr, T. A., Faulkner, S. L., Drexler, J. A. Jr. and McMullin, K. (1993). Conflicts and advantages due to working in the family business." Paper presented at the annual meeting of the Society for Industrial and Organizational Psychology, San Francisco.

Beehr, T. A. and Franz, T. M. (1987). "The current debate about the meaning of job stress." In J. M. Ivancevich and D. C. Ganster (eds), *Job Stress: From Theory to Suggestion.* New York: Haworth Press, 5–18.

Beehr, T. A. and Gupta, N. (1978). "A note on the structure of employee withdrawal." *Organizational Behavior and Human Performance, 21,* 73–9.

Beehr, T. A., Jex, S. M. and Ghosh, P. (in preparation). "The management of occupational stress." In C. M. Johnson, W. K. Redmon and T. C. Mawhinney (eds), *Organizational Performance: Behavior Analysis and Management.* New York: Springer.

Beehr, T. A., Johnson, L. B. and Nieva, R. (1989). "Coping with occupational stress among police and their spouses." In T. A. Beehr (Chair), *Coping with Work-Related Stress.* Symposium at the meeting of the Society for Industrial and Organizational Psychology, Boston, April.

Beehr, T. A. and King, L. A. (1986). "Employee occupational withdrawal". In J. S. Kim and J. D. Ford (eds), *Proceedings of the 29th Annual Conference of the Midwest Academy of Management 1986* Columbus, OH: The Ohio State University 433–7.

Beehr, T. A., King, L. A. and King, D. A. (1986). "Theoretical and empirical development of the function of uncertain expectancies in occupational stress." In D. J. Abramis (Chair), *The Past, Present, and Future of Job Stress Research: New Thoughts about Old Concepts.* Symposium at the meeting of the Academy of Management, Chicago.

Beehr, T. A., King, L. A. and King, D. W. (1990). "Social support and occupational stress: Talking to supervisors." *Journal of Vocational Behavior, 36,* 61–81.

Beehr, T. A. and McGrath, J. E. (1992). "Social support, occupational stress, and anxiety." *Anxiety Research: An International Journal, 5,* 7–19.

Beehr, T. A. and McGrath, J. E. (in preparation). "The methodology of coping research: conceptual, strategic, and operational level issues." In M. Zeidner and N. S. Endler (eds), *Handbook of Coping: Theory, Research, and Applications.* New York: Wiley.

Beehr, T. A. and Newman, J. E. (1978). "Job stress, employee health, and organizational effectiveness: a facet analysis, model, and literature review." *Personnel Psychology, 31,* 665–99.

Beehr, T. A. and O'Driscoll, M. (1990). "Employee uncertainty as a factor in occupational stress." Paper presented at the annual meeting of the Midwest Psychological Association.

Beehr, T. A. and O'Hara, K. (1987). "Methodological designs for the evaluation of occupational stress interventions." In S. V. Kasl and C. L. Cooper (eds), *Stress and Health: Issues in Research Methodology.* Chichester: Wiley, 79–112.

Beehr, T. A. and Schuler, R. S. (1982). "Stress in organizations." In K. M. Rowland and G. R. Ferris (eds), *Personnel Management*. Boston: Allyn & Bacon, 390–419.

Beehr, T. A., Walsh, J. T. and Taber T. D. (1976). "Relationships of stress to individually and organizationally valued states: higher order needs as a moderator." *Journal of Applied Psychology, 61*, 35–40.

Beutell, N. J. and Greenhaus, J. H. (1983). "Integration of home and nonhome roles: women's conflict and coping behavior." *Journal of Applied Psychology, 68*, 43–8.

Bhagat, R. S. (1983). "Effects of stressful life events upon individual performance effectiveness and work adjustment processes within organizational settings: a research model." *Academy of Management Review, 8*, 660–71.

Bhagat, R. S., McQuaid, S. J., Lindholm, H. and Segovis, J. (1985). "Total life stress: a multimethod validation of the construct and its effects on organizationally valued outcomes and withdrawal behaviors." *Journal of Applied Psychology, 70*, 202–14.

Biddle, B. J. (1979). *Role Theory: Expectations, Identities, and Behaviors*. New York: Academic Press.

Blau, G. (1981). "An empirical investigation of job stress, social support, service length, and job strain." *Organizational Behavior and Human Decision Processes, 27*, 279–302.

Bobko, P. (1987). "Utility analysis: a primer and application to organizational stress interventions." In A. W. Riley and S. J. Zaccaro (eds), *Occupational Stress and Organizational Effectiveness*. New York: Praeger, 229–44.

Borucki, Z. (1987). "Perceived organizational stress, emotions, and negative consequences of stress: global self-esteem and sense of interpersonal competence as moderator variables." *Polish Psychological Bulletin, 18*, 139–48.

Brett, J. M. (1980). "The effect of job transfer on employees and their families." In C. L. Cooper and R. Payne (eds), *Current Concerns in Occupational Stress*. Chichester: Wiley, 99–136.

Brief, A. P., Burke, M. J., George, J. M., Robinson, B. S. and Webster, J. (1988). "Should negative affectivity remain an unmeasured variable in the study of job stress?" *Journal of Applied Psychology, 73*, 193–8.

Brief, A. P., Schuler, R. S. and Van Sell, M. (1981). *Managing Job Stress*. Boston: Little, Brown, & Co.

Broadbent, D. E. (1985). "The clinical impact of job design." *British Journal of Clinical Psychology, 24*, 33–44.

Bruning, N. S. and Frew, D. R. (1987). "Effects of exercise, relaxation, and management skills training on physiological stress indicators: a field experiment." *Journal of Applied Psychology, 72*, 515–21.

Buchanan, B. (1974). "Building organizational commitment: the socialization of managers in work organizations." *Administrative Science Quarterly, 19*, 533–46.

Burke, R. J. (1984). "Beliefs and fears underlying Type A behavior: what makes Sammy run — so fast and aggressively?" *Journal of Human Stress*, Winter, 174–82.

Burns, T. and Stalker, G. M. (1966). *The Management of Innovation*, second edn. London: Tavistock.

Caplan, R. D. (1987). "Person–Environment Fit in organizations: Theories, facts, and values." In A. W. Riley and S. J. Zaccaro (eds), *Occupational Stress and Organizational Effectiveness*. New York: Praeger Press, 103–40.

Caplan, R. D., Cobb, S., French, J. R. P. Jr., Harrison, R. V. and Pinneau, S. R. (1975). *Job Demands and Worker Health: Main Effects and Occupational Differences*. Washington DC: US Government Printing Office.

Caplan, R. D. and Jones, K. W. (1975). "Effects of workload, role ambiguity, and Type A personality on anxiety, depression, and heart rate." *Journal of Applied Psychology, 60*, 713–19.

Cascio, W. F. (1991). *Costing Human Resources: The Financial Impact of Behavior in Organizations*, third edn. Boston: Kent Publishing.

Chadwick-Jones, J. K., Brown, C A. and Nicholson, N. (1973). "A-type and B-type absence: empirical trends for women employees." *Occupational Pyschology, 47*, 75–80.

Chisholm, R. F., Kasl, S. V. and Mueller, L. (1986). "The effects of social suppport on nuclear worker responses to the Three Mile Island accident." *Journal of Occupational Behaviour, 7*, 179–93.

Choo, F. (1986). "Job stress, job performance, and auditor personality characteristics." *Auditing: A Journal of Practice and Theory, 5*, 17–34.

Cobb, S. (1976). "Social support as a moderator of life stress." *Psychosomatic Medicine, 38*, 300–14.

Cobb, S. and Kasl, S. V. (1972). "Some medical aspects of unemployment." In G. M. Shatto (ed.) *Employment of the Middle-Aged: Papers from Industrial Gerontology Seminars*. Springfield, IL: Thomas, 87–96.

Coburn, D. (1975). "Job-worker incongruence: consequences for health." *Journal of Health and Social Behavior, 16*, 198–212.

Cofer, C. N. and Appley, M. H. (1964). *Motivation: Theory and Research*. New York: Wiley.

Cohen, S. and Wills, T. A. (1985). "Stress, social support, and the buffering hypothesis." *Psychological Bulletin, 98*, 310–57.

Colarelli, S. M. and Beehr, T. A. (1993). "Selection out: firings, layoffs, and retirement." In N. Schmitt and W. C. Borman (eds), *Personnel Selection in Organizations*. San Francisco: Jossey-Bass, 341–84.

Colarelli, S. M., Dean, R. A. and Konstans, C. (1987). "Comparative effects of personal and situational influences on job outcomes of new professionals." *Journal of Applied Psychology, 72*, 558–66.

Cook, T. D. and Campbell, D. T. (1979). *Quasi-experimentation: Design & Analysis Issues for Field Settings*. Chicago: Rand McNally.

Cook, T. D., Campbell, D. T. and Peracchio, L. (1990). "Quasi-Experimentation." In M. D. Dunnette and L. M. Hough (eds), *Handbook of Industrial and Organizational Psychology Volume 1* (Second edn). Palo Alto, CA: Consulting Psychologists Press, 491–576.

Cooper, C. L. and Marshall, J. (1976). "Occupational sources of stress: a review of the literature relating to coronary heart disease and mental ill health." *Journal of Occupational Psychology, 49*, 11–28.

Cooper, C. L., Watts, J., Baglioni, A. J. and Kelly, M. (1988). "Occupational stress amongst general practice dentists." *Journal of Occupational Psychology, 61*, 163–74.

Corey, D. M. and Wolf, G. D. (1992) "An integrated approach to reducing stress injuries." In J. C. Quick, L. R. Murphy and J. J. Hurrell Jr (eds) *Stress and Well-being at Work: Assessments and Interventions for Occupational Mental Health*, Washington, DC: American Psychological Association, 64–78.

Crouter, A. C. (1984). "Spillover from family to work: the neglected side of the work–family interface." *Human Relations, 37*, 425–42.

Cunningham, J. B. (1989). "A compressed shift schedule: dealing with some of the problems of shiftwork." *Journal of Organizational Behavior, 10*, 231–45.

Cutrona, C. E. (1986). "Behavioral manifestations of social support: a microanalytic investigation." *Journal of Personality and Social Psychology, 51*, 201–8.

Dalton, D. R. and Mesch, D. J. (1991). "On the extent and reduction of avoidable absenteeism: an assessment of absence policy provisions." *Journal of Applied Psychology, 76*, 810–17.

Dalton, D. R., Todor, W. D. and Krackhardt, D. M. (1982). "Turnover overstated: a functional taxonomy." *Academy of Management Review, 7,* 117–23.

Danco, L. (1980). *Inside the Family Business.* Center for Family Business: Cleveland.

Dewe, P. J. and Guest, D. E. (1990). "Methods of coping with stress at work: a conceptual analysis and empirical study of measurement issues." *Journal of Organizational Behavior, 11,* 135–50.

Dougherty, T. W. and Pritchard, R. D. (1985). "The measurement of role variables: exploratory examination of a new approach." *Organizational Behavior and Human Decision Processes, 35,* 141–55.

Dubin, R. (1956). "Industrial workers' worlds: a study of the central life interests of industrial workers." *Social Problems, 3,* 131–42.

Dubin, R. and Champoux, J. E. (1975). "Workers' central life interest and personality characteristics." *Journal of Vocational Behavior, 6,* 165–74.

Dunham, R. B. (1977). "Shiftwork: a review and theoretical analysis." *Academy of Management Review, 2,* 626–34.

Dunham, R. B., Pierce, J. L. and Castaneda, M. B. (1987). "Alternative work schedules: two field quasi-experiments." *Academy of Management Journal, 40,* 215–42.

Dunseath, J. L. and Beehr, T. A. (1991). "The job stress-social support buffering hypothesis, employee gender, and collar color." Paper presented at the annual meeting of the Midwestern Psychological Association, Chicago.

Eden, D. (1982). "Critical job events, acute stress, and strain: a multiple interrupted time series." *Organizational Behavior and Human Performance, 30,* 312–29.

Etzion, D. (1984). "Moderating effect of social support on the stress-burnout relationship." *Journal of Applied Psychology, 69,* 615–22.

Feldman, D. C. (1976). "A contingency theory of socialization." *Administrative Science Quarterly, 21,* 433–54.

Fenlason, K. J. (1989). "The effects of contents of supportive communication on work stress: a replication and extension." Paper presented at the meeting of the Midwestern Psychological Association, Chicago.

Fenlason, K. J. and Beehr, T. A. (1994). "Social support and occupational stress: effects of talking to others." *Journal of Organizational Behavior, 15,* 157–75.

Ferris, G. R., Beehr, T. A. and Gilmore, D. C. (1978). "Social facilitation: a review and alternative conceptual model." *Academy of Management Review, 3,* 338–47.

Fisher, C. D. and Gitelson, R. (1983). "A meta-analysis of the correlates of role conflict and ambiguity." *Journal of Applied Psychology, 68,* 320–33.

Fleming, I. and Baum, A. (1987). "Stress: psychobiological assessment." In J. M. Ivancevich and D. C. Ganster (eds), *Job Stress: From Theory to Suggestion.* New York: Haworth Press.

Folkman, S. (1982). "An approach to the measurement of coping." *Journal of Occupational Behavior, 3,* 95–108.

Folkman, S. and Lazarus, R. S. (1980). "An analysis of coping in a middle-aged community sample." *Journal of Health and Social Behavior, 21,* 219–39.

Frankenhaeuser, M. and Gardell, B. (1976). "Underload and overload in working life: outline of a multidisciplinary approach." *Journal of Human Stress, 2,* 35–46.

French, J. R. P. Jr and Caplan, R. D. (1973). "Organizational stress and individual strain." In A. J. Marrow (ed.), *The Failure of Success.* New York: AMACOM.

French, J. R. P. Jr and Kahn, R. L. (1962). "A programmatic approach to studying the industrial environment and mental health". *Journal of Social Issues, 18* (3), 1–47.

French, J. R. P. Jr, Rogers, W. and Cobb, S. (1974). "A model of Person–Environment Fit." In G. V. Coelho, D. A. Hamburgh and J. E. Adams (eds), *Coping and Adaptation.* New York: Basic Books.

Frese, M. (1985). "Stress at work and psychosomatic complaints: A causal interpretation." *Journal of Applied Psychology*, *70*, 314–28.

Frese M. and Okonek. K. (1984). "Night and shiftwork, psychological and psychosomatic complaints: differentations in the group of former shiftworkers." *Journal of Applied Psychology*, *70*, 314–28.

Fried, Y., Rowland, K. M. and Ferris, G. R. (1984). "The physiological measurement of work stress: a critique." *Personnel Psychology*, *37*, 583–615.

Friedman, M. and Rosenman, R. H. (1974). *Type A Behavior and Your Heart*. New York: Knopf.

Friedman, M., Rosenman, R. H. and Carroll V. (1958). "Changes in serum cholesterol and blood clotting time in men subjected to cyclic variation of occupational stress." *Circulation*, *17*, 852–61.

Gaines, J. and Jermier, J. M. (1983). "Emotional exhaustion in a high stress organization." *Academy of Management Journal*, *26*, 567–86.

Galbraith, J. (1977). *Organization Design*. Reading, MA: Addison-Wesley.

Ganster, D. C. (1987). "Type A behavior and occupational stress." In J. M. Ivancevich and D. C. Ganster (eds), *Job Stress: From Theory to Suggestion*. New York: Haworth Press, 61–84.

Ganster, D. C., Fusilier, M. R. and Mayes, B. T. (1986). "Role of social support in the experience of stress at work." *Journal of Applied Psychology*, *71*, 102–10.

Ganster, D. C., Mayes, B. T., Sime, W. E. and Tharp, G. D. (1982). "Managing organizational stress: a field experiment." *Journal of Applied Psychology*, *67*, 533–42.

Glowinkowski, S. P. and Cooper, C. L. (1987). "Managers and professionals in business/industrial settings: the research evidence." In J. M. Ivancevich and D. C. Ganster (eds), *Job Stress: From Theory to Suggestion*. New York: Haworth Press, 177–193.

Gore, S. (1987). "Perspectives on social support and research on stress moderating processes." In J. M. Ivancevich and D. C. Ganster (eds), *Job Stress: From Theory to Suggestion*. New York: Haworth Press, 85–101.

Greenhaus, J. H. and Beutell, N. J. (1985). "Sources of conflict between work and family roles." *Academy of Management Review*, *10*, 76–88.

Greenhaus, J. H. and Parasuraman, S. (1987). "A work–non-work interactive perspective of stress and its consequences." In J. M. Ivancevich and D. C. Ganster (eds), *Job Stress: From Theory to Suggestion*. New York: Haworth Press, 37–60.

Greller, M. M. and Herold, D. M. (1975) "Sources of feedback: a preliminary investigation. *Organizational Behavior and Human Performance*, *13*, 244–56.

Gupta, N. and Beehr, T. A. (1979). "Job stress and employee behaviors." *Organizational Behavior and Human Performance*, *23*, 373–87.

Gupta, N. and Beehr, T. A. (1981). "Relationships among employees' work and non-work responses." *Journal of Occupational Behaviour*, *2*, 203–9.

Gupta, N. and Jenkins, D. G. (1985). "Dual-career couples: stress, stressors, strains, and strategies." In T. A. Beehr and R. S. Bhagat (eds), *Human Stress and Cognition in Organizations*. New York: Wiley, 141–76.

Hackman, J. R. and Oldham, G. R. (1975). "Development of the Job Diagnostic survey." *Journal of Applied Psychology*, *60*, 159–70.

Hackman, J. R. and Oldham, G. R. (1976). "Motivation through the design of work: test of a theory." *Organizational Behaviors and Human Performance*, *16*, 250–79.

Hackman, J. R. and Oldham, G. R. (1980). *Work Redesign*. Reading, MA: Addison-Wesley.

Hall, D. T. (1972). "A model of coping with role conflict: the role behavior of college-educated women." *Administrative Science Quarterly*, *17*, 471–89.

Hanser, L. M. and Muchinsky, P. M. (1978). "Work as an information environment." *Organizational Behavior and Human Performance*, *21*, 47–60.

Harrison, R. V. (1985). "The Person–Environment Fit model and the study of job stress." In T. A. Beehr and R. S. Bhagat (eds), *Human Stress and Cognition in Organizations*. New York: Wiley, 23–55.

Henderson, M. and Argyle, M. (1985). "Social support by four categories of work colleagues: relationships between activities, stress and satisfaction." *Journal of Occupational Behaviour, 6,* 229–39.

Hendrix, W. H. (1987). "SCN 81–115 stress assessment package (version 2)." Unpublished survey.

Hendrix, W. H., Ovalle, N. K. Jr. and Troxler, R. G. (1985). "Behavioral and physiological consequences of stress and its antecedent factors." *Journal of Applied Psychology, 70,* 188–201.

Herman, J. B. (1977). "Working men and women: inter- and intra-role conflict. *Psychology of Women Quarterly, 1,* 319–33.

Herzberg, F., Mausner, B. and Snyderman, B. (1959). *The Motivation to Work.* New York: Wiley.

Hicks, W. D. and Klimoski, R. J. (1981). "The impact of flexitime on employee attitudes." *Academy of Management Journal, 24,* 333–41.

Holmes, T. H. and Rahe, R. H. (1967). "The social readjustment rating scale." *Journal of Psychosomatic Medicine, 11,* 213–18.

House, J. S. (1974). "Occupational stress and coronary heart disease: a review and theoretical integration." *Journal of Health and Social Behavior, 15,* 12–27.

—— (1981). *Work Stress and Social Support.* Reading, MA: Addison-Wesley.

House, J. S., McMichael, A. J., Wells, J. A., Kaplan, B. H. and Landerman, L. R. (1979). "Occupational stress and health among factory workers." *Journal of Health and Social Behavior, 20,* 139–60.

House, J. S. and Wells, J. A (1978). "Occupational stress, social support and health." In A. McLean, G. Black and M. Colligan (eds), *Reducing Occupational Stress: Proceedings of a Conference* (HEW Publication No. 78–140). Washington DC: US Government Printing Office, 8–19.

House, R. J. and Rizzo, J. R. (1972). "Role conflict and ambiguity as critical variables in a model of organizational behavior." *Organizational Behavior and Human Performance, 7,* 467–505.

Howard, J. H., Cunningham, D. A. and Rechnitzer, P. A. (1986). "Role ambiguity, Type A Behavior, and job satisfaction: moderating effects on cardiovascular and bio-chemical responses associated with coronary risk." *Journal of Applied Psychology, 71,* 95–101.

Hulin, C. L., Roznowski, M. and Hachiya, D. (1985). "Alternative opportunities and withdrawal decisions: empirical and theoretical discrepancies and integration." *Psychological Bulletin, 97,* 233–50.

Hurrell, J. J. Jr and Colligan, M. J. (1987). "Machine pacing and shiftwork: evidence for job stress." In J. M. Ivancevich and D. C. Ganster (eds), *Job Stress: From Theory to Suggestion.* New York: Haworth Press, 159–75.

Ilgen, D. R. (1990). "Health issues at work: opportunities for industrial/ organizational psychology." *American Psychologist, 45,* 273–83.

Ironson, G. (1992). "Work, job stress, and health." In S. Zedeck (ed.), *Work, Families, and Organizations.* San Francisco: Jossey-Bass, 33–69.

Ivancevich, J. M. (1974). "Effects of the shorter workweek on selected satisfaction and performance measures." *Journal of Applied Psychology, 59,* 717–21.

—— (1979). "An analysis of participation in decision-making among project engineers." *Academy of Management Journal, 22,* 253–69.

Ivancevich, J. M. and Matteson, M. T. (1980). *Stress and Work: A Managerial Perspective.* Glenview, IL.: Scott, Foresman.

Ivancevich J. M. and Matteson, M. T. (1987). "Organizational level stress management interventions: a review and recommendations." In J. M. Ivancevich and D. C. Ganster (eds), *Job Stress: From Theory to Suggestion*. New York: Haworth Press.

Ivancevich, J. M., Matteson, M. T., Freedman, S. M. and Phillips, J. T. (1990). "Worksite stress management interventions." *American Psychologist*, 45, 252–61.

Jackson, S. E. (1983). "Participation in decision making as a strategy for reducing job-related strain." *Journal of Applied Psychology*, 68, 3–19.

—— (1984). "Correction to 'Participation in decision making as a strategy for reducing job-related strain.'" *Journal of Applied Psychology*, 69, 546–7.

Jackson, S. E. and Schuler, R. S. (1985). "A meta-analysis and conceptual critique of research on role ambiguity and role conflict in work settings." *Organizational Behavior and Human Decision Processes*, 36, 16–78.

Jackson, S. E., Schwab, R. L. and Schuler, R. S. (1986). "Toward an understanding of the burnout phenomenon." *Journal of Applied Psychology*, 71, 630–40.

Jamal, M. (1984). "Job stress and job performance, controversy: an empirical assessment." *Organizational Behavior and Human Performance*, 33, 1–21.

Jenkins, G. D. Jr, Nadler, D. A., Lawler, E. E. III and Cammann, C. (1975). "Standardized observations: an approach to measuring the nature of jobs." *Journal of Applied Psychology*, 60, 171–81.

Jex, S. M. and Beehr, T. A. (1991). "Emerging theoretical and methodological issues in the study of work-related stress." In G. R. Ferris and K. M. Rowland (eds), *Research in Personnel and Human Resources Management Volume 9* Greenwich, CT: JAI Press, 311–64.

Jex, S. M., Beehr, T. A. and Roberts, C. K. (1992). "The meaning of occupational 'stress' items to survey respondents." *Journal of Applied Psychology*, 77, 623–8.

Jick, T. D. (1985). "As the ax falls: budget cuts and the experience of stress in organizations." In T. A. Beehr and R. S. Bhagat (eds), *Human Stress and Cognition in Organizations*. New York: Wiley, 83–114.

Jones, J. W., Barge, B. N., Steffy, B. D., Fay, L. M., Kunz, L. K. and Wuebker, L. J. (1988). "Stress and medical malpractice: organizational risk assessment and intervention." *Journal of Applied Psychology*, 73, 727–35.

Kabanoff, B. (1980). "Work and non-work: a review of models, methods and findings." *Psychological Bulletin*, 88, 60–77.

Kahn, R. L. and Byosiere, P. (1992). "Stress in organizations." In M. D. Dunnette and L. M. Hough (eds), *Handbook of Industrial and Organizational Psychology*, Second edn. Palo Alto, CA: Consulting Psychologists Press, 571–650.

Kahn, R. L. and Quinn, R. P. (1970). Role stress: A framework for analysis." In A. McLean (ed.), *Occupational Mental Health*. New York: Rand-McNally.

Kahn, R. L., Wolfe, D. M., Quinn, R. P., Snoek, J. D. and Rosenthal, R. A. (1964). *Organizational Stress: Studies in Role Conflict and Ambiguity*. New York: Wiley.

Kane, J. S. and Lawler, E. E. III (1978). "Methods of peer assessment." *Psychological Bulletin*, 85, 555–86.

Kaplan, A. (1964). *The Conduct of Inquiry*. San Francisco: Chandler.

Karasek, R. A. (1979). Job demands, job decision latitude, and mental strain: implications of job redesign. *Administrative Science Quarterly*, 24, 285–308.

Karasek, R., Baker, D., Maryer, F., Ahlbom, A. and Theorell, T. (1981). "Job decision latitude, job demands, and cardiovascular disease: a prospective study of Swedish men." *American Journal of Public Health*, 71, 694–705.

Kasl, S. V. (1980). "The impact of retirement." In C. L. Cooper and R. Payne (eds), *Current Concerns in Occupational Stress*. Chichester: Wiley, 137–86.

—— (1987). "Methodologies in stress and health: past difficulties, present dilemmas, future directions." In S. V. Kasl and C. L. Cooper (eds), *Stress and Health: Issues in Research Methodology*. Chichester: Wiley, 307–18.

Kasl, S. V. and Cobb, S. (1970). "Blood pressure changes in men undergoing job loss: a preliminary report." *Psychosomatic Medicine*, *32*, 19–38.

Katz, D. and Kahn, R. L. (1978). *The Social Psychology of Organizations*, second edn. New York: Wiley.

Kaufmann, G. M. and Beehr, T. A. (1986). "Interactions between job stressors and social support: some counterintuitive results." *Journal of Applied Psychology*, *71*, 522–6.

Kaufmann, G. M. and Beehr, T. A. (1989). "Occupational stressors, individual strains, and social supports among police officers." *Human Relations*, *42*, 185–97.

Keita, P. and Jones, J. M. (1990). "Reducing adverse reaction to stress in the workplace: psychology's expanding role." *American Psychologist*, *45*, 1137–41.

Kelly, J. R. and McGrath, J. E. (1988). *On Time and Method*. Newbury Park, CA: Sage.

Kessler, R. C., Price, R. H. and Wortman, C. B. (1985). "Social factors in psychopathology: stress, social support, and coping processes." In M. R. Rosenzweig and L. W. Porter (eds), *Annual review of psychology*, Vol. 36. Palo Alto, CA: Annual Reviews, 531–72.

King, L. A. and King, D. W. (1990). "Role conflict and role ambiguity: a critical assessment of construct validity." *Psychological Bulletin*, *107*, 48–64.

Kuhlmann, T. M. (1990). "Coping with occupational stress among urban bus and tram drivers." *Journal of Occupational Psychology*, *63*, 89–96.

Lane, I. M., Mathews, R. C. and Presholdt, P. H. (1988). "Determinants of nurses' intentions to leave their profession." *Journal of Organizational Behaviour*, *9*, 367–72.

La Rocco, J. M. and Jones, A. P. (1978). "Co-worker and leader support as moderators of stress–strain relationships in work situations." *Journal of Applied Psychology*, *63*, 629–34.

La Rocco, J. M., House, J. S. and French, J. R. P. Jr. (1980). "Social support, occupational stress, and health." *Journal of Health and Social Behavior*, *21*, 202–18.

Latack, J. C. (1986). Coping with job stress: measures and future directions for scale development." *Journal of Applied Psychology*, *71*, 377–85.

Latack, J. C. and Foster, L. W. (1985). "Implementation of compressed work schedules: participation and job redesign as critical factors for employee acceptance." *Personnel Psychology*, *38*, 75–92.

Lawler, E. E. III (1973). *Motivation in Work Organizations*. Monterey, Ca.: Brooks/Cole.

Lawler, E. E. III and Suttle, J. L. (1973). "Expectancy theory and job behavior." *Organizational Behavior and Human Performance*, *9*, 482–503.

Lawrence, P. R. and Lorsch, J. W. (1967). "Differentiation and integration in complex organizations." *Administrative Science Quarterly*, *12*, 1–47.

Lazarus, R. S. (1966). *Psychological Stress and the Coping Process*. New York: McGraw-Hill.

Lazarus, R. S. and Folkman, S. (1984) *Stress, Coping and Adaptation*. New York: Springer.

Lazarus, R. S. and Launier, R. (1978). "Stress related transactions between person and environment." In L. A. Pervin and M. Lewis (eds), *Internal and External Determinants of Behavior*. New York: Plenum.

Levine, S. and Scotch, N. A. (eds) (1970). *Social Stress*. Chicago: Aldine.

Lin, N., Ensel, W. M., Simeone, R. S. and Kuo, W. (1979). "Social support, stressful life events, and illness: a model and an empirical test." *Journal of Health and Social Behavior*, *20*, 108–19.

Locke, E. A. (1978). "The ubiquity of the technique of goal-setting in theories of and approaches to employee motivation." *Academy of Management Review, 3*, 594–601.

Locke, E. A., Shaw, K. N., Saari, L. M. and Latham, G. P. (1981). "Goal setting and task performance: 1969–1980." *Psychological Bulletin, 90*, 125–52.

Love, K. G. and Beehr, T. A. (1981). "Social stressors on the job: recommendations for a broadened perspective." *Group and Organization Studies, 6*, 190–200.

Lyons, T. F. (1971). "Role clarity, need for clarity, satisfaction, tension, and withdrawal." *Organizational Behavior and Human Performance, 6*, 99–110.

Mackay, C. J., Cox, T., Watts, C., Thirlaway, M. and Lazzarini, A. J. (1979). "Psychological correlates of repetitive work." In C. Mackay and T. Cox (eds), *Response to Stress*. Guilford: IPC Science and Technology Press.

Marcelissen, F. H. G., Winnubst, J. A. M., Buunk, B. and de Wolff, C. J. (1988). "Social support and occupational stress: a causal analysis." *Social Science and Medicine, 26*, 365–73.

Martocchio, J. J. and O'Leary, A. M. (1989). "Sex differences in occupational stress: a meta-analytic review." *Journal of Applied Psychology, 74*, 495–501.

Martin, R. and Wall, T. D. (1989). "Attentional demand and cost responsibility as stressors in shopfloor jobs." *Academy of Management Journal, 32*, 69–86.

Maslach, C. (1982). "Understanding burnout: definitional issues in analyzing a complex phenomenon." In W. S. Paine (ed.), *Job Stress and Burnout: Research, Theory, and Intervention Perspectives*. Beverly Hills: Sage Focus Editions, 29–40.

Maslach, C. and Jackson, S. E. (1981). *The Maslach Burnout Inventory*. Palo Alto, CA: Consulting Psychologists Press.

Mason, J. W. (1975). "A historical view of the stress field. Part I." *Journal of Human Stress, 1*, 6–12.

Mattimore, L. K. (1990). "Family support inventory: a measure of perceived family social support for workers". Unpublished Masters thesis, Central Michigan University.

Mayes, B. T. and Ganster, D. C. (1988). "Exit and voice: a test of hypotheses based on fight/flight responses to job stress." *Journal of Organizational Behavior, 9*, 199–216.

McGee, G. W., Ferguson, C. E. Jr. and Seers, A. (1989). "Role conflict and ambiguity: do the scales measure these two constructs?" *Journal of Applied Psychology, 74*, 815–18.

McGrath, J. E. (1970). "Introduction." In J. E. McGrath (ed.), *Social and Psychological Factors in Stress*. New York: Holt, Rinehart & Winston, 1–9.

—— (1976). "Stress and behavior in organizations." In M. Dunnette (ed.), *Handbook of Industrial and Organizational Psychology*. Chicago: Rand McNally, 1351–96.

McGrath J. E. and Beehr, T. A. (1990). "Some temporal issues in the conceptualization and measurement of stress." *Stress Medicine, 6*, 93–104.

McGrath, J. E. and Kelly, J. R. (1986). *Time and Human Interaction: Toward a Social Psychology of Time*. New York: Guilford Press.

Meichenbaum, D. H. (1975). "A self instructional approach to stress management." In C. D. Spielberger and J. H. Sarason (eds), *Stress and Anxiety*, Vol. 1. New York: Halstead Press, 237–63.

Meissner, M. (1971). "The long arm of the job: a study of work and leisure". *Industrial Relations, 10*, 239–60.

Mettlin, C. and Woelfel, J. (1974). "Interpersonal influence and symptoms of stress." *Journal of Health and Social Behavior, 15*, 311–19.

Mobley, W. H., Horner, S. O. and Hollingsworth, A. T. (1978). "An evaluation of precursors of hospital employee turnover." *Journal of Applied Psychology, 63*, 408–14.

Motowidlow, S. J., Packard, J. S. and Manning, M. R. (1986). "Occupational stress: its causes and consequences for job performance." *Journal of Applied Psychology,* *71,* 618–29.

Muchinsky, P. M. (1977). "Employee absenteeism: a review of the literature." *Journal of Vocational Behavior, 10,* 316–40.

Murphy, L. R. (1983). "A comparison of relaxation methods for reducing stress in nursing personnel." *Human Factors, 25,* 431–40.

—— (1984). "Stress management in highway maintenance workers." *Journal of Occupational Medicine, 26,* 436–42.

—— (1987). "A review of organizational stress management research: methodological considerations." In J. M. Ivancevich and D. C. Ganster (eds), *Job Stress: From Theory to Suggestion.* New York: Haworth Press, 215–27.

Murphy, L. R. and Hurrell, J. J. Jr. (1987). "Stress management in the process of occupational stress reduction." *Journal of Managerial Psychology, 2,* 18–23.

Murphy, L. R. and Sorenson, S. (1988). "Employee behaviors before and after stress management." *Journal of Organizational Behavior, 9,* 173–82.

Neel, R. G. (1955). "Nervous stress in the industrial situation." *Personnel Psychology, 8,* 405–16.

Newman, J. E. and Beehr, T. A. (1979). "Personal and organizational strategies for handling job stress: a review of research and opinion." *Personnel Psychology, 32,* 1–43.

O'Driscoll, M. and Beehr, T. A. (1989). "Stress among general staff." Unpublished manuscript.

Orpen, C. (1981). "Effect of flexible working hours on employee satisfaction and performance; a field experiment." *Journal of Applied Psychology, 66,* 113–15.

Osipow, S. H. and Davis, A. S. (1988). "The relationship of coping resources to occupational stress and strain." *Journal of Vocational Behavior, 32,* 1–15.

Osipow, S. H. and Spokane, A. R. (1984). "Measuring occupational stress, strain, and coping." *Applied Social Psychology Annual, 5,* 67–86.

Palmore, E. B. (1971). "The relative importance of social factors in predicting longevity." In E. B. Palmore and F. C. Jeffers (eds), *Prediction of Life Span.* Lexington, MA: Health Lexington Books, 237–47.

Pardine, P. A. Jr. (1987). "Empirical test of a cognitive model of work stress. Paper presented at the annual meeting of the Eastern Psychological Association.

Payne, R. (1980). "Occupational stress: is it really a problem?" In T. Jick (Chair), *The Stress of Stress Researchers — Ambiguities in the Research Process.* Symposium at the meeting of the Eastern Academy of Management, Buffalo, NY.

Payne, R. and Fletcher, B. C. (1983). "Job demands, supports and constraints among schoolteachers." *Journal of Vocational Behavior, 22,* 136–47.

Payne, R. and Pugh, D. S. (1976). "Organizational structure and climate." In M. D. Dunnette (ed.), *Handbook of Industrial and Organizational Psychology.* Chicago: Rand-McNally, 1125–73.

Pearce, J. L. (1981). "Bringing some clarity to role ambiguity research." *Academy of Management Review, 6,* 665–74.

Peterson, M. F. (1985) "Attitudinal differences among work shifts: what do they reflect?" *Academy of Management Journal, 28,* 723–32.

Potter, E. H. III and Fiedler, F. E. (1981). "The utilization of staff member intelligence and experience under high and low stress." *Academy of Management Journal, 24,* 361–76.

Quick, J. D., Horn, R. S. and Quick, J. C. (1987). "Health consequences of stress." In J. M. Ivancevich and D. C. Ganster (eds), *Job Stress: From Theory to Suggestion.* New York: Haworth Press, 19–36.

Quinn, R. P. and Shepard, L. J. (1974). *The 1972–1973 Quality Employment Survey:*

Descriptive Statistics with Comparison Data from the 1969–1970 Survey of Working Conditions. Ann Arbor, MI: The Institute for Social Research.

Rapoport, R. and Rapoport, R. N. (1971). *Dual-Career Families.* Harmondsworth: Penguin.

Raynor, J. O. and McFarlin, D. B. (1986). "Motivation and the self-system." In R. M. Sorrentino and E. T. Higgins (eds), *Handbook of Motivation and Cognition: Foundations of Social Behavior.* New York: Guilford Press, 315–49.

Rizzo, J. R., House, R. J. and Lirtzman, S. I. (1970). "Role conflict and ambiguity in complex organizations." *Administrative Science Quarterly, 15,* 150–63.

Russel, D. W., Altmaier, E. and Van Velzen, D. (1987). "Job-related stress, social support, and burnout among classroom teachers." *Journal of Applied Psychology, 72,* 269–74.

Salancik, G. R. and Pfeffer, J. (1978). "A social information processing approach to job attitudes and task design." *Administrative Science Quarterly, 23,* 224–53.

Sales, S. M. (1970). "Some effects of role overload and role underload." *Organizational Behavior and Human Performance, 5,* 592–608.

Sarason, I. G., Johnson, J. H. and Siegel, J. M. (1978). "Assessing the impact of life changes: development of the Life Experiences Survey." *Journal of Consulting and Clinical Psychology, 46,* 932–46.

Sarbin, R. R. and Allen, V. L. (1969). "Role theory." In G. Lindsey and E. Aronson (eds), *The Handbook of Social Psychology,* Vol. 1, second edn. Reading, MA: Addison-Wesley, 488–568.

Schaubroeck, J., Cotton, J. C. and Jennings, K. R. (1989). "Antecedents and consequences of role stress: a covariance structure analysis." *Journal of Organizational Behavior, 10,* 35–58.

Schein, E. H. (1987). "Individuals and careers." In J. W. Lorsch (ed.), *Handbook of Organizational Behavior.* Englewood Cliffs NJ: Prentice-Hall, 155–71.

Schneider, B. (1985). "Organizational behavior." In M. R. Rosenzweig and L. W. Porter (eds), *Annual Review of Psychology,* Vol. 36. Palo Alto, CA: Annual Reviews, 573–611.

Schuler, R. S. (1980). "Definition and conceptualization of stress in organizations." *Organizational Behavior and Human Performance, 25,* 184–215.

Schwarz, N. (1990). "Feelings as information: informational and motivational functions of affective states." In E. T. Higgins and R. M. Sorrentino (eds), *Handbook of Motivation and Cognition: Foundations of Social Behavior,* Vol. 2, New York: Guilford Press, 527–61.

Scott, W. E. Jr (1966). "Activation theory and task design." *Organizational Behavior and Human Performance, 1,* 3–30.

Seers, A., McGee, G. W., Serey, T. T. and Graen, G. B. (1983). "The interaction of job stress and social support: a strong inference investigation." *Academy of Management Journal, 26,* 273–84.

Sekaran, U. (1983). "How husbands and wives in dual-career families perceive their family and work worlds." *Journal of Vocational Behavior, 22,* 288–302.

Seltzer, J. and Numerof, R. E. (1988). "Supervisory leadership and subordinate burnout." *Academy of Management Journal, 31,* 439–46.

Selye, H. (1956). *The Stress of Life.* New York: McGraw-Hill.

—— (1974). *Stress without Distress.* Philadelphia: J. B. Lippincott.

—— (1975). "Confusion and controversy in the stress field." *Journal of Human Stress,* (June), 37–44.

Shamir, B. (1983). "Some antecedents of work–non-work conflict." *Journal of Vocational Behavior 23,* 989–1011.

Sharit, J. and Salvendy, G. (1982). "Occupational stress: review and reappraisal." *Human Factors, 24,* 129–62.

Shaw, J. B. and Riskind, J. H. (1983). "Predicting job stress using data from the Position Analysis Questionnaire." *Journal of Applied Psychology, 68,* 253–61.

Shinn, M. (1981). "*Caveat emptor:* potential problems in using information on burnout." In W. S. Paine (ed.), *Proceedings of the First National Conference on Burnout,* 159–94.

Shore, R. (1979). *Servants of power." APA Monitor,* November, 2.

Short Subjects. (1990). *Journal of Irreproducible Results, 35,* 8.

Sieber, S. D. (1974). "Toward a theory of role accumulation." *American Sociological Review, 39,* 567–78.

Sinclair, R. C. (1988). "Mood categorization breadth, and performance appraisal: the effects of order of information acquisition and affective state on halo, accuracy, information retrieval, and evaluations." *Organizational Behavior and Human Decision Processes, 42,* 22–46.

Sorrentino, R. M. and Short, J. C. (1986). "Uncertainty orientation, motivation, and cognition." In R. M. Sorrentino and E. T. Higgins (eds), *Handbook of Motivation and Cognition: Foundations of Social Behavior.* New York: Guilford Press, 379–403.

Spector, P. (1987a). "Interactive effects of perceived control and job stressors on affective reactions and health outcomes for clerical workers." *Work & Stress, 1,* 155–62.

—— (1987b). "Method variance as an artifact in self- reported affect and perceptions at work: myth or significant problem?" *Journal of Applied Psychology, 72,* 438–43.

Spector, P. E., Dwyer, D. J. and Jex, S. M. (1988). "Relation of job stressors to affective, health, and performance outcomes: a comparison of multiple data sources." *Journal of Applied Psychology, 73,* 11–19.

Staines, G. L. and Pleck, J. H. (1984). "Non-standard work schedules and family life." *Journal of Applied Psychology, 69,* 515–23.

Steers, R. M. and Rhodes, S. R. (1978). "Major influences on employee attendance: a process model." *Journal of Applied Psychology, 63,* 391–407.

Steffy, B. D. and Jones, J. W. (1988). "Workplace stress and indicators of coronary-disease risks." *Academy of Management Journal, 31,* 686–98.

Strube, M. J., Boland, S. M., Manfredo, P. A. and Al-Falaij, A. (1987). "Type A behavior and the self-evaluation of abilities: empirical tests of the self-appraisal model." *Journal of Personality and Social Psychology, 52,* 956–74.

Super, D. E. (1980). "A life-span approach to career development." *Journal of Vocational Behavior, 16,* 282–98.

Sutton, R. I. and Rafaeli, A. (1987). "Characteristics of work stations as potential occupational stressors." *Academy of Management Journal, 30,* 260–76.

Sweeney, D. R. (1981). "Burnout: is it really a stress syndrome?" In W. S. Paine (ed.), *Proceedings of the First National Conference on Burnout,* 99–104.

Taylor, J. A. (1953). "A personality scale of manifest anxiety." *Journal of Abnormal and Social Psychology, 48,* 285–90.

Terpstra, D. E. (1981). "Relationship between methodological rigor and reported outcomes in organization development evaluation research." *Journal of Applied Psychology, 66,* 541–3.

Tetrick, L. E. and La Rocco, J. M. (1987). "Understanding, prediction, and control as moderators of the relationships between perceived stress, satisfaction, and psychological well-being." *Journal of Applied Psychology, 72,* 538–43.

Thompson, J. D. (1967). *Organizations in Action.* New York: McGraw-Hill.

Tracy, L. and Johnson, T. W. (1981). "What do the role conflict and role ambiguity scales measure?" *Journal of Applied Psychology, 66,* 464–9.

Van Sell, M., Brief, A. P. and Schuler, R. S. (1981). "Role conflict and role ambiguity:

integration of the literature and directions for future research." *Human Relations*, *34*, 43–71.

Vaux, A. (1988). *Social Support: Theory, Research, and Intervention.* New York: Praeger.

Vroom, V. H. (1964). *Work and Motivation.* New York: Wiley.

Walsh, J. T., Taber, T. D. and Beehr, T. A. (1980). "An integrated model of perceived job characteristics." *Organizational Behavior and Human Performance*, *25*, 252–67.

Wanous, J. P. (1980). *Organizational Entry: Recruitment, Selection, and Socialization of Newcomers.* Reading, MA: Addison-Wesley.

Weiss, R. M. (1987). "Writing under the influence: science versus fiction in the analysis of corporate alcoholism programs." *Personnel Psychology*, *40*, 341–56.

Wilensky, H. L. (1960). "Work, careers and social integration." *International Social Science Journal*, *12*, 543–60.

Williams, L. J., Cote, J. A. and Buckley, M. R. (1989). "Lack of method variance in self-reported affect and perceptions at work: reality or artifact?" *Journal of Applied Psychology*, *74*, 462–8.

Winkelpleck, J. M. (1984). "Directions EAPs move: evolvement towards organizational methods." *EAP Digest: The Voice of Employee Assistance Programs*, *4* (July/August), 18–21.

Young, P. T. (1936). *Motivation of Behavior: the Fundamental Determinants of Human and Animal Activity.* New York: Wiley.

Zedeck, S. (1992). *Work, Families, and Organization.* San Francisco: Jossey-Bass.

Zedeck, S., Jackson, S. E. and Summers, E. (1983). "Shiftwork schedules and their relationship to health, adaption, satisfaction, and turnover intention." *Academy of Management Journal*, *26*, 297–310.

Zung, W. W. K. (1965). "A self-rating depression scale." *Archives of General Psychiatry*, *13*, 63–70.

Name index

Subject index

absenteeism 27, 67, 68, 92, 96, 97, 112, 127, 133, 140–5
adaptive responses 18, 87, 205
autonomy 59, 68, 93–6, 138

buffering 151, 194–202, 204, 206, 207
burnout 42, 114–16, 119, 120, 212

cardiovascular disease 122–6, 131
conflict, interpersonal 87, 88, 112, 147
consequences, individual and organizational 67, 107–48, 154–7
coping 26, 27, 31, 99, 154, 166–71, 174, 175, 182, 203, 231

dual careers 25–7, 76–8
duration of stress 21, 34–7, 50, 51, 102, 201, 227

Employee Assistance Programs 171, 179
family business 71, 72
fit, person–environment 29, 31, 32, 86

individual differences 5, 15, 18, 19, 24, 27, 37, 60, 119, 203, 228

lateness 141, 142
life events or life stress 14, 16, 23, 24, 30, 59, 104, 194, 204

machine pacing 92–4
moderators 18, 49, 56, 58–60, 66–8, 78–81, 85, 114, 138, 223

non-work situations 23, 27, 76–8

pace of work 90, 92, 93
performance, job 6, 7, 10, 27, 32, 35–51, 65, 68, 79, 80, 98, 99, 112, 127, 132, 133, 135–9, 146, 149, 214, 216
primary targets of treatment 5, 147–61, 173–7, 181
psychological contact 88–90
psychological withdrawal 148

relocation 98
responsibility 90, 93, 94, 122
role: ambiguity 11, 13, 37–9, 42–7, 49, 51, 53, 55–68, 80–6, 97, 99, 110, 112, 113, 115, 122, 134, 137–9, 141, 144–8, 158, 203, 218, 219, 226; conflict 13, 24–6, 42–5, 47, 49, 53, 55–8, 69–86, 90, 97, 110, 112, 115, 122, 137–9, 141, 145, 147, 148, 156, 218, 219, 226; overload 83–6, 91, 92, 95, 113, 115, 116, 122, 137, 139, 144, 146, 147, 203; senders 56–8, 63, 64, 70–5, 83, 99, 112

satisfaction, job 8, 27, 42–8, 59, 67, 79, 86, 87, 96, 97, 99, 111–13, 116, 118, 120, 122, 132, 139, 142, 203
schedule of work 90, 91, 114, 215
security, job 99–104
self-report measures 8–10, 14, 57, 58, 61, 62, 79, 85, 86, 92, 93, 110–15, 119–21, 123, 130, 131, 135, 139, 141, 142, 144–7, 194, 215, 216, 224, 226–9, 231, 132
size, organizational 97
social information processing 216
social support 27, 47, 48, 59, 60, 68, 86, 99, 112, 114, 117, 138, 151, 182–207, 219, 223, 224
somatic complaints 113, 114